The Rise of Modern Japan

Peter Duus
Stanford University

Houghton Mifflin Company · Boston

Atlanta Dallas Geneva, Ill. Hopewell, N.J. Palo Alto London

Maps by Richard Sanderson

Printed in the U.S.A.

Library of Congress Catalog Card Number: 75-33416

ISBN: 0-395-20665-0

Contents

Preface

Japan does not capture the front page of newspapers as many of its neighbors do, yet it is certainly one of the most advanced and potentially one of the most powerful nations in the world today. Japan's industrial machine pours forth a flood of goods to the four corners of the globe; Japan's business men and women, diplomats, students, and ordinary citizens find their way to every major city and country in the world ceaselessly in pursuit of knowledge, profit, and pleasure; Japan's science and technology, as well as Japan's art and literature, enrich the higher culture of many other peoples. Yet to many outsiders Japan remains an unknown quantity, dimly on the edge of consciousness and hard to fit into familiar categories. The Japanese themselves are partly responsible for their relative invisibility. A generation ago they paid the price of being too truculently self-assertive, and memories of defeat and military disaster in World War II have made many Japanese reluctant to thrust themselves too boldly before the world public. Nonetheless, Japan has become increasingly visible over the past decade and will doubtless continue to be visible in decades to come.

This book is a modest attempt to bring this newly visible Japan into better focus. It tells of Japan's rise to world prominence over the past hundred years—first as an aggressively Westernizing Asian nation, then as a major imperialist power, and finally as a postwar economic giant. It is presumptuous to compress a century or so of human experience between the covers of a book in the first place, and doubly so in a book so short in compass as this one. About all an author can do is offer a guide for those who wish a quick tour of modern Japanese history—and perhaps a few signposts for those planning a more extended trip. The book deals mainly with political, social, economic, and diplomatic events. To a lesser degree it concerns the development of ideas, literature, and intellectual life not because they are less interesting or less important, but because there is not space enough to do them justice. Other idiosyncrasies in emphasis and coverage will also become apparent to the reader, making it clear that this book is a place to begin a study of modern Japan not to end it.

In writing this volume I have had the help of many others. My most important collaborators have been my students, who over the past ten years or so have forced me to clarify and refine my own understanding of modern Japanese history. Colleagues have been helpful in this respect, to be sure, but my best critics have always been my silent ones, who by a yawn or a nod, a flickering frown or a brightening face, have shown me when I have understood and conveyed my understanding—and when I have not. Other more immediate assistance has come from those who have read and commented on the contents of the book in an earlier version, especially Edwin O. Reischauer and Irwin Scheiner, whose comments and suggestions were most useful. To all who have helped me in one way or another, I wish to express my thanks.

Introduction: The Meaning of Modern Japanese History

When Commodore Matthew Perry sailed into Uraga Bay in July 1853, he carried a letter to the emperor of Japan assuring him that the United States had no intention of disturbing the tranquility of his realm. This comforting diplomatic assurance could hardly have been wider of the mark, for Perry's arrival set in motion a process of rapid and bewildering change that profoundly altered the course of Japanese history. Within the space of a generation the Japanese transformed themselves into the first country outside the West to build up a modern state, to set in motion a modern industrial economy, and to plunge into the exciting but uncertain waters of world politics. As one foreign observer noted in 1900, Japan was like a bright comet suddenly tracing a path across the sky, exploding into the vision of an outside world that for centuries had hardly taken notice of it.[1]

From its beginning the remarkable transformation of Japan following the arrival of Perry excited the interest of Americans. For those of Perry's day the "opening" of Japan was seen as an event of great moment. It held out the prospect of converting a "backward and heathen" people into a "civilized and forward-looking" nation committed to progress, liberty, free trade, and Christianity. In 1861 one American publication reported that the Japanese, even though they were "Mongols," possessed "greater mental activity and capacity for acquisition of knowledge than any other nations belonging to that race," and ten years later it noted happily that Japan was progressing toward "civilization" with "a rapidity which challenges universal admiration."[2] Later observers were often less sanguine for the intrusion of Western civilization into Japan proved to be an altogether mixed blessing. "Old Japan came nearer to the achievement of the highest moral ideal than our far more evolved societies can hope to do for many a hundred years," wrote the Western journalist Lafcadio Hearn. "The future Japan [however] must rely upon the least amiable qualities of her character for success in the universal struggle, and she will need to develop them strongly."[3] With the outbreak of the Russo-Japanese War many Americans began to feel that the opening of Japan had indeed unleashed her "least amiable qualities" and that Japan was on her way to becoming a formidable rival to the United States in the Pacific. Publicists like Homer Lea[4] predicted that the Japanese could stage a successful conquest of the whole Pacific coast of the United States, and the popular press continually alerted Americans to the danger of the "yellow peril."

All these attitudes have persisted. Well-meaning American scholars and government officials continue eagerly to proffer the Japanese lessons from their society on how to do everything from managing businesses to organizing philanthropic foundations; romantics and malcontents remain fascinated by the delicate beauty of traditional Japanese art or the higher truth of Zen Buddhism; and businessmen and politicians, if no longer concerned over the possibility of invasion by Japanese armies, still wax wrathful and anxious over the invasion of Japanese goods and Japanese capital. All this is to be expected, for over the past century and over the past generation in particular the tranquillity of Japan has become intertwined with that of the United States in ways that were not conceivable in 1853. Nevertheless, how most Americans see Japan has less to do with the realities of Japan's modern experience than with their own interests and prejudices. Instead of considering the struggles and dislocations the Japanese experienced as a result of their initial encounter with the United States, they have continued to impose their own preconceptions on Japan.

American scholars and historians have found modern Japanese history of interest for other reasons. Although it came out of a radically different cultural tradition, Japan during the past century has undergone many of the same kinds of change that the Western world experienced from the mid-eighteenth century. The interesting questions are: why and how? At first most historians, reflecting a general popular assessment, tended to regard Japan as a unique case, contrasted with China, India, and other "backward" areas of the world, which were unable to make a similar breakthrough into modernity. They tried to discover what was peculiar about Japan that enabled it to succeed in doing what these other non-Western societies had not. Sometimes their answers were silly—when they cited the Japanese "capacity for imitation," for example. But the more perceptive, such as the brilliant Canadian historian E. H. Norman, noted that the breakdown of traditional society before the advent of Perry prepared the way for the massive changes that came after it.[5] This viewpoint, which suggests the unique social circumstances behind Japan's rapid modernization, continues to be suggestive even today.

Since World War II Japan's modern experience has been placed in a slightly different perspective. The emergence of a welter of "new nations" in the postwar world made Japan seem less a unique case than as the first instance of a more general phenomenon: the modernization of the non-Western world. Some historians and social scientists tried to use the Japanese case as a testing ground for larger theories about what a "modern society" is and how it gets that way. More often than not they found these theories were an ill fit for Japan. Others, more oriented toward public policy, proposed Japan as a model or example for other non-Western nations to follow. This line of thought became pronounced as memories of World War II faded, and Japan became one of the staunchest allies of the United States in the struggle against "communist totalitarianism." Clearly there were advantages to be gained in cold war ideological debates by pointing out lessons to be learned from a country that not only had modernized itself early on but had done so within the framework of a free-enterprise economy under a non-Marxist and non-ideological leadership.

The prevailing popular image of modern Japanese history has picked up this stress on the positive aspects of Japan's modern transformation. Over the past few years, there has been a strong trend to view modern Japanese history as a kind of success story. The pages of our national news magazines are graced from time to time with feature articles on the "economic miracle" that has made

Japan the third largest industrial power in the world. To be sure, there is much to commend this point of view. The Japanese today enjoy a degree of material comfort and security unknown to their great-grandparents or to their contemporaries in Korea, China, and India. As the Japanese boom has rolled on, Japanese living standards and technical achievements have come to be measured by standards of Western experience rather than by those of the non-Western world. Indeed, many observers have begun to wonder whether the "advanced" nations might not have something to learn from Japan too.

By contrast, the postwar generation of Japanese has tended to stress the darker side of Japan's modern century. They do not deny the realities of Japan's economic growth, but they point out that other things came with it—the persistent feudal habits of mind, an authoritarian political order, an expansionist foreign policy, and the final tragedy of war. They look back beyond the remarkable Gross National Product of today to the circumstances that led to the leveling of Hiroshima and Nagasaki by atomic bombs. In the past decade, while some optimistic Americans looked forward to the emergence of a "Japanese century" in the near future, more pessimistic Japanese observers feared the re-emergence of Japanese imperialism in new and subtler forms, a turn of events they regarded as as ominous for the Japanese themselves as for the rest of the world. For them, the prime lesson of Japan's modern history is how *not* to modernize.

If one looks at the course of Japanese history during the last century, it is clear that whatever one's standards are, Japan's path to the present has been strewn with both failures and successes. To sweep aside the failures as the price inevitably paid for the long-run achievements makes no more sense than to suggest that these achievements are nothing compared with the sufferings it has undergone. But before making a final judgment on the meaning of Japan's modern experience, one ought to try to understand what happened and why. Not to do so means falling into an ahistorical praise-and-blame approach to history, which judges people and nations of the past by standards they themselves did not accept or regard as appropriate. Human history, like human life, is ambiguous, and when one moves from description and analysis to moral judgment, its meaning becomes as varied as its observers are numerous.

The pages that follow attempt no assessment of the implications of modern Japanese history for either general social theories or current American foreign policy. Nor do they attempt to sort out heroes from villains or triumphs from tragedy. Nor do they attempt a spurious objectivity. Rather they attempt to introduce those who wish to understand modern Japan to some of the central themes and events in its history. Ultimate judgments on the meaning of this history, whether for an understanding of current world politics, for an assessment of American foreign policy in Asia, or for inquiry into the larger processes by which modern societies develop, will necessarily depend on the readers themselves. In the end we all have to be our own historians.

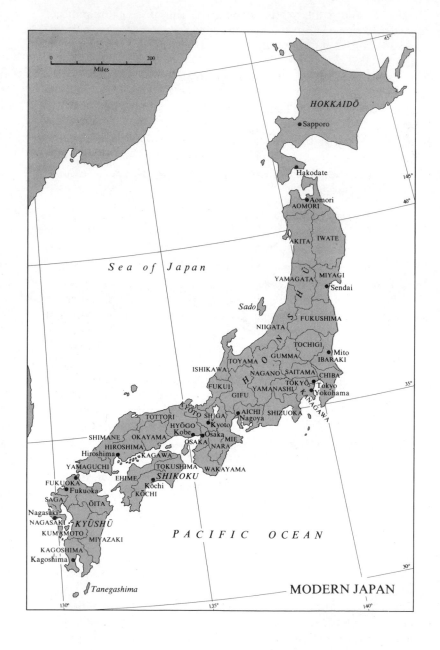

Scale: 0 — 200 Miles

HOKKAIDŌ

- Sapporo
- Hakodate
- Aomori
- AOMORI
- AKITA
- IWATE
- YAMAGATA
- MIYAGI
- Sendai
- FUKUSHIMA
- NIIGATA
- TOCHIGI
- GUMMA
- Mito
- IBARAKI
- TOYAMA
- NAGANO
- SAITAMA
- CHIBA
- ISHIKAWA
- FUKUI
- YAMANASHI
- TŌKYŌ
- Tokyo
- Yokohama
- GIFU
- KANAGAWA
- KYŌTO
- SHIGA
- AICHI
- SHIZUOKA
- Nagoya
- TOTTORI
- HYŌGO
- Kyoto
- SHIMANE
- OKAYAMA
- Kobe
- Osaka
- OSAKA
- NARA
- MIE
- HIROSHIMA
- KAGAWA
- Hiroshima
- TOKUSHIMA
- WAKAYAMA
- YAMAGUCHI
- EHIME
- **SHIKOKU**
- FUKUOKA
- Kōchi
- KŌCHI
- Fukuoka
- SAGA
- ŌITA
- Nagasaki
- NAGASAKI
- **KYŪSHŪ**
- KUMAMOTO
- MIYAZAKI
- KAGOSHIMA
- Kagoshima
- *Tanegashima*
- *Sado*
- *Sea of Japan*
- *PACIFIC OCEAN*

MODERN JAPAN

1

Traditional Attitudes

Modern Japan did not spring into being full-blown with the arrival of the West; it grew out of a historical context and a cultural heritage that continued to influence its development even after the process of modernization had begun. To be sure, the modern transformation of Japan involved an assault on traditional institutions, attitudes, and cultural patterns, but many of these persisted, often serving to facilitate the building of national wealth and strength. Indeed many Japanese were proud that they had not been inundated by Western civilization and had managed to preserve their cultural integrity without sacrificing their national independence. As the essayist Okakura Tenshin noted in 1904,

> One who looks beneath the surface of things can see, in spite of her modern garb, that the heart of Old Japan is still beating. . . . Our individuality has been preserved from submersion beneath the mighty flood of Western ideas by the same national characteristics which ever enabled us to remain true to ourselves in spite of repeated influxes of foreign thought.[1]

Even today, though the Japan of the 1970s would be nearly unrecognizable to the Japanese of the 1850s, the style or feel of Japanese society and culture is distinctly different from other modern nations. The residue of the past persists, making present-day Japan both modern and uniquely Japanese. A good way to begin a study of modern Japan is to look at some of the national characteristics or traditional attitudes on the eve of its modern transformation, bearing in mind that they were not merely traits to be overcome but also assets in the building of the new Japan.

Hierarchy and Status Consciousness

From prehistoric times Japanese culture has emphasized the importance of hierarchical status and respect for rank. As early as the third century, a Chinese chronicle reported that the Japanese showed deference to people of high rank by squatting along the roadside when they passed. In this respect the early Japanese were no different from most literate, preindustrial peoples, including those of premodern Western Europe, but such attitudes perhaps have lasted longer in Japan than elsewhere. As one contemporary Japanese observer has noted, Japan is still a "society of be-ers," not a "society of doers" as is the United States.[2] What people *do* is less important to most Japanese than who they are, where they work, what their positions are, and who their relatives are. The social distance between people of different status is also much greater than in American society, where the common man is revered in word if not always in deed.

The society of early nineteenth-century Japan was highly hierarchical, stressing the prerogatives of rank, sex, and age. The basic social division, both in theory and in law, was between two main classes, the *samurai*, or warriors, and the commoners. The samurai were an elite ruling class set apart from the commoners by special privileges and special obligations. The sharp division between samurai and commoner had its origins in the late sixteenth century when Toyotomi Hideyoshi, one of the three great unifiers of Japan, attempted to end local civil disorder and social anarchy by assigning people to their proper stations in society. The commoners were disarmed, the right to carry weapons was restricted to the samurai, and the commoners, most of whom were peasants, were forbidden to leave their fields and land for military adventure. Under the Tokugawa dynasty, founded by Hideyoshi's political successor, Tokugawa Ieyasu, these regulations were reinforced and elaborated. The right to carry two swords continued to be the principal outward badge of samurai status, but new sumptuary regulations were issued presenting meticulous distinctions separating samurai from commoners in every sphere of daily life, from hairstyles to house plans. The distinction extended even to criminal law, which established a double standard for the two classes. Samurais might cut down commoners for insolent behavior without fear of punishment, but if they were caught gambling, a mild misdemeanor for commoners, they would face severe punishment and censure for compromising the dignity of their class.

This broad class hierarchy found support in the doctrines of Neo-Confucianism, the most pervasive stream of social and political thought in Tokugawa Japan. Nearly all political theorists accepted the notion that it was in the order of things to divide society into a hierarchy of four estates or four classes, each with its own special function and each with its own special contribution to society. This view was neatly summarized by one late seventeenth-century thinker who wrote: "The peasant cultivates the fields and so nourishes the people; the artisan makes utensils and has the people use them; the merchant exchanges what one has for what one has not and so helps the people; the samurai rules so that disorders will not arise. Though each performs only his own job, he is helping the other."[3] Clearly some of these social functions were more useful than others, so the four classes were ranked according to their social utility. The samurai stood at the top of this hierarchy because they were the most dedicated to the good of the whole and the least interested in personal profit; next came the peasants who produced the basic essential, food; then the artisans who produced less necessary goods; and last the merchants who produced nothing. Naturally, the lower orders, who were seen as endowed with less virtue, were enjoined to obey those above, who always acted on the basis of moral principle, rather than personal or private interest.

In practice class status was normally hereditary. Mobility between classes was not unknown, but by the early 1800s children of samurais usually remained samurais and commoners' children remained commoners. In this respect Japan differed from Confucian China. There status was linked with ability or virtue. In China one became a member of the privileged scholar-official elite by successful passage of the civil service examination. Japanese Confucianists paid lip service to this ideology of merit,[4] but Japanese society was far more closed and aristocratic than that of its continental neighbor. The social pecking order was more rigid and the possibility of entering the ruling class more limited. By the same token, however, there was stronger motivation for all people to perform as well as they could in whatever status the fortune of birth had put them. If they could not rise to a higher status outside their class, they could at least rise to the first rank among peers.

The emphasis on keeping one's proper station was further reinforced within family groups, especially among the samurai class. From infancy most children learned to be aware of carefully shaded differences of status and authority. The family itself constituted a small hierarchical pyramid, in which one learned to show deference to social superiors. Younger brother obeyed older, sisters deferred to brothers, parents took precedence over children, and the father ruled all as the family head. Language itself was woven through with special honorific words used toward those above and familiar ones used toward intimates and those below. Children called their older siblings by special words meaning "elder brother" or "elder sister." A mother addressed her child with the familiar form of *you,* like the French *tu,* but when she spoke with her husband (and master) she used a more formal second-person pronoun like the French *vous.* Nonverbal language underlined the meaning of spoken language. A bowed head and averted eyes were the proper posture for a wife being lectured by her husband or a naughty child scolded by her or his parents.

Family morality, like social theory, drew heavily on the doctrines of Confucianism. The *Classic of Filial Piety,* the main Confucian text for this morality, was a well-read volume. It was filled with instructive tales of model children who went to the grossest extremes of self-sacrifice to show respect for their parents. One paragon of filial piety, even though well into middle age, gamboled like an infant in front of his seventy-year-old parents so they would think themselves still young, and another drenched himself with rice wine (sake) and lay naked by his parents' bed at night to draw the mosquitoes away from them. Similarly, Kaibara Ekken, author of a classic work on child-rearing, enjoined parents,

> The way of man is to observe the virtues of filial piety and obedience, and the children must be taught that all goodness in life emanates from these two virtues. . . . If parents permit their children to hold other people in contempt, and take pleasure in their antics, the children will lose a sense of distinction between good and evil . . . and will not shed their bad habits even after they become adults.[5]

In short, model behavior was submissive behavior.

The emphasis on hierarchy was unchecked by any notion of the equality of people, so familiar in American universalistic society, and people varied their behavior toward others according to their rank in society. The result, as Fukuzawa Yukichi, a later critic, noted, was a kind of authoritarian situational ethic. "[The Japanese] make a clear distinction between the moral codes that apply to people above them and to people below, and an equally clear distinction in the field of rights and duties. As a result every individual is in one capacity the victim of coercion, while in another he metes out coercion to his fellow men."[6] Such an authoritarian status structure sounds grim indeed to most Americans, since there is no room in it for the concept of personal rights or personal freedom. But it would be wrong to characterize early nineteenth-century Japan as a place of untrammeled social tyranny. For one thing, hierarchy counted for little in some relationships, for example between friends. Even more important, irresponsible use of authority was held in check by the notion that superiors had duties even if inferiors did not have rights. According to Confucian doctrine people were to be regarded as deserving respect or authority only if they fulfilled the ethical obligations of their social roles. In theory, a feudal lord could be blamed if he was a coward and a father could be criticized if he was a brute. In practice, of course, it was difficult to achieve redress against superiors who shirked their duty. Courts would entertain suits by people of low status against their superiors only with the superiors' consent. But since the idea of obligation to inferiors was drilled into people's minds along with a belief in the sanctity of status, Confucian ideas did help to contain the temptations to oppress those below and spurred the impulse to act with benevolence. Authoritarianism was not checked by rights, but it was mitigated by a web of mutual and interlocking social obligations.

It is also wise to remember that the status ethic was most highly developed among the samurai and perhaps among the more affluent commoners. Officers usually are more concerned with fine-grained distinctions of rank than first-class privates are. Although the lower orders submitted to the samurai and those in positions of authority, they were often inclined to measure people on their merits rather than on their social rank. "Birth and lineage mean nothing," proclaimed one tract for eighteenth-century merchants. "Money is the only family tree for the townsman. A man may be descended from the noblest of the Fujiwara (an ancient aristocratic family), but if he dwells among shopkeepers and lives in poverty he is lower than a vagabond monkey-trainer."[7] Relations among members of a peasant community were also marked by much more informality, freedom from constraint, and equality than among the samurai class. Peasants earned the respect of their neighbors less by their parents' pedigrees than by display of hard work. In sum, alongside the official hierarchy of birth and status there existed a humble hierarchy of talent and ability.

Community and Social Harmony

If the late Tokugawa respect for hierarchy seems peculiar to those nurtured on a diet of egalitarianism, so too does the willingness of most Japanese to subordinate their personal interests to the claims of group interest. Rugged individualism was not highly regarded in early nineteenth-century Japan. On the contrary, independent individuals stubbornly sticking to their own interests or following the dictates of their consciences were apt to be regarded as criminals or rebels rather than as culture heroes. They faced all the sanctions society could bring to bear on them. A popular saying went, "The nail that sticks out gets hammered down." Ideal individuals obeyed what the sociologist R. P. Dore has called a "collectivity ethic,"[8] which made the goals of their group, whether family, village, or domain, more important than their own. Individualism, in the sense of pursuing one's own desires in defiance of group demands, was so alien a concept that a word had not yet been invented for it. If the idea existed at all, it was equated with personal selfishness.

The most explicit and extreme form of "collectivity ethic" was to be found in the samurai class, whose members were bound to their lord and their domain by strong ties of personal loyalty. By precept and example young samurais learned that people's worth was measured not by their independence, but by their willingness to sacrifice themselves to the demands of their lords. The military romances and moral tracts they read took as their heroes medieval warriors who fought to the death in the services of their lords, throwing away without hesitation the precious gift of life. The tale of the forty-seven samurai retainers of the lord of Akō, who devoted their lives to avenging the unjust execution of their young lord in the early eighteenth century, was one of the favorite dramas of the time.[9] The theme of self-sacrifice in the name of feudal loyalty was repeated in other less well-known historical plays as well. Few samurai in the early nineteenth century were called on to make the ultimate sacrifice, death, and most regarded their lords less as personal masters than as leaders of their domains. Nonetheless, the idea of "duty to one's lord" remained a powerful moral imperative at the center of the samurai's outlook on life.

The collectivity ethic of the samurai, meshed as it was with the hierarchy of status and authority, had strong authoritarian overtones. But there was another less hierarchical collectivity ethic within the village, a tightly woven community knit together not by feudal bonds of lord-retainer but by common economic interests, the need to cooperate in many areas of daily life, and a sense of togetherness over generations. This "little tradition" of individual conformity to group pressures was perhaps as important in the long run as the "great tradition" of samurai loyalty, since the bulk of Japan's population were peasant villagers.

Unity within the village community showed itself in many ways. Groups of neighboring households often cooperated to help each other out. Sometimes they joined in thatching each others' roofs or took care of a family stricken by the death of one of its members, and sometimes they pooled their cash to send one of their number off on a pilgrimage to a distant shrine or temple. The village as a whole usually shared a common annual cycle of festivals from communal rice planting in the spring to harvest celebrations in the fall, and often the villagers shared a common local deity (*ujigami*), worshipped at a village shrine taken care of by all. All of those activities encouraged a common sense of purpose and a strong sense of community.

The sense of belonging that bound the villagers to their village community was reinforced by social and economic factors. Population movements among the rural population were slight. Most families had lived in their village as far back as memory could stretch, and membership in the village was a kind of birthright. This population stability over generations created a sense of local roots that is now unimaginable in highly mobile American society, where people change jobs and houses at the drop of a hat. At the same time, the wet-field system of rice agriculture made for a high degree of economic interdependence among all the villagers. The need to share limited water resources placed a premium on village cooperation. The proper flow of water into the family rice paddy plots was a mat-

ter of prosperity or hardship for most peasant farmers. Too little
water in the paddy could spoil the harvest, and a peasant family that
got more than its fair share could hurt the welfare of its neighbors.
In most villages a rigid custom governed the flow of irrigation water
and the order in which each field received its share so that no family
gained at the expense of others.

Under these circumstances pressures toward community solidarity
and personal conformity to village opinion were strong indeed.
Villagers usually regarded outsiders with suspicion and deviants with
intolerance. They felt that decisions affecting the interests of the
village as a group should be based on a consensus of all concerned,
and that once taken decisions should be obeyed by all. The sanctions
for defying the village consensus were often harsh. In extreme cases
families or individual villagers who breached the village code were
faced with ostracism (*mura-hachibu*), which cut them off from all
normal human contact even if they chose to remain in the village.

Village custom and consensus often affected the most minute
aspects of daily life, from the number of cups of sake someone
could drink at a village wedding to the decision whether a farmer
could convert a piece of dry field land to rice paddy. The oppressive-
ness of life in the village in contrast to the relative freedom of anony-
mous city life was later well described by the novelist, Tokutomi
Kenjirō, who wrote,

> There's as much freedom in the country as in a prison, believe
> me. Drop a pebble in a bowl and you set up a tidal wave.
> Stretch your arms in the country, and you bump old Tagobei's
> front door—your legs, and they get caught in Gonsuke's back
> gate. If your daughter so much as changes the neckband of her
> kimono, the whole village must be talking about it. A hermit
> can live in the middle of any town, and in the capital nobody
> bothers about anything—but in the country you can't even
> sneeze without wondering what people will say.[10]

General acceptance of the need for cooperation, cohesiveness, and
consensus did not make Tokugawa society immune to competition
or conflict. Economic competition among villagers over possession
of land was common and so was conflict over status, especially when
newly prosperous families began to vie with declining older ones for
village honors. Rarer but no less important were village riots or risings, when villagers defied samurai authorities or plundered rich
peasant storehouses over some grievance. But on the whole conflict

and competition were not seen as creative, an attitude common in our own society, which is dominated by adversary relationships. Rather they were regarded as bad and destructive. The good society was a harmonious society and the presence of conflict meant all was not well with the world. Every effort was bent to resolve potential conflict without resort to law or litigation (really a continuation of conflict by other means.) Conciliation through negotiation and go-between were used most often. Peasants angry at the unfairness of local samurai officials sometimes appealed albeit illegally over their heads by petition to the domain lord, and merchants involved in a dispute over debts negotiated through some third party to achieve a reasonable compromise. Only when there was no redress of griev-ances or resolution of differences did violence occur and then it was almost always punished severely.

Work and Achievement

A firm belief in the value of diligence, frugality, and achievement was central to the outlook of most Tokugawa Japanese, whatever their class. "Work much, earn much, and spend little," wrote the peasant-philosopher Ninomiya Sontoku.[11] For the ordinary peasant, such advice was a matter of daily hard necessity. Wet-rice agriculture put a premium on the intensive use of human labor. Unlike farmers in Western Europe and the United States who relied heavily on the use of draft animals and machinery, Japanese peasants had to rely for the most part on the labor of their own hands and muscle. Labor saving devices were difficult to introduce into the raising of rice in irrigated fields and every farming operation from planting rice seed-lings in the spring to harvesting the ripe grain in the fall was done by human labor. Hard work could lead to prosperity and laziness to ruin. Frugality was important too since even the most rigorous labor could squeeze only so much from the land. Indulgence and extrava-gance were shunned as vehemently as indolence.

Such a work ethic is common in many peasant societies, but in Japan it was shared as well by the samurai and the town commoner. For all classes, as sociologist Robert Bellah has pointed out, the work and frugality ethic was not linked to the idea of personal suc-cess or well-being but to the well-being or success of the group. Diligence and frugality were encouraged as ways of ensuring the prosperity of the collectivity and of repaying the blessings bestowed by ancestors, parents, or lord. As Ninomiya wrote, "The wealth of our parents depends on the industry of their ancestry, and our wealth depends on the accumulated good deeds of our parents. Our descendants' wealth depends on us and our faithful discharge of duty."[12] Similar sentiments were expressed in the family constitutions of merchant families or in the writings of samurai moralists who described hard work and frugality as a means of showing loyalty and service to one's lord.

Personal achievement was identified with group achievement and subordinated to it. Successful merchants were praiseworthy not because they were self-made but because they were good stewards of the family fortune. Rich peasants who expanded the family landholdings did so not to enjoy material comforts for themselves but to provide for their descendants. Ambitious samurai officials, though they might be rewarded with a higher rank or stipend, saw themselves working for the cause of the feudal lord. All this is not to say that such people were without self-interest, but that social approval was forthcoming only if the pursuit of self-interest were clothed in the garb of repaying obligations.

At the same time, since status was hereditary in Tokugawa Japan personal achievement was not so closely linked with upward social mobility as it is in American society. Given the strong legal and customary restraints on rising above one's station, ambition meant doing one's best in one's own walk of life. Carpenters could not hope to become samurai but they could hope to become master artisans whose work was admired by all. It was this kind of success in which the Japanese took pride. "No matter how poor you are, you must not be beguiled into another trade," warned a book of advice to craftsmen. "If you ply your craft unchangingly and with complete devotion, the time may come when you will prosper."[13] All people had their own places in society and they were expected to do their best within those places. Confucian writers spoke of this place as a *shokubun* ("calling"). Each calling had its own set of duties and functions to be fulfilled and people's worths were measured by the extent to which they succeeded in fulfilling them.

Reward for achievement in Japan was measured in immediate benefits in the here-and-now. Despite centuries of Buddhist influence most people were "this worldly" in outlook. Reward for hard work and diligence lay not in treasures stored up in heaven but in the good opinion of one's fellows or in hard material terms. As in any society there were ascetics and pietists who strove to suppress their worldly cravings. Zen monks pursued enlightenment to set them above the desires that claimed most people and Confucian purists held pursuit of personal profit to be contemptible. But most people were exercised over more immediate daily concerns. The folk religion practised in most villages, for example, centered around praying for good harvests and expressing thanks for the beneficence of nature's gods. Relief from sickness, hunger, and other hardships rather than a glorious afterlife enticed most people.

It would be a mistake to regard early nineteenth-century Japan as a nation of grim-faced drones. The work ethic was not at all incompatible with a penchant for play and release from routine obligations. Despite all the injunctions to hard work and frugality Tokugawa society offered many opportunities for indulgence and free spending. Village festivals were usually free and unrestrained affairs, well lubricated with sake and sometimes marked by sexual license. Town merchants and samurai were not at all reluctant to frequent the "gay quarters" of the towns and cities, in search of wine, women, and song. Just because people were diligent did not mean they had to be abstemious. Enjoyment was not to be repressed, a notion associated with traditional American attitudes toward work and achievement, but rather to be put in its proper place. The pursuit of pleasure, sexual and otherwise, was regarded as natural and inevitable, to be condemned only when it threatened to put diligence and frugality behind it. Thus it was possible, as one recent observer has noted, for the Japanese to be Protestant by day and Mediterranean by night, an enviable cultural compromise.[14]

Insularity and Provinciality

To a degree unusual in most literate societies the Japanese were cut off from contacts with outside peoples. A formidable maritime barrier made it difficult for Japan to make easy contact with its continental neighbors Korea and China. The Straits of Tsushima separated northern Kyushu from the tip of Korea by a distance of 115 miles, about five times the width of the English Channel, and Korea itself placed a considerable land barrier between Japan and China, traditionally the center and spawning ground of East Asian civilization. This maritime barrier was not insurmountable for trading and merchant sailing vessels but it was sufficient to protect Japan from outside invasion. Indeed, save for two abortive invasions by Mongol armadas in the late thirteenth century no foreign power had ever attempted establishing its authority on Japanese soil. No foreign monarch had ever ruled Japan as Norman kings ruled England or Mongol and Manchu emperors ruled China. Nor, except for an influx of Koreans and Chinese in the fifth, sixth, and seventh centuries, had Japan ever known massive immigration by alien peoples. The only ethnically alien peoples in Japan were the Ainu, a Caucasoid group that may have migrated from Siberia in prehistoric times. By the early nineteenth century, however, they lived segregated from the main centers of Japanese population on the cold and then remote northern island of Hokkaido (then called Ezo).

·The lack of major migrations or outside invasions in the millenia before 1800 kept Japan free of many of the religious, linguistic, and ethnic differences that historically have troubled its Asian neighbors. The Japanese people, by and large, shared a common racial heritage, spoke the same language, and worshipped the same gods. There was no conflict between religions, as with Hindu and Moslem in India, no mix of ethnic groups and peoples as in the Indonesian archipelago, no sharp differences in dialect as between Cantonese and Mandarin in China. In contrast to these multicultural societies with widely variant local traditions Japan was monocultural, marked by a highly homogeneous population and a relatively even distribution of culture traits throughout the islands. The country's physical boundaries were also unambiguous, defined by its coastline. Together with cultural homogeneity, this made it easy for the Japanese to distinguish who was Japanese and who was not.

The insularity of the Japanese was further heightened by a deliberate policy of the Tokugawa dynasty to shut off contacts with the outside world. In the early seventeenth century the first Tokugawa rulers had adopted a "closed country" policy designed to quarantine the islands from foreign influences, especially from contact with the Europeans, who had first found their way to Japan in the 1540s. Ironically, the Japanese, then in an expansive phase, at first welcomed the "southern barbarians." Feudal lords (*daimyō*) in the western part of Japan had cultivated contacts with the Portuguese and the Spanish, whose ships brought highly coveted firearms and a profitable trade. A number of these lords had even accepted the foreigners' religion, Catholicism, in a canny effort to monopolize trade with them. But the influx of the "southern barbarians," particularly zealous missionaries who made large numbers of converts, began to excite suspicion and distrust. When the Protestant English and Dutch arrived on the scene at the turn of the seventeenth century they suggested to the leaders of the newly established Tokugawa regime that the Spanish conquest of the Philippines was a true measure of the intention of the Catholic powers. From the first decade of the seventeenth century the Tokugawa slowly began to cut off contact with the Europeans, first expelling the missionaries, then persecuting native converts, and finally refusing Spanish and Portuguese ships entry to Japanese ports.

The seclusion policy took final form in the late 1630s following the Shimabara rebellion in western Kyushu in 1637. The rising, which began as a peasant disorder, enjoyed the support of a local Christian daimyo and it was rumored that the rebels also got help from the Europeans. As a result, after suppressing the rebellion the Tokugawa regime placed restrictions on the volume of foreign trade and put foreign merchants under the rigid scrutiny of Tokugawa officials. The only foreign traders allowed into the country were the Dutch and Chinese, who were confined to the remote Western port of Nagasaki. At the same time, laws were promulgated to prevent Japanese from traveling abroad, for fear they might have contact with sinister foreign influences there. No one was allowed to leave the country without the consent of the government officials, and those who left without it were allowed to return only under pain of death. Even in 1800 the original defensive and political purpose behind the closed-country policy still remained fresh in memory and was also defended on the grounds that foreign trade drained the country of its basic wealth in exchange for useless luxuries. It remained an ancestral policy of the Tokugawa dynasty, by and large unquestioned by any but a handful of foreigners and a few Japanese scholars.

Despite the physical quarantine the Japanese had come to realize the utility of some aspects of Western civilization, especially its technical achievements. From the early eighteenth century when the government lifted the ban on the import of nonreligious books there emerged a small group known as "Dutch scholars" (*rangakusha*), who studied Western astronomy, medicine, mathematics, botany, and other practical sciences from Dutch books brought into Nagasaki. For the most part their studies were remote from the mainstream of intellectual life and they remained a narrow coterie with little social influence, occupying roughly the same position as Egyptologists or Buddhologists in our own society. Most of them had no interest or admiration for Western social and political institutions or for Western values, which seemed bizarre, repellent, and in flagrant violation of common sense and normal ethics. Like most educated Japanese, the Dutch scholars dismissed the Westerners as "barbarians" beyond the pale of morality and civilization, and regarded their own culture as superior to that of the West.

The blithe assumption of Japanese superiority was more difficult to sustain when the Japanese looked at China, the other major civilization with which they had contact. Much of Japanese civilization was Chinese in origin. Their writing system used Chinese characters; many aspects of their material culture, from kimono to chopsticks, had come from China; and so had Buddhism, Indian in origin but modified in China before its influx into Japan. The same was unequivocally true of Chinese Confucianism, the dominant intellectual influence on Japanese attitudes on society and morality. The Confucian classics were written in Chinese, as were Japanese commentaries on them. They referred to events in Chinese history and they made allusions to China's cultural heroes such as Yao and Shun, mythical founders of the Chinese state. The founders of the Confucian tradition, Confucius and Mencius, as well as its major interpreters, Chu Hsi and Wang Yang-ming, were also Chinese.

The way in which educated Japanese dealt with Confucianism reveals the strength of their sense of cultural identity. To be sure, some Japanese Confucian scholars accepted the Chinese evaluation of the world, namely that Chinese wisdom and morality, embodied in the Confucian tradition, were the apex of civilization and that the rest of the world consisted of "barbarians" who might be brought within its fold. Hayashi Razan, who played a central role in securing official Tokugawa patronage for Confucianism in the seventeenth century, argued that Japan was founded by refugees from the court of Chou-dynasty China, and even the less orthodox Confucianist Ogyū Sorai was wont to refer to himself as a "stupid Eastern barbarian." But on the whole this kind of Confucian fundamentalism was rare and idiosyncratic by the late eighteenth century. Far more typical were those who ascribed moral superiority to Japanese civilization despite its heavy dependence on China and on Confucius. Some did this by detaching Confucianism from its Chinese base and others by rejecting Confucianism and Chinese civilization completely.

The first approach was that of eclecticism, represented by the seventeenth century Confucian, Yamazaki Anzai, who combined an intense commitment to "the way of Confucius" with a firm belief in a "Japanese Way." When some of his students asked him what he would do if China attacked Japan "with Confucius as general and Mencius as lieutenant-general," he replied without hesitation that he would put on his armor, take up a spear, and capture the two sages for the sake of Japan, for this is what Confucius taught one to do.[15] What he was really saying was that the truth Confucius taught was independent of the country of its source and that being a universal truth it was as much Japanese as Chinese. Some, however, went further and suggested that Confucianism worked even better in Japan than in China. Matsudaira Sadanobu, a Tokugawa official who sought to ban all points of view but the Chu Hsi version of Confucianism, once remarked, "Even in the days of Yao and Shun (the mythical founders of the Chinese state) and the three ancient dynasties, I doubt if China can be compared with Japan in the unsurpassed harmoniousness and benevolence of government."[16] If such an orthodox Confucian could make such a pronouncement it is clear that a sense of Japanese moral superiority ran strong and ran deep indeed.

An even more extreme expression of this strong cultural provinciality was to be found in the development of nativism, an eighteenth-century reaction to the heavy influence of Confucian thought. Nativist thinkers tried to discover an authentic and superior Japanese Way that predated the influx of ideas and institutions from China. They drew their evidence from a body of myth, legend, and semilegendary history set down in the *Kojiki* ("Record of Ancient Matters") and the *Nihongi* ("Chronicle of Japan"), works that described Japan before the first introduction of Chinese civilization in the seventh century. This body of literature became the basis for *kokugaku* or the "school of national learning" in the eighteenth century. Kokugaku thinkers like Motoori Norinaga emphasized the spontaneous, emotional, and aesthetic sensitivity of the Japanese Way in contrast to the hard, rational moralism of the Confucianism.

At the same time, Motoori and other nativists stressed the notion of the Japanese as a kind of chosen people, whose country was founded by the Sun Goddess (Amaterasu) and enjoyed the special blessing and protection of the gods (*kami*). They pointed out that in contrast to China, where one dynasty succeeded another, Japan had been ruled by one Imperial family, "one line unbroken from time immemorial," since its founding. For nativist thinkers this was the strongest proof of the superiority of the Japanese Way. Nativist thought reached perhaps its most extreme expression in Hirata Atsutane, who declared in no uncertain terms, "Our country, as a special mark of favor from the heavenly gods, was begotten by them, and there is thus so immense a difference between Japan and all other countries of the world as to defy comparison."

In sum, Japan's insularity and unfamiliarity with alien ways combined with a strong sense of Japan's uniqueness or sacredness gave many educated Japanese a highly provincial view of the outside world. It gave them a strong and sharply defined sense of cultural identity. But paradoxically this provinciality in the long run proved a greater asset than the spongelike cosmopolitanism of the Chinese, who took long to realize that their civilization was not so universally valid as they might think. Though most Japanese might believe in the superiority of Japanese spirit they were also aware that there were other peoples and cultures in the outside world more powerful than they. Living on an island exposed at every point to the sea, they realized that they could not retreat into a vast continental interior, like the Chinese, to escape a seaborne threat. Their sense of cultural identity and moral superiority was always tempered by a strong sense of vulnerability.

2

The Political Heritage

In many ways Japan, with her well-defined natural boundaries and her homogeneous culture, might seem to be a "natural nation," but modern nations, like heroes, are made not born. Each one is the product of conscious decisions to build a political community where none existed before. People owe their loyalty to the modern nation state not simply because they share a common language or a common tradition with their fellow nationals, but because they believe that the nation will safeguard their personal welfare and security. In 1800 many Japanese may have had a common sense of cultural identity but few had a sense of common interest or common dependence as a nation. Authority and allegiance were fragmented. There was no culturewide political authority able to guarantee the public order, nor any political center to which all Japanese gave their undivided political loyalty. Japan remained a geographical expression rather than a political one—and in this sense was not a nation.

Emperor and Shogun

The fragmentation of political loyalties reflected the peculiar character of the Tokugawa political order. At the very highest level, political leadership was divided between two authorities bound together in a symbiotic relationship that prevented either from monopolizing the allegiance of the Japanese people. One was the emperor (*tennō*), the semidivine civil monarch who lived remote and isolated at the old imperial capital at Kyoto. The other was the *shōgun,* or military monarch, based in the capital at Edo (later Tokyo). The shogun served as the feudal suzerain of the two hundred fifty or so daimyo who occupied most of the country.

The imperial institution had been defunct as an effective governmental force for centuries. The emperor had been the pawn first of ambitious factions of court aristocrats (*kuge*) and later of great feudal barons. In 1800 he served mainly a symbolic religious function. As lineal descendant and chief priest of Amaterasu, the putative founder of the country, he provided a link between the world of the divine and the human world. His most significant political role was to legitimize the de facto power of the shogun, who as chief feudal lord of the realm more clearly controlled the country. In theory, the shogun was the deputy of the emperor's authority, exercising the sovereign powers that the emperor had long since lost. In fact, the shogun was the patron of the emperor, for the Tokugawa family had in the early seventeenth century granted the imperial family landed income to rescue it from poverty and enable it to maintain a court and aristocratic retinue. Most men realized the duties of the emperor did not involve political leadership. Even kokugaku thinkers, who most vehemently touted the imperial institution as embodiment of Japan's unique virtues, never challenged the authority of the shogun for they recognized that it was the feudal authorities who had the power to keep order, promulgate law, and control society. For most of the people the emperor remained remote, known mainly through literature and drama, never as a close political presence.

Despite his considerable legal powers, the shogun was equally handicapped as a potential focus for national political allegiance. The political system over which he presided was a highly fragmented and divided one. Just as the emperor delegated authority to the shogun, so the shogun in turn left many basic functions of government to the local daimyo. The power to raise taxes, issue laws, raise military forces, and dispense justice, which in western Europe was concentrated in the hands of kings and parliaments, were widely dispersed among the daimyo domains (*han*). The shogun had no monopoly of state power as the territorial monarchs of early modern Europe did.

This fragmentation of power resulted from the way in which the Tokugawa dynasty originally came to power. In 1600, after nearly two centuries of chronic feudal disorder and local warfare, Toku-

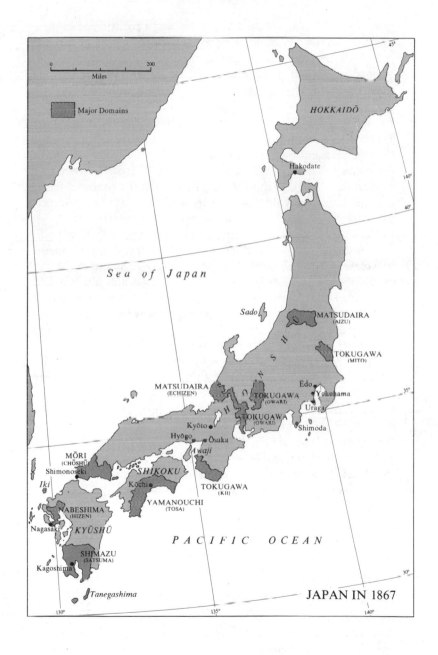

0   200
Miles

Major Domains

HOKKAIDŌ

Hakodate

Sea of Japan

Sado

MATSUDAIRA
(AIZU)

TOKUGAWA
(MITO)

MATSUDAIRA
(ECHIZEN)

Edo

Yokohama

TOKUGAWA
(OWARI)

Uraga

TOKUGAWA
(OWARI)

Kyōto

Shimoda

Hyōgo

Ōsaka

Awaji

MŌRI
(CHŌSHŪ)

Shimonoseki

SHIKOKU

Iki

Kōchi

TOKUGAWA
(KII)

NABESHIMA
(HIZEN)

YAMANOUCHI
(TOSA)

Nagasaki

KYŪSHŪ

PACIFIC   OCEAN

SHIMAZU
(SATSUMA)

Kagoshima

Tanegashima

JAPAN IN 1867

gawa Ieyasu, founder of the dynasty, had led a coalition of daimyo
to victory over a rival coalition at the battle of Sekigahara. Three
years later, to crown his military triumph, Ieyasu assumed the title
of shogun, an office first conferred by the emperor on a successful
warrior leader in the late twelfth century. In effect, it gave Ieyasu
the mandate to bring the local daimyo under his political control.
But Ieyasu's military and political triumphs had not meant the destruction of daimyo power. The ranks of their samurai retainers had
been thinned, but they had not been disarmed. Moreover, save for a
few of the losers at Sekigahara, the daimyo still had effective control
of local territorial domains they had built up in the course of feudal
warfare. Individually the daimyo were weak vis-à-vis the preponderant power of Ieyasu, who controlled perhaps a quarter of the
country's landed wealth, but collectively they were a force to be
reckoned with. In consolidating their position Ieyasu and his successors chose not to centralize further but merely to minimize the
possibility of a rebellion by the daimyo, either as individuals or as a
coalition. The Tokugawa regime, which remained intact in its broadest outline in 1800, was therefore largely negative in intent, leaving
the local domains intact but checking and emasculating their power
as much as possible. The resulting political order was an uneasy
compromise between feudal fragmentation and central unification.

Despite the aspirations of the Tokugawa to rule the whole country,
the political loyalties of most people bound them to local entities,
the domain and perhaps the village, rather than central authorities
such as the shogun or emperor. Although people spoke of Japan as
"our country" (*wagakuni*), "the realm" (*tenka*), "the land of the
gods" (*shinshū*), or some other abstract term, they knew that their
social and economic welfare ultimately depended on the domain
(*kuni*) and its government (*kokka*). It was only with the advent of a
massive outside threat, the West, that people began to think of either
the shogun or the emperor as a bulwark and protector of the whole
people against foreign invasion and loss of independence.

The Bakuhan System

The Tokugawa political system is usually known as the *bakuhan*
system, linking the *bakufu,* the government of the shogun, and the
han, the domains of the local daimyo. In origin, its central mechanisms were feudal in character, since Ieyasu consolidated his power by

applying to the whole country the same practices he had used as a local daimyo to govern and check his own band of vassals. Throughout the Tokugawa period, the shogun exercised power over the daimyo as a feudal suzerain. All the daimyo, whatever their size or origin, were treated as the personal vassals of the shogun, bound to him by an oath of personal allegiance that was renewed each time a new shogun was installed. When the heirs of daimyo took office, they likewise were obliged to go through a kind of investiture ceremony in the shogun's presence. In return for their pledges of loyalty, the daimyo held their domains as fiefs from the shogun, even though their ancestors might have won them in battle centuries before. In practice, of course, this feudal contract between shogun and daimyo was largely pro forma, since the shogun normally acceded to whatever heir the daimyo family proposed as a legitimate heir. Nonetheless the shogun had considerable legal powers over the daimyo as the result of this feudal tie.

The daimyo were subject to whole series of regulations designed to prevent them from expanding their power at the shogun's expense or plotting against his interests. The daimyo were enjoined to keep surveillance on one another's domains, they were allowed to maintain only a certain number of samurai retainers, they had to request permission from the bakufu in order to repair their castles, they had to receive permission for marriages with other daimyo families, and so forth. All these restrictions reflected a fundamental suspicion of the latent power of the daimyo. At the same time the sanction for disobedience to the shogun's regulations was the shogun's right as feudal lord to transfer a daimyo from a large domain to a smaller, to reduce a daimyo's domain in size, or to confiscate a daimyo's lands altogether. By the early nineteenth century punitive transfers or confiscations were rarer than they had been in the turbulent half-century following the battle of Sekigahara, but this reflected not so much a weakening of the shogun's powers as the growing political docility and passiveness of the daimyo.

In part the political docility was due to the passage of generations, which laid ancient antagonisms to rest. It was also fostered by the *sankin-kōtai* or alternate attendance system instituted by Ieyasu in the early 1600s. At first by custom and then by law all the daimyo were required to spend half their time in Edo and to leave their families as well as a specified number of domain officials, retainers, and guards there at all times. This practice probably grew out of the use of hostages by many daimyo in order to control their powerful vassals in the age of feudal disorder. It also rested on the feeling that the daimyo as vassals of the shogun should pay personal attendance on him. In the long run the sankin-kōtai system helped to convert the daimyo from fractious provincial warlords into free-spending courtiers of the shogun, cut off from concern for the administration of their own domains and involved in the protocol and pleasures of life at Edo. Equally important, the sankin-kōtai system also drained much of the financial resources of the daimyo's domain into non-military expenditure. The need to maintain a large mansion at Edo, the costs of an elegant progress to and from the capital every other year, and the rising levels of daimyo luxury spurred by life in the great city kept the daimyo financially off balance.

The daimyo were not a unified group by any means. The size of their domains varied widely and so did their political interests and their influence with the bakufu. Since the seventeenth century the daimyo had been divided into three main groups: the *fudai* or vassal daimyo, the *shimpan* or collateral daimyo, and the *tozama* or allied daimyo. This division reflected not wealth, strength, or prestige of the individual daimyo but rather the bakufu's view of his political reliability. The fudai daimyo were most closely identified with the interests of the shogun and the Tokugawa dynasty. They sprang from families originally part of the Tokugawa's vassal band or families that had been made daimyo by Ieyasu and his successors. Their territories frequently abutted bakufu lands, protecting their flanks militarily, and most of the bakufu's top officials were drawn from their ranks. While retaining a strong sense of their own domain interests, the fudai daimyo tended to be the most loyal supporters of the bakufu. Indeed, as one historian has pointed out, they were more Tokugawa than the Tokugawa themselves.

The tozama daimyo, by contrast, were kept at arm's length by the bakufu. Most of the tozama houses were descended from daimyo allies of Ieyasu who were too strong to be considered his direct vassals or who submitted to his suzerainty only after the battle of Sekigahara. They usually controlled relatively larger domains than the fudai. In 1867, for example, the average size of a tozama domain was 87,000 koku of rice while the average size of a fudai domain was 42,000 koku, or about half as large. Because they were large, and less the creatures of the Tokugawa dynasty, the tozama daimyo were not permitted to participate in the administration of the bakufu or occupy any high posts in it. Though occasionally a "friendly" tozama daimyo would be used to guard some strategic location or act as a buffer to bakufu territory most of the tozama domains were located on the periphery of the archipelago, at a distance from the capital and less easily able to mount an attack on it.

The shimpan daimyo occupied a position somewhere between the fudai and the tozama in terms of their political influence. All the shimpan daimyo houses were newly created by the Tokugawa. In effect there were branch families of the Tokugawa dynasty, given domains confiscated from other daimyo in order to ensure successors to the main branch or to placate those children of the early shoguns who did not inherit the office. The shimpan daimyo were formally excluded from office in the bakufu, but since they were related to the incumbent shogun they often had much informal influence. The opinions of the shimpan daimyo, particularly the older and more prestigious houses such as Mito, Kii, and Hitotsubashi, carried great weight in making bakufu policy.

On the whole, the division of administrative power between shogun and daimyo coupled with the divided interests of the daimyo themselves meant that the bakuhan system was not well geared to concerted action. Its parts were stronger than the whole. At the same time, in many domains, especially the larger tozama domains, residual feelings of hostility or resentment toward the Tokugawa family remained. How widespread they were is unclear but there is no question domain interest was often a more powerful motive behind the actions of daimyo or domain officials than concern for the interest of the whole realm. Sectionalism, both administrative and psychological, was continually a factor in Tokugawa politics.

The Web of Government

With such a clutter of local jurisdictions and bailiwicks one might think that government in late Tokugawa Japan was in a state of unimaginable confusion. But paradoxically, political fragmentation did not weaken the power of government. Rather it enabled political authority to reach far deeper into the population and far closer to daily life than in most premodern societies. Despite its outwardly feudal structure Japan was in many respects a model bureaucratic state, a situation that was to stand it in good stead when it began to modernize. The territories of most daimyo were small enough that every village and every peasant lived within two or three days' journey from the castle town. The same was true of Tokugawa lands that lay in the immediate hinterland of Edo. Government offices were stacked high with records and documents of every conceivable kind, from land surveys to population registers, which recorded the existence of most of the population in some way or other. (In the domain of Nambu, a horse breeding area, even the pregnancies and deaths of horses were recorded.) Checkpoints (*sekisho*) were set up along all the main highways to scrutinize the comings and goings of travelers, and peasants had to carry permits when they went on pilgrimages to distant temples or shrines. "Few people in pre-modern times have lived under such a heavy load of official regulation and supervision," comments the historian John W. Hall. "The Tokugawa Japanese lived out his life with his head constantly bowed to higher authority."[1]

The institutions of government were relatively uniform throughout the country. The daimyo domains were, on the whole, small-scale reproductions of the bakufu. This resulted partly from the common origin of both and partly from bakufu pressures on daimyo to model their domain administration on bakufu practice. The same uniformity was true of political leadership. For the most part, political leadership was conciliar and oligarchic rather than personal and charismatic. Neither the daimyo nor the shogun normally made major political decisions by themselves, but instead relied on small groups of advisory officials whose policies they sanctioned and legitimized. In the bakufu, this role was played by the *rōjū* (council of elders), a body made up of middling-size fudai daimyo, informally dominated by a chief elder (*rōjū shūseki*). In the domains it was played by the domain elders (*karō*), recruited from the highest ranks of the daimyo's retainers. This conciliar style of leadership protected the bakufu (and the domains as well) against the possibility of a weak or incompetent shogun, of whom there were not a few after the first century of Tokugawa rule.

The politics of the bakufu, like those of the domains, tended to be court politics: cliquish, secretive, and resting on personal influence and persuasiveness. In the bakufu, for example, the prestige and the power of the rōjū, especially the rōjū-shūseki, to control bakufu finances, promote and demote lower officials, and make critical policy decisions enabled them to build up personal cliques and factions resting on friendship, patronage, or marriage. Astute clique leaders gathered round them able and reliable cohorts and secured their influence by organizing coalitions of backers among the other fudai daimyo, the shimpan houses, and even the shogun's harem. Although this style of politics was highly undemocratic, the struggles of cliques to control the council of elders did provide a turnover in leadership. It gave some flexibility to bakufu policies and allowed the regime to adapt to changing circumstances. The same was true of domain government, where similar cliques were common.

The day-to-day business of government, both for the bakufu and the domains, was carried on by a body of civil officials recruited from the shogun's petty liege vassals (*hatamoto* and *gokenin*) or by the samurai retainers of the daimyo. It was they who collected taxes, managed finances, settled civil disputes, enforced criminal laws, managed economic enterprises, maintained roads and military forti-fications, and so forth.

The most important of these functions was the collection of taxes, which the daimyo used to support their retainers and maintain their aristocratic style of life. The main tax was levied on land and was collected in rice, which was the staple crop of the peasantry, the basic source of wealth in the country, and the main standard of value for the ruling class. The size of domains, the ranks of retainers, and the salaries of officials were all reckoned in so many koku of rice. The machinery for collecting taxes was small, efficient, and econom-ical. Instead of taxing individual farmers or households the shogun and daimyo levied from each village a regular quota of tax rice and let the villagers decide among themselves how much each household should pay. Local samurai intendants (*daikan*) received the taxes and as long as the proper total quota was delivered the authorities in Edo or the castle town were unconcerned with how it was assembled. The local intendant usually worked with a small staff of clerks, recorders, and guards drawn from the lower samurai ranks and paid for their services. This system avoided the abuses of tax-farming common in other Asian countries like China and India, where taxes were collected not by paid officials but private individuals or con-tractors, who made personal profit by squeezing as much as possible from the peasants and forwarding as little as possible to the govern-ment. Save for a small amount subtracted for administrative costs nearly all of the taxes reached bakufu or domain treasuries. The result was not only a high level of honesty in government but also a very high effective tax rate, perhaps 25 to 30 percent of the harvest by 1800.

Alongside the hierarchy of civil officials was a military hierarchy.

Both bakufu and domain continued to rely on their samurai vassal band for military forces. The shogun maintained guard forces made up of the hatamoto and gokenin and also required each daimyo to maintain a military force and an arsenal of weapons. In theory, at least, the shogun could raise a feudal levy of several hundred thousand in time of emergency. In fact, however, since the two centuries before 1800 were unbroken by a major war, these military forces really served as a kind of constabulary. The liege vassals stood guard at the shogun's castles or manned small garrisons at key strategic points. The forces of the large fudai daimyo and the shimpan daimyo performed a vestigial function of protecting the outer perimeters of the Tokugawa domain against attacks from domestic rivals. But since attacks never came, membership in the guard forces was by 1800 mostly a matter of hereditary prestige, with little relation to military skill or prowess. Rutherford Alcock, first English minister to Japan, noted in the 1850s that the guard houses throughout Edo were "generally occupied by boys or superannuated old men, who spend their whole time squatting on their knees and heels and either dozing or smoking the pipe of apathetic idleness."[2]

Generally speaking, the processes of government were heavily bound by tradition and precedent. Despite the thoroughness and efficiency of the administration a meticulous concern for privilege, protocol, and prerogative prevailed among the highest officials of both bakufu and domain. Most political leaders saw themselves as stewards of ancestral traditions stretching back to the days of Ieyasu. One eighteenth-century daimyo, for example, enjoined his officials that administration should "rest upon the respectful adherence to the laws of the previous generation and to their elaboration."[3] Policies might change, he said, and old usages might no longer fit new situations, but still every effort should be bent that "basic laws and important precedents shall not be put aside." Given the prevalence of this kind of attitude, the majority of officials tended to be rather conservative, unwilling to make major changes and inclined to garb them in the guise of tradition when they did.

The Samurai Elite

Apart from the daimyo, the ruling class in late Tokugawa Japan was the samurai class, from whom most officials and military officers were recruited. In medieval times the samurai had been feudal warriors, living on landed fiefs and answering the summons of their lords in time of war. By 1800, however, the samurai were no more swashbuckling fighters than their lords were battle-hardened generals. Ever since the end of the sixteenth century, most samurai had been moved out of the countryside and into the castletowns of their daimyo. In the process most had been "de-fiefed." Instead of living off income from land granted to them by their lords they were given annual stipends of rice, the size of which indicated their rank. As the fires of feudal warfare faded to ashes most daimyo no longer needed their samurai retainers as fighters, but since the daimyo were still obliged to support their retainers, they found other uses for them in jobs as officials.

The samurai class, though a privileged group set off by birth and law from the rest of the population, was neither a petty aristocracy nor a landed gentry class. It was a class of hereditary officials, relatively large in size. If one includes their families, the samurai class amounted to about 6 percent of the population, a proportion very much larger than any European aristocracy and larger even than the nonaristocratic scholar-official class in China. The range of its members' wealth and prestige was wide, stretching from the great retainers of the shogun and the large daimyo, who often enjoyed incomes as large as those of small daimyo, to country samurai (*gōshi*) or groundling footsoldiers (*ashigaru*), whose incomes were barely sufficient to sustain their families. In some domains high-ranking samurai families had retainers or rear-vassals (*baishin*) of their own, adding further complexity to the character of the class. In many cases the social distance between the lower samurai ranks and the upper was as great as it was between lower samurai and commoners. (In the domain of Nakatsu groundling footsoldiers, when they met a high ranking retainer, were required to prostrate themselves on the ground, and children of lower samurai families used different and less elegant language from that of upper samurai children.)

Historians are not agreed on the controversial issue of where the breaks between upper, middle, and lower samurai should be made in terms of rank and income. The important thing to note is that members of the class were aware that such distinctions existed and that they signified enormous differences in wealth, political influence, access to office, opportunities for education, and feelings of self-respect. The upper samurai were usually a tiny minority, a handful of families in most domains. It was they who usually served as domain elders, it was they who lived in splendid residences at the center of the castle town, and it was their sons and daughters who intermarried with the daimyo's offspring. By contrast, the lower samurai, far and away in the majority, lived in crowded dwellings on the edge of the samurai quarters, often with little or no contact with the daimyo, serving as petty guards, runners, messengers, or clerks. Somewhere in between lay the middle ranks who had the right of audience with their lord and who occupied posts as officers in the daimyo's guard (*bangata*), as magistrates in the central domain administrative offices, or as local or district intendants.

Although a samurai's rank was hereditary, passed on from father to son, there were some opportunities for mobility within the samurai -class. Normally office was linked to rank, with the higher posts reserved for the upper and middle samurai. But within this frame-work there was some room for competition and the recruitment of talent. Usually there were more samurai in a particular rank than offices to fill, a circumstance which allowed for a certain amount of selectivity in recruiting. Moreover, if individual samurai showed special talent they could often work their way a step or two beyond the offices normally open to them. Such a rise on the ladder of pre-ferment meant a rise in income, since extra stipends (*tashidaka*) went with certain offices. Sometimes it also meant temporary promotion to higher rank, for the individual samurai if not for his family. Con-sequently, although the samurai class never became a meritocracy like the Chinese scholar-official class or the modern civil servant, there were opportunities for a person with special skills or talent to rise in the world.

The ethos of the samurai, sometimes called "the way of the war-rior" (*bushidō*) or "the way of the samurai" (*shidō*), reflected the dual character of the class. On the one hand, the original concept of the samurai as a fighter, constantly faced with prospect of death on the battlefield in the service of the lord, persisted into Tokugawa times. This aspect of bushidō celebrated all the virtues the samurai had needed in medieval times—courage, physical prowess, magna-nimity toward subordinates, and willingness to give one's life for one's leader. Moral tracts for samurai, such as the *Hagakure*, con-tinued to call upon the samurai to "educate themselves for death." This older conception combined with, and sometimes competed with, a newer concept of the samurai as a kind of Confucian gentle-man, a "man of virtue" whose moral qualities and character justified his paramount position in society. This side of bushidō stressed the pacific virtues—literacy, industry, fortitude, prudence, and austerity needed by most samurai to survive in their role as officials. It stressed public service rather than mere military service and called on the samurai to set a moral example for the commoners. The older ideology of violence was combined with a newer ideology of merit.

As many have pointed out, the samurai ethic was a tremendous asset for mid-nineteenth-century Japan since it meant that the ruling class was not only keenly sensitive to military threat, but was also equipped with a strong sense of public service. Yet at the time it was also the source of some self-questioning. It was hard for most samurai to be either fighters or moral exemplars for the masses in any complete sense. Samurai were rarely if ever called upon to display the virtues of fearlessness and bravery in battle enjoined by the education for death. The military skills they acquired—archery, swordsmanship, and the like—were more a sport or accomplishment than skills needed for survival. The majority of samurai, as the historian Thomas Smith has pointed out, lived "aimless and routine lives"[4] punctuated only by a trip to Edo in the daimyo's van or by pompous official ceremonies. This bothered many samurai who saw the quiet and routine life of the castle towns as a sign of samurai decadence, a falling away from their authentic and original role. As one writer noted in the late eighteenth century, most samurai had lost the "true martial spirit" and in time of crisis "seven or eight out of ten would be as weak as women and their morale as mean as merchants."[5]

The notion that the samurai was a man of virtue especially qualified for his position in society by his moral character likewise seemed out of kilter with social reality. It was clear that in practice the highest positions of power and authority went not to the virtuous and the talented but to the well-born. The domain elders, the daimyo, the shogun were often as not people of threadbare morality and no particular capacities. By 1800 complaints that the highest leaders of the land were weak, ignorant, stupid, ostentatious, self-indulgent, extravagant, and arrogant were common among samurai writers and thinkers. Like those who complained that the samurai had lost their will to fight, they felt that the most able and virtuous people in society were not accorded the influence they should be. This loss of confidence in the legitimacy of hereditary leadership doubtless reflected a serious weakness in Tokugawa society, the existence of a vague and not always articulate uneasiness over the discrepancy between the samurai's ideal self-image and actual condition.

Still, such doubts about their society probably were not sufficient to bring most samurai to the point of rebellion, as some historians have suggested. In the final analysis most samurai realized their dependence on the bakuhan system and its leaders for both income and status. Unlike the rebellious gentry in seventeenth-century England they were cut off from the land, and unlike the restive bourgeosie of eighteenth-century France they were an established class enjoying hereditary privilege. Although discontent might move a minority of them to a "revolutionary rage" (to use Professor Harootunian's phrase),[6] the majority accepted their lot in life, consoled by family pride, a sense of pedigree, and their outward badge of status. Far from wanting to overthrow the bakuhan system, even those samurai who criticized their society wanted it to live up to its stated ideals. They were not future-oriented radicals but backward-looking fundamentalists.

3

Economic and
Social Change

By modern standards the economy of late Tokugawa Japan, like
any preindustrial country, was backward and underdeveloped.
By the standards of the time it was prosperous and thriving. In 1796
C. P. Thunberg, a doctor stationed at the Dutch trading post in
Nagasaki who had seen a good bit of the world, was so impressed
that he wrote, "Of all the countries that inhabit the three largest
parts of the globe, the Japanese deserve to rank the first, and to be
compared with the Europeans."[1] Many economics historians today
agree. They argue that preindustrial economic growth, sometimes
called a commercial revolution, produced during the Tokugawa
period institutions and attitudes that served to facilitate the task of
building a modern economy rapidly once Japan imported modern
technology and the factory system. In 1800 the economy was
already in a state of gestation or potential change which needed only
an outside trigger to produce full-blown modern economic growth.
At the same time the social dislocations resulting from economic
change made easier the emergence of a new group of political leaders dedicated to economic innovation and industrialization.

The Commercial Revolution

Officials in Tokugawa Japan were not as assiduous as their great-great-grandchildren in assembling economic statistics, so the actual scale of economic growth during Tokugawa times is hard to measure with any precision. Population censuses, land registers, and tax records, however, do indicate that both population and agricultural production, two basic indices of growth in premodern economies, greatly increased between 1600 and 1800. According to one estimate the population grew from around 18 million in 1590 to around 25 million in 1804, and the amount of land under cultivation from around 1,635,000 *chō* (one *chō* equals 2.45 acres) in the early 1600s to around 3,050,000 chō by the early 1800s. Equally remarkable was the growth of great urban centers, such as Edo and Osaka, each a metropolis by contemporary world standards. In the 1780s Edo, a small castle town and fishing harbor when Ieyasu arrived there in 1590, had achieved a population of around 1.3 million, making it one of the largest cities in the world. To be sure, economic, demographic, and urban growth was not steady. The greatest spurt of development came in the seventeenth century. From the 1720s there set in a period of relative slowdown and stability punctuated by occasional fluctuations. Some have suggested that this early eighteenth-century slowdown represented the onset of stagnation, but it is clear that growth of agriculture and other production continued, albeit at a slower rate than before.

Economic development was doubtless promoted by changing political conditions and institutions after 1600. For one thing, the establishment of peace and security brought to an end the destructive warfare that had taken lives and destroyed property before the Tokugawa unification. Much of the economic growth during the seventeenth century represented a recovery from the conditions of feudal warfare. Unification of the country also ended local hindrances to trade such as tariff barriers set up on main highways by local daimyo to exact taxes on goods traveling through their domains. The Tokugawa bakufu abolished these internal tax barriers and created the institutional infrastructure for the development of a national market. They attempted to replace a welter of local weights and measures with units standard throughout the country; they created a countrywide currency; they promoted the construction of highways that linked the remotest extremities of the islands to the shogun's capital at Edo. This economic national unification, which took place despite the lack of a similar political one, meant that merchants and goods could travel from one part of Japan to another in relative security and that business transactions could be carried on under relatively uniform conditions in all parts of the country. These institutional changes forged the ligatures of a national economy and provided stimulus to economic growth as well.

Perhaps the most positive stimulus to the growth of trade was the urbanization of the samurai class. The movement of the samurai into castle towns produced new kinds of economic demand. Deprived of landed fiefs and no longer able to live on their own, the nonproductive samurai had to be provided with the food, clothing, and other goods in earlier ages supplied from their own land or peasants. The developing castle towns required supplies from hinterlands producing economic surpluses, and they also had to develop local routes and marketing mechanisms to bring them to town.

What happened locally in the domains happened on a countrywide scale with the institution of the sankin-kōtai system. The daimyo, who were obliged to maintain residences and large staffs in Edo, were forced to increase their consumption. They also had to convert the tax revenues collected in rice on their domains into the cash they needed to pay for their expenditures at Edo. Both forces worked to stimulate the growth of an embryonic national economy revolving on the two great cities of Edo and Osaka.

At the center of the national economy was the rice trade. In terms of volume and value it was probably the most important single part of the commercial economy down to 1800. To convert tax revenues into money most daimyo were forced to market their tax rice outside their domains, where there was neither a demand for surplus rice nor anyone with sufficient capital to purchase it. From the 1620s most domains in western Japan began to send their rice to market at Osaka and those in the east to Edo. At first these marketing transactions were handled by senior retainers, but increasingly they fell into the hands of private merchants. The merchant houses involved in the rice trade soon became the merchant princes of Tokugawa Japan. The wealth they accumulated in the rice trade they used to invest in other kinds of ventures, usually of a financial sort. The most lucrative, if not the most secure, was lending money to the daimyo or the bakufu. Usually these loans took the form of advances on payments against tax rice. Often these advances, in effect long-term loans, amounted to several years' worth of rice revenue. Since interest rates usually amounted to 15 to 20 percent per year, profits were enormous. Many of the merchant princes at Osaka, and to a lesser extent in Edo, also acted as money changers, converting the silver currency of the rice market into the gold currency normally used in official transactions in Edo. They also became involved in long-distance transfer of credit through paper notes or served as deposit bankers for people with large sums.

There were other kinds of countrywide interregional trade besides the rice trade. Both Edo and Osaka, with their enormous nonproductive, nonagricultural populations, created huge markets for a wide variety of goods. Most of the supply of these goods came from the hinterland of both cities, but much came from farther away as well. Every conceivable kind of consumption good began to flow into Edo and Osaka, from vegetables and pickles to crockery and ironware. The well-known wood block prints of Hokusai and Hiroshige illustrate richly and in detail the welter of products for sale in the shops and markets of Edo, from the teeming fish market at Nihonbashi to the vast drapery showrooms of the Echigoya. This interregional trade was usually handled by wholesale merchants or jobbers specializing in one kind of good or product, such as oranges or medicine or cloth. Often these wholesalers became embryonic investors in production. Many wholesale drapiers or clothiers, for example, set up purchasing establishments in Kyoto to buy up the production of whole districts of silk weavers. Sometimes they would advance working capital or raw materials to craftsmen. The most successful, such as the Mitsui family, controlled the whole process of production and marketing from the making of cloth goods to their distribution through retail shops in Edo.

By the beginning of the nineteenth century, the economy was characterized by a great volume of trade, a national marketing network, and fairly sophisticated commercial institutions. But if the commercial revolution had created all these, it had done little to alter the traditional modes of manufacturing production. The manufacture of most common consumption goods, as well as the production of luxury products like porcelain and lacquerware, was carried on in small workshops. There were no factories in the modern sense of the word. In the 1840s there existed a workshop in Ashikaga city that assembled as many as a hundred weavers under one roof but this was the exception, not the rule. Most goods were made in small workshops, often simply a room in the home of a master craftsman who might hire apprentices or assistants but usually relied on the labor of his family. Concentration of large numbers of workers was unnecessary because most things were made with hand tools or simple machines propelled by human power rather than water, steam, or some other inanimate form of energy. Similarly, the manufacture of some goods, especially cloth, was done in agricultural off-season by peasant families. If the process was complicated, sometimes different stages in production might be done in different places. Raw cotton might be carded in the clothier-merchant's warehouse, the carded cotton spun into yarn in the house of one peasant, the yarn woven into cloth in the home of another, and the cloth dyed or finished in the home of a third. In place of the assembly line of a modern factory was a chain of small workshops, linked by the clothier-capitalist entrepreneur but basically following the pattern of cottage industry common to most preindustrial economies.

By the mid-eighteenth century the great mercantile houses of Osaka and Edo, the well-to-do bankers and moneylenders, and the large wholesale merchants had become a well-entrenched mercantile elite, more interested in security of profits than in innovation. Most of them enjoyed political protection and monopoly privileges that gave them advantages over possible competitors. Beginning in the 1720s, for example, groups of wholesale merchants began to secure charters from the bakufu establishing them as trade associations called *kabu-nakama,* with exclusive rights to carry on a particular type of trade in Edo. These associations did not act to pool funds for investment in new enterprises, like the joint-stock organizations that developed in Europe. Rather they worked to protect the security of profits by price fixing, maintaining the quality of products sold, enforcing their members' honesty, and sometimes advancing to members loans of working capital. Naturally this limited the freedom of kabu-nakama merchants to develop as independent entrepreneurs. But the advantage of membership in these monopolistic trade associations was so highly regarded that from the late eighteenth century there grew up an active market for the rights of members, or *kabu,* which were normally hereditary.

The outlook of established merchant houses tended to be prudent and cautious. The heads of merchant houses regarded their enterprises not as personal ventures but as family concerns, and they saw themselves less as entrepreneurs than as stewards of the family fortunes. A sense of obligation to forebears, reinforced by custom, made them reluctant to jeopardize or dissipate the fortunes bequeathed to them. The cautionary literature written for merchants by men like Ihara Saikaku, as well as the house constitutions of many merchants' families, naturally stressed the work ethic of diligence and frugality. More important, they placed a high premium on following family tradition. As the Mitsui family code put it simply, "Do not put your hand to any type of activity that has not been done before."[2] Consequently few of the great merchant houses were psychologically equipped to display the innovative entrepreneurship needed for industrialization. (Indeed, once industrialization began many of them sank rather quickly in importance in contrast to bold and adventurous new businessmen, less bound by the constraints of conservatism.)

At the same time, in contrast to contemporary Europe Japan was technologically backward. The economy had not experienced the technical breakthroughs that took place in eighteenth-century England. The failure to develop forms of energy alternative to human labor, such as steam or water power, and to harness such energy to the production process through the use of machinery continued to hold the economy in check. Without such technical breakthroughs, which on the whole were not much in sight in 1800 save perhaps in the work of the Dutch scholars, the Tokugawa economy lacked the fundamendal basis for an indigenous industrial revolution of the kind that transformed Europe in the early nineteenth century.

The Impact on the Countryside

If the commercial revolution did not provide the makings of an industrial revolution it did have a profound impact on the countryside, setting in motion forces of social change. At the outset of the Tokugawa period the peasantry had been regarded by the rulers as tax-producing machines whose surplus crops were to be gobbled up by those in power. Taxes were to take as much of the peasants' harvest as possible, leaving just enough for subsistence. As one of Ieyasu's closest advisors put it, "It is fit that the peasants be treated so that they have neither too much nor too little."[3] If they tried to improve their lot by keeping aside some of their crops for capital the social equilibrium would be upset. The rulers would be deprived of revenue and invidious distinctions between rich and poor in the villages would create conflict and disorder. Consequently peasants were forbidden by law to buy or sell land and taxes were usually fixed at high rates.

By the early nineteenth century, however, this exploitative view of the peasantry no longer accorded with social reality in the country-side. Although agricultural production grew, tax rates did not change radically over the years. Peasants resisted official attempts at new surveys and assessments, often by force. As Thomas Smith has shown, by the middle of the nineteenth century taxes in many areas were based on assessments a century and a half old, even though the productivity as well as the amount of land under cultivation had increased enormously in the meantime.[4] Since the rural population remained relatively stable and in some areas declined, by 1800 many peasants were no longer at the subsistence level. They were producing surpluses well over and above what they needed to feed themselves and pay taxes.

All these developments were most marked in the more highly commercialized regions of Japan: in the hinterlands of Edo and Osaka, near the main highways over which goods and daimyo processions traveled, and along the Inland Sea, a heavily traveled water route. In these areas peasants were increasingly drawn into commercial economy both as producers and consumers. On the one hand the emergence of great urban markets provided nearby populations with opportunities for cash cropping. Peasants could grow rice and other agricultural products such as vegetables, cotton, medicinal herbs, indigo dye, and the like for eventual sale in castle town or city markets. Even in villages where land was poor and barely able to support subsistence farming prosperity was possible if peasants had some local products for sale in city markets. At the same time the commercial revolution also reduced the self-sufficiency of villages in these areas. Peasants began to buy with cash goods that they no longer could or would make by themselves. Small village shops sold everything from incense and inkstones to salt and soy sauce, and in less accessible hamlets peddlers and traveling hawkers of goods made their regular rounds. The growth of the interregional trade thus drew the village increasingly into it, not only by offering the acquisitive peasant new opportunities for money income, but also by forcing on all peasants a greater need for ready cash.

The commercialization of the rural economy coupled with the growth of agricultural surpluses had precisely the effects the founders of the Tokugawa order had feared. The village experienced a growing gap between rich peasants and poor. In contrast to the early Tokugawa period, when villages tended to be made of families holding more or less the same amounts of land, by 1800 there were marked differences of wealth and poverty within the peasant class. The more aggressive and enterprising began to improve the yields from their fields by better farming techniques. By the early eighteenth century there had already accumulated an extensive body of literature on how to improve crops and improvement was aimed at making more intensive use of the land. Most of the literature showed how to make two stalks of rice grow where one grew before through small improvements such as using better fertilizers, using treadmills instead of buckets to haul water to the fields, planting winter crops of rice or some other grain, and finding more efficient ways to thresh the ripe grain in order to make possible earlier winter plantings.

At the same time land came to be regarded not simply as a means of supplying one's needs but as useful for making a profit as well. Many of the improving peasants began to use the profit from their increased yields to accumulate more land. Sometimes they acquired new land by clearing new fields or terracing hillsides for new rice paddies but they also acquired it from their less enterprising or less fortunate neighbors. Despite the legal prohibitions on the sale of land various legal devices developed to accommodate the more or less permanent transfer of land from one household to another. An astute and acquisitive peasant who had managed to put aside a small money reserve would make loans to fellow villagers, often at rates as high as 20 percent a year. In return the borrower would put up his land as collateral for the loan or promise to pay a portion of his harvest to the lender over an agreed period of years. Often borrowers found themselves unable to repay loans—a crop failure, a drop in the rice price, death or sickness in the family left them without wherewithal to repay their debts. When this happened the lenders would either take the borrowers' land in payment for the debt or make the borrowers into sharecroppers on their own land. Through this kind of process, sustained by an active land market, in many village communities land holdings increasingly concentrated in the hands of a few families and the number of small holders or tenant farmers and sharecroppers grew. In many villages there were a handful of peasants with more land than they could farm by themselves, a very great many with too little land to survive on alone, and a dwindling group of the middling-size landholders who had been so numerous in early Tokugawa times.

The wealthy peasant landlords who profited most from rural prosperity and the commercialization of agriculture often became small rural entrepreneurs as well. Apart from moneylending or pawn-broking, they used their money to set up sake breweries, to invest in presses for making vegetable oil, or to buy silk weaving looms for putting out work to other villagers. These small manufacturing operations were usually modest in scale, supplying a few neighboring villages or perhaps even the castle town. But some more ambitious rural entrepreneurs began to break into interregional trade, shipping cloth loomed in the village to neighboring domains or to the great national market centers of Edo and Osaka. Patterns of trade became increasingly complex. Not only did neighboring domains establish more and more trade that by-passed the national entrepots, but the rural entrepreneurs began to resent the official urban monopolies dominated by the kabu-nakama merchants. The newly arisen rural entrepreneur-landlord class not only challenged the privileged merchants of Edo and Osaka economically, but on occasion also protested to the authorities about the unfair monopoly practices of the associations.

The rise of a well-to-do peasant class was disruptive in other ways as well. Many began to adopt a lifestyle like that of the samurai class. They educated their sons, took up polite pursuits like callig-raphy and painting, kept concubines, and made pleasure trips to the city. Many samurai observers deplored this. "The most lamentable abuse of the present day among the peasants," noted one anony-mous writer, "is that those who have become wealthy forget their status and live luxuriously like city aristocrats."[5] Such samurai critics were alarmed that the strict distinction between samurai and rich peasants were beginning to blur, and that the wealth of the rich peasants was bought at the expense of their neighbors.

The well-to-do landlord-entrepreneurs were often upstarts whose status-seeking led to conflicts with the established village leaders over precedence and protocol. The resentment of the mass of small cultivators and tenants toward the well-to-do peasants also led to village conflict, often of a violent sort. In the early days of the Toku-gawa period, when peasant riots and village disorders were usually provoked by the exactions of corrupt officials or rapacious daimyo, the whole village rose united in protest against them. By the late eighteenth century, however, peasant riots or rebellions became more frequent, especially in times of bad harvests or famine, and they were directed less against samurai authorities than against well-to-do peasants within the villages. Led by middling-size or poorer peasants, the villagers vented their hostilities by looting and burning the storehouses and homes of the village landlords and money-lenders. Despite these symptoms of social unrest, which were especially prevalent during the famines of the 1780s and the 1830s, the bakufu did little to check the rise of the wealthy peasants. On the contrary, both bakufu and domain governments often found it useful to raise money from wealthy peasants by levying forced loans (*goyōkin*) from them or by selling them the privilege of wearing swords or taking surnames. This accelerated the blurring of class lines already seriously eroded as the result of the commercial revolution and it accelerated the aspirations of many wealthy peasants as well.

The Role of Government

The ruling authorities watched the growth of trade with alarm or confusion. Intellectually, their Confucian training made them ill prepared to cope with the great expansion in trade and production. To be sure, there was widespread recognition that material prosperity was important in a well-ordered society. (Indeed, the modern Japanese word for economics [*keizai*] at the time meant "governing the realm and assisting the people.") But the Confucian concept of material prosperity lacked any notion of economic progress and it was also profoundly antimerchant. The wealth of the realm was seen as basically fixed and the role of benevolent government, the Confucian ideal, was to see that it was distributed equitably among the people. The good ruler was enjoined to interfere in the economy not so much to expand the country's wealth as to keep production and consumption in balance. The traditional goal of economic policy was to encourage production as far as possible but to discourage consumption as well since there were limits on what the land could produce.

Confucian beliefs were of little practical use in face of the commercial revolution, since the market economy posed a series of practical problems for bakufu and domain authorities more complex than those dealt with in Confucian economic theories. First, there was much instability in government revenues. The price of rice, subject as it was to the vagaries of the market in Osaka and Edo, fluctuated from one year to the next. The amount of tax rice collected remained fairly steady but its value did not and hence daimyo might find their incomes sufficient one year but not the next. Second, although government income tended to remain fixed, the household and other expenditures of the daimyo, saddled with the obligations of the sankin kōtai system, grew more lavish over the years. The same was true of the bakufu, which, as Conrad Totman has pointed out, was "caught between a more or less fixed income and a practically unlimited capacity for consumption."[6] Third, given the gap between income and outgo, the bakufu and daimyo were often forced to tide themselves over by going into debt with the rich merchant-financiers of Edo and Osaka as their creditors. The need to pay interest on these loans placed new burdens on their exchequers and compounded the problem of finances even further. Finally, the financial difficulties of the shogun and daimyo naturally resulted in financial difficulties for their retainers. Aside from the expenses of the sankin-kōtai system, the major item in most domain budgets was the payment of samurai stipends. Daimyo often rescued themselves from personal financial straits by reducing these stipends. Usually this took the form of borrowing perhaps a third or a quarter of their samurai-retainers' stipends, but in practice the "borrowing" became a permanent loan since no term was specified for repayment.

The bakufu response to the problems created by the commercial revolution was on the whole unimaginative, negative, and restrictive. In the early eighteenth century bakufu leaders had shown some recognition of the new social realities by exercising direct administrative supervision over the financial and commodity markets of Osaka. The main institutional breakthrough was the granting of official recognition to monopoly merchants through the issuance of charters to kabu-nakama merchants. The benefits of the arrangement to the merchants have already been discussed, but there were benefits for the government as well. It was easier for the bakufu authorities to deal with the merchants as a group, and the fees merchants paid in order to secure association charters provided additional revenue for the bakufu. This amounted to an indirect commercial tax, but the bakufu stopped short of systematic taxation on trade. In part failure to adopt trade taxes reflected the administrative difficulty of collecting them and in part it reflected the persistent notion that profits from trade were unseemly.

In any event, throughout the eighteenth and early nineteenth centuries the bakufu seemed unable to cope with the difficulties produced by the commercial revolution. For the most part, it complacently tolerated the rice trade, the rise in rice prices, and the financial power of the great merchant princes. The bakufu authorities tried to make ends meet by extracting forced loans from rich merchants and wealthy peasants or by debasing bakufu currency in order to pay off debts with cheap money. Occasionally there were also attempts at reform, such as those of Matsudaira Sadanobu in the 1790s and those of Mizuno Tadakuni in the early 1840s. These reforms, however, were essentially reactionary in character. They aimed at righting the social equilibrium through issuing sumptuary laws, price-fixing, curtailing of merchant privileges, and general austerity in bakufu spending. At best such reform measures were weak palliatives and at worst they were serious disruptions to the movement of trade, actually making the rise of prices even more acute.

The bakufu also failed to exploit another possible policy that might have alleviated their financial difficulties: direct official involvement in trade and manufacture. By contrast, many of the larger domains resorted to such methods to shore up their finances. By the early nineteenth century many of these domains had set up official monopoly organizations to market a particular commodity within the domains or to export some special local product to the national market centers of Osaka and Edo. These domain monopolies were intended to augment rice tax revenues, which were no longer sufficient to make ends meet. The monopolies profited from buying up goods at prices fixed arbitrarily by domain officials, usually as low as possible, and by selling them at much higher ones. Sometimes the domain monopolies were run directly by domain officials who engaged in the buying and selling operations themselves and sometimes they were run by local merchants or entrepreneurs operating under patents or licenses from the daimyo. In any case the domain monopolies were often extremely successful. In domains that were the sole producers of a product, such as Satsuma, which imported sugar cane from the Ryukyus, profits were enormous. The operation of such a profitable monopoly allowed Satsuma to balance its budget without resort to the demoralizing and disruptive practice of cutting samurai stipends.

Samurai Discontent and Social Criticism

Needless to say, economic growth created difficulties for the samurai. In contrast to the wealthy town merchants or well-to-do peasant landlord-entrepreneurs, the samurai class as a whole suffered a relative decline in income and in some cases an absolute decline as well. Their family stipends were fixed at levels far less than their needs in 1800 and they benefited little if at all from the prosperity produced by the commercial revolution. Many samurai found it impossible to maintain a lifestyle congruent with their station in life. Some even had difficulty in making ends meet. Fukuzawa Yukichi reported that in his small domain an income of twenty to thirty *koku* of rice per year was necessary just to get along, but that many samurai families had incomes of less than fifteen koku. By the early nineteenth century many samurai, particularly those in the middling and lower ranks, were seriously scrambling to find ways of supplementing their incomes.

The more fortunate often found some sort of genteel occupation to earn extra money—teaching calligraphy, giving instruction in swordsmanship, taking in roomers, or perhaps raising *bonsai* ("dwarf trees") for sale, half as hobby, half as business. Others tried to marry their daughters into well-to-do commoner families. In Edo, it is said, there were even marriage brokers who would arrange such misalliances for a fee. Still others sold family heirlooms or ran up debts with town merchants in the hope, perhaps, that domain government would eventually cancel their indebtedness by fiat. But for the lower ranks of the samurai, regarded by money lenders as poor risks for loans, the only alternative was to earn money through handicraft labor, making paper fans or umbrellas, spinning silk into cloth, or some other menial work. This was particularly distasteful since it meant haggling over prices and pay with the commoner merchants for whom they were obliged to work. Little wonder that the impecunious but pretentious samurai was becoming a stock figure in popular satire and that commoner respect for the class, if not for its authority, had begun to dwindle.

Naturally the sagging status of the samurai class produced some discontent within its ranks. It is difficult, however, to say exactly how much. For one thing, the decline in the samurai's economic position was slow, not sudden, and conditions varied from domain to domain. At the same time many samurai, however impoverished, could still find solace in the dignity and tradition of their class. But it is also true that a vocal minority of samurai expressed a feeling that the times were out of joint and the world of men was in disarray.

Most social criticism in early nineteenth-century Japan was couched in conservative Confucian terms. Many expressed resentment that everywhere the relentless pursuit of profit, the cardinal Confucian sin, was beginning to upset the delicate balance of the social hierarchy. Economic change, the growth of trade, the rise of the cities, and the growing prosperity of well-to-do commoners reflected a general decline in public morals. As Fujita Yūkoku, an advisor to the Mito daimyo, noted, "High and low compete in ostentation and luxury while government becomes more and more lax. This is an age when money buys anything."[7] This sort of criticism became particularly pronounced from the 1780s, when a sudden and dramatic wave of peasant riots and local rebellions broke out. Such outbursts of peasant discontent were taken as a sign that all was not well within the realm as a result of declining public morality. "If there is good government," observed the nativist scholar Motoori Norinaga, "there will be no rioting, no matter how poverty-stricken the peasants may be."[8]

If the pursuit of profit seemed to many samurai critics the main cause of troubles within the realm, the declining quality of political leadership contributed as well. In the Confucian view only virtuous rulers could guarantee political stability and social harmony. When the ruler no longer practiced benevolent government, rebellion was at hand. "Whose fault is it that the people starve and good fields turn to waste?" wrote one reformer in the late eighteenth century. "These evils can not be blamed on laziness or disloyalty [of the people] but are owing to the crimes of the rulers."[9] Some critics attributed the failure of leadership to the long peace, which had sapped the vigor of the shogun and daimyo. Instead of tending to affairs of state the leaders of domains and bakufu closeted themselves in their mansions, surrounded by sycophants, with little concern for their people or their retainers. Others blamed the daimyo and the shogun for failing to rely on true men of talent or men of virtue as their advisors and ministers. In any case many critics were agreed that the restoration of benevolent government to Japan required an end to the domination of politics by a purely hereditary leadership and that it required greater reliance on men of ability.

By the late eighteenth century there were a few samurai critics here and there who advocated very fundamental changes in the institutions of society and the role of government policy. The most significant development was the emergence of a group of thinkers who suggested that the authorities take advantage of the growth of trade instead of trying to hold it in check. Kaihō Seiryō argued that profit was not to be disdained or disparaged and that in fact the whole structure of society rested on the principles of exchange and profit. Rice tax was a form of profit for the daimyo, and the samurai's stipend was a wage paid for service. Consequently, he said, the samurai should be encouraged to work in trade and production, and unproductive elements in society should be eliminated. Honda Toshiaki advocated an aggressive policy of internal and external economic development, including a program of foreign trade and overseas colonization. Satō Nobuhiro urged a total reorganization of government from a feudal structure into a centralized bureaucratic state dedicated to building up the national wealth and the national strength.

For the most part men like Kaihō, Honda, and Satō remained isolated voices in the wilderness, significant less for their direct influence than for their foretelling of things yet to come. The outlooks of most discontented would-be reformers were fundamentally conservative, based on traditional Confucian notions of the good society rather than on any new set of social or political principles. Reformers criticized the present-day rulers of Japan not in the name of some new vision of society but in the name of received morality. They did not feel that older political standards were no longer valid, but rather that society did not live up to them. Hence most critics did not call for the overthrow of the bakuhan system or even of its constituted leaders. Instead they attacked the people in power for moral failings and urged them to return to ancient standards. It was only with the increasing intrusion of a recalcitrant and aggressive West that this general discontent was converted into radical political action. The arrival of the West not only added the problem of threat from without to troubles within, but also provided some discontents with an alternative model for organizing the country.

4

The Fall of the Old Order

The social stresses created by the impoverishment of the samurai, the growth of a market economy, and the emergence of new social classes had begun to strain credibility and confidence in the existing social and institutional structure by the early nineteenth century. Many historians believe that these basic changes were pushing Japan in the direction of radical, perhaps even revolutionary change. Whether such was the case is a conundrum not easily answered since the pressures toward revolution from within were suddenly overwhelmed by a decisive revolutionary shock from without, the arrival of the Western powers demanding that Japan open to the outside world. The demonstrated failure of the bakufu to handle this crisis revealed grave weaknesses in the bakuhan system and cast doubt on the nerve and imagination of bakufu leaders, who seemed more concerned with Tokugawa dynastic interests than with the interests of Japan as a whole. To be sure, long-standing grievances and discontent with the Tokugawa order contributed to the downfall of the old order and perhaps shaped the way in which the end came, but such discontent served mainly to facilitate what the arrival of the West made inevitable, the transformation of Japan into a modern state.

The Foreign Threat

The seclusion policy worked as well as it did for nearly two centuries because the Westerners had as little interest in getting into Japan as the Japanese had in letting them in. In contrast to India and China, Japan remained outside the imagination of most Westerners, a little-known country with no exotic appeal and hardly any practical significance. It was only in the last decade of the eighteenth century that, largely for economic and commercial reasons, the expanding horizons of the Western world began to converge on Japan. To the north Russian explorers began to chart the icy waters off Hokkaido and Russian trappers to settle on the sparsely inhabited islands of Sakhalin and the Kuriles chain. To the south aggressive British merchants were plying a prosperous and expanding trade in tea and opium at the port of Canton in China. To the east American sea captains from New England were pushing into the western Pacific in pursuit of whales or profits from the China trade. As a result many Japanese leaders and thinkers had begun to worry again about the threat from without.

The new "red-haired barbarians" were very different from those who had first reached Japan in the sixteenth and seventeenth centuries but the Japanese view of them remained deeply tinged with hostility and suspicion. The old fears of Christianity and foreign invasion remained strong. "When those barbarians plan to subdue a country not their own, they start by opening commerce and watch for a sign of weakness," commented one early nineteenth-century writer. "If an opportunity is presented, they will preach their alien religion to captivate the people's hearts."[1] To some extent the Japanese fear of the Westerners as predators was a self-fulfilling prophecy and to some extent justified. Beginning in 1793 the Russians sent three peaceful expeditions to Japan in an attempt to open up normal commercial relations. The bakufu, alarmed at what they called the northern threat, turned all away empty-handed. Frustrated members of the last expedition, under the leadership of Rezanov, attacked Japanese settlements on Sakhalin in 1806 and 1807. Shortly afterward, in 1808, the British frigate *Phaeton* entered Nagasaki in pursuit of Dutch merchant ships, then enemies in the Napoleonic wars. Its nineteen-year-old captain, a hotheaded adolescent, threatened to burn all the Chinese and Dutch ships in the harbor if he were not supplied with provisions and water. These incidents, though of no great significance in indicating the true nature of Western intentions toward Japan, which for the most part were peaceful and commercial, deepened the apprehensions of bakufu officials and other political leaders.

In the face of new pressures from the outside the official policy was to hold the line in defense of the seclusion. In the 1790s and early 1800s bakufu officials met the Russians with evasive firmness, offering courtesy but not concessions, leaving one of them to note in his diary that the Japanese were "a strange mixture of geniality and craftiness."[2] As more and more Western vessels appeared in Japanese waters and inevitably more and more foreign sailors were shipwrecked on Japanese shores, the bakufu's position hardened. In 1825, following an armed raid for supplies by English sailors on the island of Hirado off Kyushu, the bakufu issued an expulsion order that enjoined local authorities to destroy all foreign vessels that came close to Japanese shores and to arrest or kill any surviving crew members without hesitation, discussion, or second thoughts. Shooting first and asking questions later was admirably inspiring but increasingly unrealistic as a practical policy and it was not enforced with any particular rigor.

Any easy confidence that the Westerners might be put off by force was rudely shaken in the late 1830s by news of the Opium War in China. Beginning in 1839 alarming reports of British gunboat attacks on Macao, the blockade of Amoy and Ningpo, the bombardment of Canton, and the signing of the Treaty of Nanking were brought to Japan by Dutch and Chinese traders at Nagasaki. By the mid-1840s accounts of the war were well circulated in Japan. The defeat of the Chinese by a small British naval and military force was a tremendous shock. It shattered the image of Chinese centrality and strength. It also raised the question of whether a similar fate might be in store for Japan. "How can we know," remarked one writer, "whether the mist gathering over China might not come down as frost on Japan."[3]

The sense of threat from without, smouldering since the 1790s and now fanned into more urgent fear by the Opium War, provoked debate among scholars, officials, and concerned political leaders over how best to deal with the "barbarians." Their general stance was antiforeign. Nearly all who participated in the debate were agreed that the Westerners were either inferior or up to no good or both. But there was far less agreement on how best to deal with their predatory intentions.

At one end of the spectrum were men like Aizawa Seishisai and Fujita Tōko, scholars under the patronage of Tokugawa Nariaki, daimyo of Mito, one of the great shimpan houses. These men, moved in part by Confucian economic theory and in part a visceral nativist xenophobia, urged a rigid policy of seclusion. Should Japan open herself to trade with the outside, they said, foreign commerce would not only drain Japan of her gold and silver, it would also enrich profit-grubbing merchants and townsmen and encourage the habits of luxury, moral laxity, and social corruption already much too evident in the country. They argued on more emotional grounds that foreigners in Japan would pollute and corrupt "the divine land" by their contaminating presence. The foreigners, being violent in their actions and absorbed in the pursuit of profit, were ignorant of "true morality" and adhered to the "false doctrines" of Christianity, whose beliefs could subvert the whole society.

These radical seclusionists, moved very much by the Confucian notion that morality was the pivot of politics, urged that the Western threat be met by a moral rearmament of the country. The Westerners, they argued, posed a threat not simply because of their violent character but also because they arrived in a Japan made flabby and weak by two centuries of peace and idleness. Unless the samurai class regained its old spirit of frugality, discipline, and martial vigor and the people their old spirit of obedience, nothing could save Japan from being overwhelmed by its enemies nor from slipping into moral decay following exposure to the Westerners. In good Confucian fashion, the Mito writers called on the bakufu leaders as well as the daimyo to set an example for the rest of the country by cleaning up official laxity, putting an end to corruption, showing more concern for popular welfare, and not spending money lavishly on concubines and entertainments. Troubles within made Japan more susceptible to dangers from without. Equally striking, the Mito writers urged the restoration of the imperial institution. By this they did not mean overthrowing the bakuhan system, but rather making the emperor, already regarded with affection, loyalty, and respect by the people, into a kind of rallying point or national symbol.

At the other end of the spectrum from the seclusionist Mito writers were men like Takashima Shūhan, Sakuma Shōzan, and Takano Chōei, all Dutch scholars. These men had an acute appreciation of Japan's military backwardness vis-à-vis the West. They were no less antiforeign than the seclusionists and no less convinced of Japan's moral superiority, but they disagreed that Japan could maintain her independence by moral or political means. To be sure, they agreed that domestic reforms were necessary—few men did not—but they urged that the main task in dealing with the foreign threat was to acquire Western science, Western technology, and Western guns. Without these, no matter how valiant and determined its people Japan would be incapable of defending itself. As Sakuma Shōzan put it, "Why did an upright and righteous great country like China lose to an insolent, unjust, and contemptible country like England? It is because the [rulers of China] prided themselves on their superiority, regarded the outside world with contempt, and paid no heed to the progress of machinery in foreign countries." However distasteful Western morals might be, Sakuma concluded, it would be necessary to bring Western science to the defense of Japanese spirit or Eastern morality.[4]

The pamphleteers' debate was echoed and amplified in the council chambers of the larger domains, especially those in strategic positions along the coast such as Satsuma, Tosa, Echizen, and Mito. Moved by the same concern and anxiety as the Mito writers and their opponents, a number of leading daimyo, the "able daimyo," became active in looking for ways to deal with the foreign threat. The main advocate of militantly defending seclusion was Tokugawa Nariaki, the blunt, persistent, near fanatical lord of Mito. Already in the 1830s, under the influence of men like Fujita Yūkoku and Fujita Tōko, he began a reform program ranging from smallpox inoculations to forging cannon from temple bells in preparation for a military clash with the foreigners. He fell out of favor with the bakufu when in an excess of zeal he suggested that the shogun cut down his household spending and abandon his effete life of luxury in Edo castle but his fortunes rose once more after the Opium War. There were other daimyo, however, who felt the need for a more flexible response to the problems. One was Shimazu Nariakira, daimyo of Satsuma, who was not only well acquainted with British activities in China but also had a consuming interest in Western science. Unlike Tokugawa Nariaki he felt that it would be impossible to keep the country closed as it had been in the past. He argued that the only realistic policy for the country was to build up military and economic strength to keep the foreigners in line once they came into the country for trade. When in 1846 British and French ships demanded that the kingdom of the Ryukyus, an unofficial dependency of Satsuma, sign treaties of friendship and commerce, Shimazu Nariakira urged the bakufu to give permission to do so.

By the early 1850s then, many Japanese had taken measure of the foreign threat. The contrast with other Asian countries, particularly China, is striking. To some extent, the Japanese profited from the bad example of China and they were beginning to cash in their paradoxical asset of vulnerability to outside threat. But most important of all, in the debate over the foreign problem the notion of national interest as opposed to national identity was already beginning to stir. Whatever their differences, men like Mito Nariaki and Shimazu Nariakira, Aizawa Seishisai and Sakuma Shōzan all conceived of Japan as a political entity rather simply as a way of life or style of civilization. Modern nationalism had begun.

The Opening of Japan

While the debate over the foreign threat went on the bakufu began to shift away from its rigid defense of the seclusion policy. Although Edo continued to put off overtures by the Western powers for opening normal trading relations, it retreated from a position of obscurantist militance to one of greater caution. In 1842 the "no second thought" expulsion order was rescinded. An even greater shift in bakufu policy came under Abe Masahiro, the chief elder of the bakufu from 1843 to 1855, who undertook military and institutional reforms to deal with the foreign problem realistically. In July 1845 Abe set up a new office of coastal defence headed by himself to serve as a combination foreign office and maritime defense ministry. He also attempted to build up coastal defense fortifications. His efforts along these lines were hamstrung by meagre finances and the conservatism of other high bakufu officials loathe to imitate Western weaponry.

In the long run the most significant element in Abe's policy was his attempt to rally the "able daimyo," both shimpan and tozama, behind him. The debate on the foreign threat had shown a considerable lack of consensus among the daimyo and there was danger that the country might fly apart under foreign pressure. To prevent this Abe broke the long-standing practice of keeping the daimyo divided and weak. He not only tried to win the personal trust and confidence of men like Mito Nariaki and Shimazu Nariakira, he also permitted Satsuma, Saga, Kamaishi, and other domains to build new coastal fortifications or to experiment with Western technology. He realized that Japan could not hope to face the Westerners successfully unless the inherent weaknesses of the decentralized bakuhan system were overcome, and he encouraged the able daimyo to undertake self-strengthening programs like the one he had attempted to implement in the bakufu with little success.

The arrival of four American gunboats in July 1853 was hardly a surprise to the Japanese authorities. It was an open secret in the treaty ports of China that the Americans were on their way to Japan to open negotiations and local authorities there had already put off two earlier American efforts in 1846 and 1849. But this time the tactics of obfuscation and delay, so often useful in deflecting diplomatic overtures from the Westerners in the past, had no effect. The dogged, humorless, and imperious American commander, Commodore Matthew Perry, was determined to succeed in browbeating the Japanese, whom he viewed as vindictive and deceitful.[5] He sailed his "black ships" under the guns of forts guarding the entrance to Edo Bay, plunging the city into consternation and implying his willingness to use force in negotiating a treaty with Japan.

Faced with Perry's firmness and their own lack of military preparedness the bakufu leadership under Abe chose not to fight in order to defend seclusion. To be sure, it did so with the tacit acquiescence of the daimyo. Shortly after Perry's arrival Abe Masahiro, pursuing his policy of building political support in all quarters, sent queries to all the daimyo as to how to respond to the American demands. The replies still extant, sixty one out of two hundred odd, indicate that most of the daimyo felt that the bakufu should reject the American demands for trade but that it should also avoid hostilities. Only a handful of daimyo were willing to go to war in defense of seclusion. Given this mandate the bakufu leaders felt they had no choice but to compromise with the Americans. In March 1854 the bakufu signed a treaty opening the remote ports of Shimoda and Hakodate to American ships and providing for the repatriation of shipwrecked sailors, the provisioning of American ships, and the establishment of American consulates at the newly opened ports. This "wood and water treaty" was not entirely satisfactory to the Americans, who also wanted to open commercial relations, and it was not entirely satisfactory to antiforeign daimyo like Tokugawa Nariaki, who were shocked at the extent of the concessions to the Americans. But the bakufu leadership under Abe was happy to have weathered the crisis without resort to war and without having to make any clearcut recognition of the foreigners' right to trade.

As might be expected, the Perry treaty was merely a first step for the foreign powers, who now began to put greater and greater pressure on the bakufu. In the wake of Perry's expedition the other Western powers, acting in concert toward Japan as they had toward China in the 1840s, extracted from the Japanese treaties similar to the one they had made with the United States. With continuing vigor they also pressed for trade relations, the fundamental motive behind attempts to open Japan in the first place. The main initiative was taken once again by the Americans, represented now by Townshend Harris, the first American consul. Arriving at Shimoda in late 1856, Harris almost immediately opened negotiations to persuade the bakufu to agree to trade. Although unlike Perry he had no fleet to back him he proved a persuasive advocate. At once cajoling and intimidating, Harris argued that, contrary to Confucian economic theories, trade would be more beneficial to Japan than harmful and that it would be better for the Japanese to reach an agreement with him than with a fleet of British gunboats, as the Chinese had. The bakufu, now led by Hotta Masayoshi, was more and more inclined to accept the inevitable. So were most of the daimyo. In late 1857, after soliciting the opinions of the daimyo on the question of trade, the bakufu found most agreed that neither trade nor diplomatic relations with the foreigners could be avoided. With a much clearer mandate than Abe, Hotta therefore agreed in January 1858 to a draft treaty with the United States that provided for the opening of a new set of treaty ports, the establishment of custom duties by treaty, the right of American traders and other nationals to be tried by consular courts rather than Japanese courts, and the right of the Americans to dispatch a minister to Edo. These were essentially the same terms the foreigners had earlier extracted from the Chinese in order to ensure unobstructed trade and the opening of Western-style diplomatic relations.

Although there was general agreement among the daimyo on the need to accept the Harris treaty, lines of fracture were beginning to show at the highest levels of politics. The attempt to secure a general consensus behind the bakufu by consulting with the daimyo had begun to break down. On the one hand the fudai daimyo, especially those eligible for the highest offices in the bakufu administration, began to feel their position threatened as influence over bakufu decisions was being more widely shared. On the other hand the able daimyo from domains such as Satsuma, Echizen, Mito, and Date began to have a greater appetite for power. In large measure this was prompted by a feeling that in such critical times there was need for new blood in the bakufu leadership. The reforming daimyo became more and more outspoken in their demand that the bakufu set its house in order and develop military strength. Acting in collaboration they urged that Tokugawa Keiki, the promising young daimyo of Hitotsubashi (Tokugawa Nariaki's seventh son), be named as heir to the shogun. They felt that under such strong leadership the country would be more likely to avoid civil upheaval. The result was a dangerous polarization between the fudai daimyo who stood for internal status quo and the reforming daimyo now known as the Hitotsubashi party who stood for some kind of internal reform.

These tensions came to a climax in the spring of 1858 when Hotta, again anxious to ensure a consensus behind the bakufu's foreign policy, decided to submit the Harris treaty to the emperor for ratification. Confident that imperial approval would be forthcoming Hotta in an unprecedented move traveled personally to Kyoto, bearing lavish gifts for the court nobility, to make the request. The move proved disastrous. Not only were the emperor Kōmei and the court nobles around him antiforeign, but they also were being urged by conservatives like Tokugawa Nariaki to reject the treaty and by reformers such as Shimazu Nariakira and Matsudaira Shungaku to support the Hitotsubashi candidacy. In reply to Hotta the emperor expressed disapproval of the treaty and urged the bakufu to reconsider it after consulting with the other daimyo. He also obliquely supported the Hitotsubashi candidacy. This reply, a radical departure from the emperor's usual custom of tamely submitting to the bakufu's requests, was a blow to Hotta and to the influence of the fudai in general.

Faced with this kind of constitutional crisis Hotta fell from power. In his place the shogun appointed Ii Naosuke, daimyo of Hikone, to the office of Great Elder (*tairō*), a position usually appointed in times of crisis. A strong and intelligent man, Ii Naosuke, backed by the rest of the fudai officials, was determined to reassert bakufu initiative both in foreign policy and domestic politics. In July 1858 when Townshend Harris sent word that the British and French, just victorious in a second opium war with China, were preparing a naval expedition to Japan, Ii resolved to go ahead and sign the Harris treaty without imperial approval. Similar agreements with the Dutch, the Russians, the British, and the French soon followed. At the same time Ii also tried to put bakufu decision-making back on traditional tracks by declaring the matter of shogunal succession a purely internal affair of the Tokugawa house, with which neither tozama daimyo nor emperor had a right to interfere. He declared the daimyo of Kii, rather than Hitotsubashi Keiki, would be the shogunal heir. To put down domestic opposition he forced into retirement most of the reforming daimyo who had backed the Hitotsubashi candidacy, including Tokugawa Nariaki, Matsudaira Shungaku, Yamauchi Yōdō, and Hitotsubashi Keiki himself. A number of their retainers who had expressed opposition either to the Harris treaty or to the fudai's candidate for shogunal succession were also arrested and punished. Like the able daimyo, Ii was aware of the need for strong leadership, but he was not prepared to accept it on untraditional terms.

Although the bakufu had managed to avoid a confrontation with Western military strength the events of 1858 seriously weakened the bakufu's political position. The ancestral law of seclusion, a keystone of the Tokugawa order, was dead and the bakufu had killed it. By contrast, the emperor, who had taken a forthright and resolute stand against the Harris treaty, emerged as a rallying point for antiforeign elements. Equally important, the bakufu, in defying the emperor's wishes by signing the Harris treaty, had betrayed its trust as delegate of the imperial power. With some justice the shogun could be branded as traitor or rebel. In short, although the bakufu had adopted a foreign policy that was generally approved by the daimyo and probably saved Japan from a clash with foreign gunboats, it did so only at the tremendous cost of putting the legitimacy of its leadership in jeopardy. People now began to consider new ways to lead the country.

"Revere the Emperor and Expel the Barbarians"

Declining confidence in bakufu leadership did not lead immediately to demands for its overthrow, but there was strong sentiment in favor of altering the regime in order to cope better with the foreign problem. A small group of young Western experts, many of them in the employ of the bakufu, urged a crash program of self-strengthening, the adoption of Western military science and technology, and a shift from the principle of hereditary office-holding to recruitment of men of talent. The large able daimyo, led by Satsuma, sought greater involvement in affairs of state, especially in dealing with the foreigners and building the country's defenses. Finally, a group of antiforeign loyalist young samurai, recruited from all over Japan, urged expulsion of the foreigners from Japan under the leadership of the emperor of Kyoto. The interplay of these forces shaped the politics of the early 1860s.

At the highest level of politics the most important group was the able daimyo, most of whom had been members of the Hitotsubashi party, but also including new men such as the daimyo of Chōshū. Having failed to secure a change in bakufu leadership they now proposed a reconciliation between Edo and Kyoto, estranged over the treaty ratification question. The initiative for new policy, known as "the union of court and bakufu" (*kōbu-gattai*), at first came from the bakufu. In 1860 the bakufu leadership proposed to cement such a union by a marriage between the shogun, Iemochi, and the emperor's sister, Kazunomiya. Like the earlier bakufu attempt to secure approval of the Harris treaty, the move was intended to bolster the authority of the bakufu. But the reforming lords used the same slogan to increase their own influence. After an unsuccessful bid by Chōshū to bring court and bakufu together the leadership of the kōbu-gattai movement gravitated to Shimazu Hisamatsu, the new daimyo of Satsuma. In 1862 the kōbu-gattai daimyo, in return for putting down antiforeign agitation and mediating between the Court and the bakufu, extracted from the bakufu leadership a promise to appoint Shimazu, Matsudaira Shungaku, and Hitotsubashi Keiki (all normally denied access to bakufu office) to special posts as high advisors to the bakufu. They also achieved a relaxation of the sankin-kōtai regulations so that daimyo could divert funds usually spent on their processions and Edo residences to building up local military defenses.

The bakufu was willing to make these concessions not simply because it needed allies in its continuing confrontation with foreign pressure but also because it was apprehensive over the rise of the *sonnō-jōi* ("revere the emperor and repel the barbarians") or loyalist movement. The loyalist movement had begun in the late 1850s as an antiforeign movement, drawing into its ranks men roused by the contamination of the "divine land" by the "barbarian" foreigners or by fear for the country's independence. When the emperor took his stand on the Harris treaty in 1858 Kyoto became a gathering place for antiforeign elements. For some loyalists the emperor was a rallying point because he was the divine embodiment of Japanese identity. For others he was the apex of a chain of loyalty stretching from the domains through the shogun and his antiforeign wishes had to be given precedence over the policy of the shogun, his "rebellious" vassal. In either case by the early 1860s a firm link had been forged between antiforeignism (*jōi*) and "veneration for the emperor" (*sonnō*).

Fairly typical of loyalist movement membership was Yoshida Shoin (1830–1859), a young samurai from Chōshū, who had shown early concern for Japan's foreign threat by traveling the country to study coastal defenses and to make the acquaintance of technical Westernizers like Sakuma Shōzan even before the Americans arrived. After an abortive attempt in 1854 to stow away on one of Perry's vessels to study the West first-hand Yoshida became more and more contemptuous of both shogun and daimyo for their failure to stand up to the foreigners. By the time of his execution in the purge of 1859 he had come to respect and trust only the emperor and called for a rising of "low ranking heroes," able to transcend their domain loyalties, who would serve the emperor in struggling against the foreigners without and the corrupt leaders within.

The loyalist movement attracted many men like Yoshida from the middle and lower ranks of the samurai class. It also attracted an admixture of commoners, especially those most heavily influenced by samurai ideals and lifestyle, such as sons of wealthy peasants or well-to-do townsmen. More significant than class background were a number of other characteristics common to the loyalist movement membership. First, most loyalists came from the large domains, such as Satsuma, Chōshū, or Mito, whose daimyo had been active in the high-level disputes of the 1850s. Second, most were young, in their late teens or twenties, angered and frustrated by the failure of older and more responsible men to deal with the foreign problem or with the country's weakness. Finally, the majority came from a station in society with little influence on domain politics. They condemned "black-hearted officials" partly out of frustration at their own political impotence. In some domains, notably Satsuma and Mito, the daimyo or high-ranking domain officials were often sympathetic to loyalist views but there were also conservatives who feared the emergence of a vocal and undisciplined element that challenged tradition and precedent.

The loyalists thought that the pusillanimous posture of the bakufu toward the foreigners resulted from the long-run decline in the morale and martial vigor of the samurai class. Unlike the able daimyo, they did not simply advocate reform. They tried to embody in their own lives and political action the ideals of the samurai ethic. They found inspiration in the original samurai virtues of decisiveness, daring, and indifference to death, and they took as their heroes men like Kusunoki Masashige, the epitome of the religion of loyalty and of devotion to the emperor. Many loyalists underwent something like a religious conversion, cutting themselves off from ties to the domains and abandoning pro forma loyalty to their daimyo for a more intense and personal commitment to the emperor. Reckless, confident in their own virtue, and committed to a cult of action, the loyalists became a formidable disruptive element in politics.

The loyalist movement was a violent and bloody one. Its tactics were putschism and terror and its members hoped acts of violence and heroism would bring the bakufu and the daimyo to their senses. The most dramatic act of terrorism was the assassination in 1860 of Ii Naosuke, a potent symbol of the arbitrary attitude of the bakufu and of its concessions to the foreigners. Other attempts on high bakufu officials soon followed. Beyond this the loyalists also attempted to provoke a bakufu confrontation with the hated barbarians by direct attacks on the foreigners and their lackies. In 1861 Hendrik Heuskens, Townshend Harris's interpreter, was killed in Edo and loyalist samurai attacked the British legation there, killing several of its staff. At the foreign settlement in the new treaty port of Yokohama foreign merchants and officials slept with pistols and swords by their bedsides, ever fearful of attack. In 1862 an English tourist by the name of Richardson was cut down when he rode in front of the Satsuma daimyo's procession and allegedly proforeign officials and merchants in Kyoto were attacked and harassed. When these efforts failed to wreck the treaty settlement, in June 1863 loyalist leaders in Chōshū managed to persuade the domain government to fire on ships passing through the Straits of Shimonoseki, in accordance with an edict issued by the emperor Kōmei. The climax of the loyalist movement came in September 1863, when loyalist samurai from Satsuma, Chōshū, and Tōsa staged an attempted coup d'état in Kyoto. Their hope was to "free" the emperor from his gilded cage to lead a military expedition expelling the foreigners from Japan. But this bold attempt was put down with troops from

Satsuma and Aizu, whose daimyo had put their hopes on the kōbu-gattai policy.

The loyalist movement was, as the intellectual historian Harry Harootunian has said, merely "a rehearsal for Restoration," for in the end it proved a failure.[6] First of all, the movement lacked concrete future goals other than expulsion of the barbarians. Some loyalist leaders expected the bakuhan system to remain intact while others envisaged the creation of a new institutional structure modeled on the precepts from the Confucian classics. Second, its goal of expelling the barbarians was a practical impossibility. A few loyalists like Itō Hirobumi and Takasugi Shinsaku became convinced of this as the result of visits outside Japan, where they saw the fullness of Western power before their very eyes. But even the most obtuse loyalist realized the futility of expulsion after the British bombarded the Satsuma capital of Kagoshima in September 1863 to force payment of reparations for the murder of Richardson and the joint Western fleet bombarded Chōshū shore batteries in September 1864 in retaliation for attacks on Western vessels in the Straits of Shimonoseki. Finally, the loyalists found few sympathizers among the able daimyo, most of whom regarded the movement as a threat to the delicate game of compromise between court and bakufu and as a violation of the bureaucratic samurai ethic of loyalty to superiors.

The coup de grace for the loyalist movement came in the summer of 1864 when the rump of the loyalist movement, many of whom had taken refuge in the domain of Chōshū, clashed with troops of kōbu-gattai daimyo, Satsuma, Aizu, and Kuwana. Taking advantage of this act of insubordination the bakufu managed to have the emperor declare the domain of Chōshū an enemy of the court and mounted a military expedition against it with samurai levies from domains all over Japan. In late 1864 Chōshū surrendered without a fight and the loyalist movement, its leadership decimated and its influence at Kyoto destroyed, was effectively at an end. The action shifted from acts of heroic violence in Kyoto and Edo to new efforts to build an organized antibakufu movement using the domains as a base.

The Meiji Restoration

Ironically, the crushing of the loyalist movement proved no salvation for the bakufu, whose prestige had been eaten away not only by

its inability to put down internal dissent by itself but also by the
steady extraction of political concessions by the reforming daimyo.
In Satsuma, Chōshū, and Tosa many former loyalists, chastened by
the failure of terrorism and expulsion, now began to pursue a more
realistic program. They aimed at using the domains as a political and
strategic base for curbing the feckless and aimless bakufu leadership. Controlling key positions in their domains as the result of civil
war (in Chōshū) or enjoying personal influence with the daimyo (in
Satsuma), they began to gird themselves for a final showdown with
the bakufu. The antibakufu forces began a program of vigorous self-
strengthening, designed to build up self-sufficiency in the event of a
domestic trial of strength. Since both Chōshū and Satsuma had succeeded in righting their finances during the early nineteenth century
both had funds to buy foreign arms and ships from foreign merchants
at Nagasaki. The antibakufu forces became increasingly convinced
that the great domains should somehow unite politically to counter-
vail the power of the bakufu. Such activists as the Tosa samurai
Sakamoto Ryōma envisaged a consultative assembly of daimyo acting as advisors to the bakufu. Others argued for a political alliance
between the strong domains as protection against bakufu power.
In March 1866 Satsuma and Chōshū made a secret agreement to help
each other if attacked by the bakufu. The alliance, soon tested when
the bakufu sent a second expedition against Chōshū, succeeded in
thwarting bakufu attempts to reassert its authority.

While these developments went on in the domains the bakufu made
a last desperate effort to shore up its position. It attempted a last
gasp reform program of the kind that so often precedes the downfall
of a crippled regime. The resurgence of the bakufu came, strangely
enough, under the leadership of Hitotsubashi Keiki, former member
of the kōbu-gattai party. After the death of shogun Iemochi in
August 1866 Keiki was named as his successor. Apparently still
attached to the idea of some sort of conciliar government, Keiki at
first proposed an election of a new shogun by a council of daimyo,
which would then assist in initiating a reform program. But there
was little response from most daimyo, now increasingly suspicious of
the bakufu because of its two attempts to crush Chōshū. Frustrated
in this gesture, Keiki himself, aided by a number of Western experts
among the high bakufu officials but determined not simply to be a
figurehead like his predecessors, began a vigorous attempt at self-
strengthening. Like the efforts of Satsuma and Chōshū these were

directed against internal enemies as much as against the foreigners. The bakufu was fighting for dynastic survival, not simply for national survival.

The sweeping reform plans contemplated by Keiki went beyond mere military self-strengthening. They included a major institutional overhaul. The council of elders was to be recast into a Western style cabinet with functional ministries; bakufu finances were to be restored through the levy of new taxes, the opening of mines, and the promotion of industry; and the military forces of the bakufu were to be transformed from a feudal samurai levy into a professional standing army, armed with Western weapons and partly financed by money taxes on the gokenin and hatamoto. In effect, Keiki was planning to transform the bakuhan system into a highly centralized modern-style state. Little wonder that Kido Kōin, an antibakufu leader in Chōshū, commented his emergence as bakufu leader was like "the rebirth of Ieyasu." Such massive changes not only threatened vested interests within the bakufu, they also were predicated on financial aid from France, whose minister, Leon Roches, had suggested many of them.

This belated attempt at bakufu reform was the last straw for its opponents in the strong domains. By mid–1867 the antibakufu forces in control of Chōshū, Satsuma, and Tosa were determined to overthrow bakufu rule and create a new government centering on the emperor. The idea had already been put forward by men like Iwakura Tomomi, a loyalist court noble, who wrote in 1866, "To [reassert our national prestige and overcome the foreigners] requires that the country be united. For the country to be united, policy and administration must have a single source. And for policy and administration to have a single source, the Court must be made the center of the national government."[7] The remaining problem was how to achieve the restoration of imperial power.

In July 1867 activist samurai from Tosa, led by Sakamoto Ryōma, put forth a plan for a peaceful transfer of power: the abolition of the shogunate, the demotion of the Tokugawa family to mere daimyo status, and the establishment of a bicameral assembly made up of an upper house of court nobles and daimyo and a lower house of samurai and even of commoners. The Tosa plan meshed with the ideas of reformers within the bakufu like Katsu Awa, and even with the hopes of Keiki himself. In November Keiki finally agreed to a formal return of sovereign powers to the emperor. The change, however, was more formal than substantive. Under the new regime Keiki continued to hold considerable powers, serving as head of both the executive and legislative branches of the new government and retaining the power to appoint judicial officials as well. The new arrangement also left the Tokugawa family in control of its ancestral house lands. With this extensive domain as a political and economic base the Tokugawa still remained an *imperium in imperio,* powerful enough to challenge imperial authority.

The leaders of Satsuma and Chōshū, fearing that the bakufu intended to pursue its own selfish interests, now decided to pursue another plan of action—a military coup to end both the authority of the shogun and the economic power of the Tokugawa. Troops from Satsuma and Chōshū began to move into Kyoto in small contingents in early December 1867, ready for a final move. On January 3, 1868, while military units from Satsuma, Chōshū, and Tōsa seized control of the palace gates, the young emperor Meiji issued a decree formally abolishing all the traditional offices of the court and bakufu, establishing a new imperial government staffed with a number of high ranking court nobles, daimyo, and their retainers, and promising to sweep away past evils. The Tokugawa bakufu had come to an end, after two and a half centuries.

Typical of the secretive style of traditional politics, this cataclysmic declaration was kept from the daimyo for nearly a week. The implications of the palace revolution were soon clear enough to the former shogun Keiki. At the urging of certain retainers he decided to put up a fight. The civil war that followed demonstrated how completely Tokugawa authority had collapsed. An imperial army under the command of Saigō Takamori had little difficulty in forcing Keiki's retreat to Edo despite the fact that both forces moved through domains traditionally friendly to the bakufu. In April 1868 the bakufu army finally surrendered Edo castle to Saigō, albeit on rather generous terms. Amnesty was granted to Keiki's retainers, many of whom subsequently joined the new government; and Keiki himself was forced merely to retire. His successor as head of the Tokugawa family was granted a domain of 700,000 koku, about equal in size to Satsuma and twice as large as Chōshū. Resistance to the new imperial government continued for several months in the northeast, especially in the domains of Aizu and Nambu, which earlier had decided to cast their lot with the bakufu. Their resistance, however, was less inspired by traditional loyalty to the Tokugawa than by fear at the new power acquired by the southwestern daimyo. Provincial loyalty and sectionalism died harder than the authority of the Tokugawa, and fighting in the north did not end until six months after the fall of Edo.

Few had rallied to the cause of the Tokugawa. All those who might have been expected to defend the dynasty—the direct retainers, the fudai daimyo, and the great collateral houses—had remained neutral in the fighting. The reasons for the general lack of support are not hard to guess. Basic, of course, was the long-term decline in bakufu prestige. Despite Keiki's last minute efforts the bakufu had shown itself incapable of fending off foreign pressure or putting its own house in order. Then too there was the long-run economic decline of the samurai class, including the bakufu's own direct retainers, whose loyalty to the Tokugawa had eroded and who had lost their confidence in the capacity of the Tokugawa for benevolent rule. Finally, of course, the leaders of the Satsuma and Chōshū had wisely wrapped themselves in the "brocade banner" of imperial sanction, as founders of new dynasties and new government had done in the past. Had the overthrow of the Tokugawa been simply the work of a few disgruntled daimyo it probably would not have gone so smoothly. But "seizure of the jewel [i.e. the emperor] " made it possible to declare Keiki an enemy of the court and gave his traditional supporters justification to cast off their bonds of allegiance.

Although the last of the Tokugawa did not lose his head and general bloodshed was minimal, the restoration of the Meiji emperor was a revolutionary event. To be sure, it was, as Thomas Smith has pointed out, "an aristocratic revolution" led by disgruntled members of the old ruling class alarmed at the discrepancy between the pretensions of the bakufu and the realities of its power.[8] In this respect it was no different from most modern revolutions. It differed only in that the revolutionaries used traditional language and traditional slogans—the "restoration of imperial rule"—to justify their actions. But it was soon to become clear that behind this apparently conservative goal was to emerge a fundamental commitment by the new imperial government to reshape Japan from top to bottom.

5

Revolution from Above

The goals of the men who came to power in 1868 were not so very different from those of the regime they had just overthrown. Beneath all the complex maneuvering of the 1860s there had emerged a consensus among all camps, whether for the bakufu or against it, that Japan would have to become a modern nation state if she were to retain her independence and enjoy full sovereignty. Antiforeign sentiment remained smouldering beneath the surface but it no longer took the form of a crude expulsionist position. Rather it was now embodied in a determination to make Japan rich and powerful like the Western nations by borrowing their technology and by reforming its own institutions along Western lines. These ideas had lain behind Tokugawa Keiki's belated reforms no less than behind the Satsuma-Chōshū alliance that overthrew him and the Restoration had merely determined they would be pursued by the latter instead of the former. Except for a few recalcitrant loyalists most political leaders and activists were committed to a policy of building a "rich country and a strong army" (*fukoku kyōhei*) in order to meet the Western challenge. But it was not always clear how best to do this. As a result the first steps toward modernity were marked by piecemeal experimentations, many false starts, and considerable debate.

The New Government

The imperial government that came into being in 1868 was basically a coalition of revolutionary factions from the imperial court and the western domains of Satsuma, Chōshū, and Tosa. Born in conspiracy, it was a narrow group of men, enjoying neither broad popular support nor representing a cross section of society. In the highest ranking positions were court nobles like Iwakura Tomomi and Sanjō Sanetomi, veterans of the loyalist movement of the 1860s, and a number of reforming daimyo sympathetic to the antibakufu cause. Most of the real decision-making lay in the hands of middle and lower ranking officials, who took most of the initiative in shaping the government policies. Among them were men like Ōkubo Toshimichi, Saigō Takamori, Kido Kōin, and other former officials from Satsuma, Chōshū, and Tosa, who had dominated the politics of their domains in the late 1860s. Finally the new government also included a number of outsiders not directly involved in plotting the Restoration who were recruited primarily because of their reputation as Western experts—men like Ōkuma Shigenobu, Etō Shimpei, and Yokoi Shōnan.

The new government at first was neither very cohesive nor very stable. As one perceptive foreign journalist noted, "There was a restlessness, I might almost say an irritability perceptible in the management of public business that showed all was not working smoothly. Men had not yet found their proper grooves."[1] Much of this restlessness stemmed from continuing provincial hostilities and jealousies. In 1868 rumors swept Tokyo (the new name for Edo, now the imperial capital) that fighting would shortly break out between Satsuma and Chōshū now that the bakufu had been overthrown. At the same time within the new government strong rivalries persisted between the personal cliques of the chief Restoration leaders, further adding to the uncertainty. But perhaps most important, much of this restlessness resulted from discussion and uncertainty over what Japan's future should be. The coalition that overthrew the bakufu had been united by a common enemy, but once the Tokugawa were gone members of this coalition began to struggle among themselves over what to do next.

The conspirators who overthrew the bakufu had done so on practical, not ideological, grounds. They had no utopian vision of a new and perfect social order. Utopias rest on faith in things unseen,

and the Western cannon and gunboats that had so agitated them in
the first place were quite visible. Their goals were very few and very
simple, set forth in the Imperial Oath of 1868 (usually called the
Charter Oath).[2] This document committed the new government to
convocation of an assembly and "public discussion" on matters of
state, unity of "all classes high and low" in promoting the national
welfare, abandonment of "absurd customs of olden times" and
conformity to "the principles of international justice," and an effort
at "seeking knowledge from all over the world." All of these goals
were unexceptionable, reflecting the consensus that had gradually
emerged out of the struggles of the 1860s, but at the same time they
were ambiguous enough to permit reasonable men to differ over how
best to realize them. It was such differences of opinion that gave the
politics of the 1870s not only a great deal of instability, but also a
spirit of experimentation and improvisation.

The basic issue over which differences arose was the problem of
how much of the old society had to be jettisoned in order to strengthen
the foundations of the Imperial polity. A minority of officials,
particularly a number of nativist ideologues surrounding the court,
believed in a literal restoration of the monarchical way with direct
rule by a divine priest-monarch, but their ideas did not prove persuasive. Far more important was the debate over the future of the
domains and the samurai class, both still intact despite the change in
government. On the one hand men like Saigō Takamori, the com-
pelling military leader of the Restoration, contemplated no fundamental change in the old society or its institutions other than greater
domain involvement in national politics. At the other extreme were
younger men like Itō Hirobumi (Chōshū), Yamagata Aritomo (Chōshū), and Ōkuma Shigenobu (Hizen), who wished to push ahead
rapidly, dismantling as much of the old regime as necessary to
achieve national unity and strength. Somewhere in between were
men like Ōkubo Toshimichi and Iwakura Tomomi, canny pragmatists
who urged caution less because they were opposed to radical institutional change than because they felt the need for circumspection. It
was only after much turmoil and debate that the choice became
clear: either Japan had to become a highly centralized bureaucratic
regime indifferent to the interests of the old ruling class or it would
remain no stronger than it had been when Perry first sailed into
Uraga Bay.

The Centralization of Power

Like all revolutionary governments the new imperial regime first had
to solve the fundamental problem of consolidating its control over
the rest of the country. The new government had a firm territorial
base only in Tokyo and the domains confiscated from the Tokugawa but in the rest of the country the domains remained intact,
collecting taxes, controlling the peasants, and maintaining samurai
fighting forces as before. All the divisiveness of the bakuhan system
remained. Unsure of itself, the government was cautious at first,
letting the domains retain their traditional autonomy. It attempted
some degree of national unity by establishing a bicameral national
assembly (*kōgisho*) with an upper house made up of court nobles,
daimyo, and certain of their highest retainers, and a lower house
made up of representatives from each domain. The powers given to
this body were considerable. The upper house, for example, had
responsibility for the establishment of a constitution, the enactment
of laws, the supreme judicial power, the conclusion of treaties, and
the making of war and peace. The purpose of this body was not
representative government, however, so much as the creation of a
federal and conciliar system of rule like that suggested by Tosa leaders in 1867.

The government's attempt to rule through the domains proved
unsatisfactory. Administrative procedures varied from domain to
domain and the resulting confusion was enormous; officials in some
domains were loathe to follow the decrees sent out by the new
government while officials in others began rather sweeping reforms
that ran ahead of the government's program; and there lingered the
fear that as long as the domains remained intact, the loyalties of the
people would remain divided and the sense of national unity weak.
Consequently the imperial government led by Ōkubo and Kido
began to reduce provincial autonomy. As Kido Kōin noted, "A single
rod, even though a stout one, may be broken by a young child, but
if ten rods, though all are weak, are made into a bundle, they cannot
be broken even by a full grown man."[3]

In March 1869, after months of hard bargaining and persistent
negotiation, government leaders persuaded the daimyo of Chōshū,
Satsuma, Hizen, and Tosa to return their land and population registers to the emperor. This curious halfway measure, more symbolic
than practical, was meant to demonstrate that daimyo domains were

ultimately the land of the Emperor and their populations were the subjects of the emperor rather than subjects of the lords. Soon other daimyo followed suit voluntarily. In August 1869 the return of land registers was made mandatory. The daimyo were converted into local governors. They still retained their powers to raise taxes and so forth, but now, in principle at least, they exercised these powers as servants of the emperor. Other measures aimed at administrative rationalization and simplification soon followed—elaborate status distinctions within the samurai class were simplified to two classes (*shizoku* and *sotsu*), the stipends of retainers were reduced, all remaining fiefs were made public land, and uniform procedures for tax collection and the like were established. The government's final move came in August 1871. After organizing the Imperial Guard, a military force made up of 8,000 troops from Satsuma, Chōshū, and Tosa, the emperor gathered together the former daimyo to announce the abolition of the domains, the division of the country into prefectures, and the end of administrative localism. A month later the domain armies were also disbanded.

The abolition of the domains at the time seemed to be a radical move. The British minister, astonished that it was achieved by the issuance of an edict, remarked that in Europe such a move could have been accomplished only after years of warfare; he concluded that it succeeded only through an act of Providence. But the hand of God was less at work than certain practical considerations. Many of the former daimyo and their advisors feared that resistance would provoke civil war, and most of them wished to avoid that. Even more important, there was already a fair degree of sentiment in the country favoring the abolition of the domains. During a debate in the Kōgisho in the early summer of 1869 nearly half the representatives of the domains favored establishing some sort of new centralized administrative system. Many of the domains were in debt not only as the result of long-standing obligations but also because of expenses incurred during the civil war. They were anxious to shift their debts to the new government. A few domains even surrendered their land registers before being ordered to. At the same time the imperial government, though it wished to end the political autonomy of the domains, agreed to continue paying the stipends of the daimyo and the retainers. Samurai retainers received only a third of their former stipends, but the daimyo did rather well. They received stipends equal to one tenth of their former domain taxes, a rather good living, considering that they now had no political responsibilities, administrative or ceremonial expenses, nor any need to support their former retainers. This comfortable economic settlement doubtless eased the final transition from the domain system to the centralized administrative structure.

The abolition of the domains, seen by some as a second Restoration, was followed by an all-round tightening of the central government's authority. All tangible traces of the domains soon were obliterated. The former daimyo were ordered to live in Tokyo, presumably to prevent them from becoming rallying points for local discontent, and in their place new prefectural governors, usually ex-samurai from other areas, were appointed. The old domain boundaries vanished. The country was divided by newly drawn political boundaries into seventy-two prefectures. At the same time officials of the central government became less and less concerned about local interests. With the domains gone their priority was the interest of Japan as a whole and domain loyalties now ceased to have any but a tangential influence on government policy.

The Agrarian Settlement

The abolition of the domains unlocked the floodgates of reform. Once the government committed itself irrevocably to centralization the way to solving other problems became clear. One problem was government finances. Until the abolition of the domains the imperial government lived from hand to mouth, relying on a makeshift arrangement to meet expenses that continually exceeded income. About three-quarters of its revenues came from taxes on old bakufu domains under its control. It squeezed these lands with such vigor that in many areas peasants accustomed to the laxer ways of bakufu intendants rose in protest. The government also relied on forced loans from great merchant houses such as the Mitsui, Ono, and Shimada, and its printing presses issued a flood of poorly backed paper notes. One possible source of funds was loans from foreign banks and financiers, but the leaders of the government were reluctant to put themselves under the financial wing of the foreigners or to pay the rather high interest rates they demanded. Except for a few small railroad construction loans floated in London the government relied solely on domestic sources of income.

All these were temporary expedients. The government's leaders realized they needed a financial base that was substantial, stable, and uniform throughout the country. The obvious solution was suggested by Kanda Kōhei, a Western expert who proposed turning the land over to the peasants who cultivated it and taxing them as its owners. His ideas were shared by Matsukata Masayoshi, a young Satsuma man, with a reputation as an able administrator. But others saw tax reform as the occasion for shoring up the economic position of the ex-samurai class. Some proposed to raise new land taxes, turn them directly over to the samurai, and let them buy the land. Others suggested a variety of arrangements for turning over land tax revenues directly to the court nobility and the samurai. Mutsū Munemitsu suggested that the government buy all the land from the peasants and put it on public sale, a land reform program aimed at putting much of the land into the hands of the stipended ex-samurai rather than the poorer cultivators.

Not too surprisingly, victory in the land tax debate went to the officials who favored bureaucratic rationalization and the interests of the central government over those of the former samurai. New tax laws promulgated in 1873 provided a land tax uniform throughout the country producing revenues equal to that of the former domains and bakufu combined. Unlike feudal taxes, the new land tax, which made up about 80% of the government's revenues down to the 1880s, was to be collected in money rather than in rice. It was assessed on the value of the land, not the size of the harvest. This made the new tax structure more rigid than the old. The new peasant landowners were obliged to pay the same amount of tax, year in year out, regardless of the vagaries of weather or natural blight. In the old days peasants often had received tax reductions from their daimyo in years of bad harvest but under the new system they were obliged to meet their tax bills whether the harvest was good or bad. At the same time, since the new laws kept taxation at pre-Restoration levels, the peasants' tax burden remained the same.

If the tax laws provided no lightening of the peasants' economic burden, they did have the side effect of increasing their personal and legal freedom. Old restrictions on the sale of crops or the type of crop raised were lifted in 1871 and the following year similar restrictions on the right to sell land were lifted. After the promulgation of the land tax law, peasants not only received title to the land, but they could also buy and sell land as they pleased, grow vegetables or fruit instead of rice as they saw fit, and even abandon their land if they wished. Naturally the beneficiaries of these changes were not the poorer peasants and certainly not the landless ones (about 25 percent of the total). The main gains went to well-to-do peasants, who now could do freely and openly what they had done by legal fictions in pre-Restoration times. If the agrarian settlement engineered by the government served the interests of administrative convenience at the expense of samurai welfare, it also served the interests of the well-to-do or acquisitive peasants at the expense of the poorer ones. Such was not the intent behind the change but it did encourage, perhaps at an accelerated rate, a continuing concentration of economic power within the villages into the hands of landlords.

Conscription and the Fall of the Samurai

The same issues that animated the debate over land reform likewise underlay the question of building a new army. In the long run military reform meant strengthening the defenses of the country against the outside world but in these early uncertain years the need for military forces to maintain internal order was an equally pressing concern. The imperial government could not expel the barbarians, who were there to stay, but it did have to protect itself against domestic enemies, real or potential. The question was not whether to have an army, but what kind it should be.

At first the leaders of the new government relied on levies of samurai from their old domains. Many of them regarded arming the common people as ridiculous or dangerous, and they had trouble conceiving of anything but a samurai army. In late 1870, when the government began girding its loins for the final assault on the domain autonomy, it assembled an Imperial Guard made up of separate samurai units brought in from Satsuma, Chōshū, and Tosa. But this force soon proved unsatisfactory. It was hard for the samurai soldiers to submit to Western-style military discipline and many of them were basically adventurers interested mainly in their pay and given to roistering in the barracks.

Within the Ministry of War a debate raged over army reorganization. As early as 1869 Ōmura Masajirō (Chōshū), a Chōshū expert on Western military practice, championed the idea of a conscript army drawing on samurai and commoner alike. After Ōmura's death by assassination the main advocate of this position was Yamagata Aritomo (Chōshū), who had fought with mixed peasant-samurai militia forces in Chōshū during the 1860s and found the commoners capable of holding their own in battle with samurai. Yamagata, who had accompanied Saigō Tsugumichi on a foreign tour to observe military systems in France and Prussia, favored the conscription systems he saw there. He also saw military training for commoners as a way of mobilizing the population behind the government. A conscript system would make the army a "great civil and military university."

Against Yamagata were arrayed those who clung to the idea of an army recruited mainly from samurai. Men like Tani Kanjō (Tosa), Maebara Issei (Chōshū), and Torio Koyata (Tosa) argued that since the commoners had no martial *élan* they would not make fighting men of high caliber. Itagaki Taisuke (Tosa) argued for a volunteer army on the assumption that it would draw mainly on the old samurai class. But the views of Yamagata, backed by Ōkubo and others, prevailed. In January 1873 the government promulgated a conscription law requiring every male regardless of social rank to spend three years on active service followed by four in the reserves. Exemptions were provided for government officials, students, adopted sons, household heads, and the like, but in principle the whole population was liable for military service.

The conscription law was a rude jolt to the former samurai for it called into question their *raison d'être*, the meaning of their existence as a privileged class. The conscription edict, in rather strong language, offered a sweeping attack on the samurai class. It accused the obdurate samurai of "having lived a life of idleness for generations" at the expense of others and of having "in extreme cases put people to the sword." "Neither the samurai nor the common people will have the status they were accustomed to in the past," said the edict, "nor will there be any distinction in the service they render to their country, for they will all be alike as subjects of the Empire."[4] The most immediate objections to the decree came from members of the Imperial Guard, many of them heroes who had fought in the wars of the Restoration. One dissident general attacked Yamagata for taking "grimy peasants and their ilk, and turning them into puppets."[5]

The creation of the conscript army coupled with the abolition of the domains before it raised anew the most ticklish question of all what to do with the old samurai class. The samurai class was not only bereft of its old functions but also enormously expensive to maintain. In 1873, for example, the government spent as much on payments to the samurai as it did on all its administrative expenses, and it was clear that disbursements on such a grand scale could not continue indefinitely. In December 1873 the government decided to tax the stipends, taking with one hand what it gave with the other. At the suggestion of Ōkuma Shigenobu (Hizen) it also tried to extricate itself by offering to commute annual pensions less than 100 *koku* into interest-bearing government bonds. The hope was that energetic samurai would use these negotiable bonds as capital to invest in land and industry or to set up small business ventures of their own. In the end only a few former samurai, perhaps a fifth of the class, chose to convert their stipends.

By late 1873 the runaway reform program, including the conscription law, had begun to weed out those less committed to change and to bring into prominence experts and pragmatists committed mainly to the central government. The process was accelerated by the Iwakura mission, dispatched in 1871 to observe conditions in the West first-hand. The government leaders who led the mission—Iwakura, Ōkubo, and Kido—returned with an acute realization that Japan had far to go in order to catch up with the West and that sentimental attachment to the old institutions was a luxury it could not afford.

A major split in the ranks of the government leadership finally occurred in late 1873 over the issue of whether or not to send a military expedition to chastise Korea for alleged diplomatic insults toward Japan. Saigō Takamori, along with Itagaki Taisuke, Gotō Shōjirō, and Etō Shimpei, backed the project in hopes that it would offer members of the samurai class a chance to achieve glory on the battlefield that might compensate for the privileges being stripped of them at home. Saigō even volunteered to serve as ambassador to Korea in the hopes he might be assassinated, providing Japan with an unambiguous *casus belli*. The members of the Iwakura mission, especially Ōkubo, opposed the idea on the grounds it would dissipate the fragile financial and military resources of the government. When the final decision went against the war party they resigned from the government, leaving it in the hands of those who favored continued centralization and rationalization of society.

Under these circumstances it was merely a matter of time before the former samurai were stripped of their last privileges. In 1874 optional commutation was extended to stipends over 100 *koku;* in

1875 all payments were converted to cash; in 1876 all stipends were made compulsory and the samurai were finally forbidden to wear the two swords that for centuries had set them apart from the commoners. The abolition of the samurai as a class was complete.

The social effects of the elimination of the samurai class were mixed. On the one hand the loss of stipends spelled financial ruin for many samurai families. Interest on government bond payments amounted to only half the money value of their former pensions, which in any case had been steadily reduced since the Restoration. Even relatively well-off middle and upper samurai families were forced to the edge of subsistence. Since prices rose swiftly in the late 1870s the purchasing value of income from the bonds fell. Many samurai were forced to sell them for cash just to make ends meet. On the other hand many samurai, now forced to make their way in the world without the benefit of a guaranteed income, began to turn their education and skills to new use. Some went into business. Others found jobs as policemen, teachers, military officers, and petty officials, for which their background had prepared them. Though the abolition of the class created hardship, it did make possible channeling the energies and talent of the former samurai into the task of building the new Japan from below.

"Increasing Production and Promoting Industry"

If centralization of power was the main political goal of the imperial government in the 1870s, the building of industrial and commercial power was its main economic goal. The Westerners had demonstrated not only the superiority of their gunboats, but also the superiority of their manufactured goods and skill at trade. The old idea that a country's strength rested on its agricultural base no longer seemed valid. As Kanda Kōhei wrote, "The nations that depend on business are always rich while those that depend on agriculture are always poor. Therefore, the eastern countries are always poor and the western ones always rich." It was time, he concluded, for Japan's leaders to "learn the ways of business and open the way to trade."[6] This realization had touched most of the imperial government even in 1868, but any lingering doubts were dispelled by the Iwakura mission. As Ōkubo noted in a letter on his travels in England, "There is nowhere we have not been. And everywhere we go, there is nothing growing in the ground, just coal and iron. . . . Factories have increased to an unheard-of extent, so that black smoke rises to the sky from every possible kind. . . . This is a sufficient explanation of England's wealth and strength."[7]

It was clear that the government would have to play a major role in building a modern commercial and industrial economy. The task was beyond the resources and imagination of the old merchant class. The great city merchants had neither the capital resources nor the new knowledge necessary to understand the technical complexities of modern manufacturing or foreign trade. Profits were still high in traditional enterprises, such as money-lending and trade, and they offered the old merchant class a familiarity and security that investing in railroads or new factories did not. In 1869, when the government, working through the house of Mitsui as its agent, tried to induce local merchants to invest in a Kyoto-Osaka railroad line, the project failed for lack of interest, even though the government offered a guaranteed return of 7 percent on invested capital plus half the profits over 7 percent. Given such reluctance by the merchants to engage in modern enterprises, the government had little choice but to assume a major portion of the responsibility. Fortunately it could rely on the skills of many officials who even before the Restoration had worked to establish foreign trading companies or rudimentary arsenals and factories within their domains as part of local self-strengthening policies.

From the early 1870s, under the initiative of Ōkubo, Itō, Ōkuma, and others, the government embarked on a policy of state capitalism. It served as the principal (though not sole) entrepreneur, manager, and financier of modern industry. It began a number of pilot plant operations, buying whole factories abroad, assembling them in Japan, and bringing in foreign technicians and workmen to get them started. Naturally a good many of these government enterprises were strategic industries—shipyards, arsenals, and mines—directly related to military needs. Others were intended to supply the government's needs without relying on foreign goods. Cement and glass factories were built to provide materials for new government office buildings or woolen mills to produce cloth for army uniforms. The government also realized the need to import modern industrial technology and mechanized techniques for the manufacture of goods already produced by traditional native cottage-industry operations. The Tomioka silk reeling mill built in 1872, for example, showed that it was possible not only to turn out more silk thread, but also thread of better quality by the new machine methods. At first these factories, arsenals, and shipyards relied heavily on the guidance of foreign experts, not only high level technicians and engineers but also workmen with common skills such as drafting, carpentry, and metalworking. But once native Japanese had mastered both managerial and technical skills, the foreigners were released and the Japanese workers became the nucleus of a new technocracy who scattered throughout the rest of the country to spread knowledge of their new skills.

The ultimate goal of the government was not permanent involvement in modern industry but rather the growth of a private enterprise economy such as prevailed in the advanced Western countries. They pursued a kind of paternalistic policy, intervening in the economy only to import the new technology in the hopes that independent and aggressive native entrepreneurs would eventually play the major role in modern manufacturing. While continuing both to establish and operate government enterprises the government also sought to create an institutional environment agreeable to the emergence of a modern entrepreneurial capitalist class. On the one hand the government tried to encourage the growth of joint stock companies, the chief organizational technique for pooling of private entrepreneurial capital in the West. (Shibusawa Eiichi, the main advocate of this policy, after retiring from the government became the Johnny Appleseed of Meiji capitalism, helping to found over six hundred joint stock companies in his lifetime.) At the same time the government tried to foster the growth of a modern banking system to provide funds and a stable credit system for the financing of new enterprises. In 1876, following the model of the American national banking system, the government began to issue charters to private banks enabling them to issue notes against government bonds in their holdings. The banking system was also intended to encourage the former daimyo and samurai whose stipends had been converted into cash and government bonds to invest funds in banking. Between 1876 and 1880 148 new national banks were organized.

The government's policy of encouraging the growth of a native capitalist class had mixed results. By the late 1870s the establishment of national banks and the promulgation of joint stock company regulations produced a wave of bubble companies, often started by former samurai anxious to pool their bonds and meager cash resources. Often they failed owing to the unscrupulousness or incompetence of their promoters. But a number of the early Meiji entrepreneurs were enormously successful. Most did not belong to the old merchant class, but were newcomers to business, willing to plunge into the uncertainties of enterprise and to reinvest their profits in new ventures. Some were profiteers, often men of humble origin with an eye for the main chance, who took advantage of the unsettled conditions of the 1860s and 1870s to accumulate personal fortunes as dealers in the burgeoning silk and tea trade at Yokohama, as arms merchants for the contending political forces in the 1860s, or as manipulators of currency. Others were "political merchants," to use the contemptuous term applied to them, who used connections with government officials to build profitable companies.

The government quite consciously favored certain of the new businessmen through direct subsidies, long-term low-interest loans, granting of government contracts without competitive bidding, deposit of government funds, or sale of government properties at bargain prices. All these practices, which smacked of an unsavory intimacy between government officials and private entrepreneurs, resulted not so much from official corruption as from the government's desire to help those who were bold enough to venture in the development of modern industry. The policy of government favoritism was reminiscent of the Tokugawa period, when both bakufu and daimyo had relied on privileged and monopoly merchants for supplies. But there was economic justification for it as well. Since infant industries could not be protected by tariffs the government had to use more direct means of defending them against foreign competition. The businessmen and companies given special favors were usually those that had already showed they could succeed. The government was merely backing the winners, a few key firms whose activities in the long run would build up national economic strength.

Ultimately, of course, the policy of increasing industry and promoting production meshed with the general trend toward the centralization of the country's institutional structure. The entire government enterprise policy, as well as the special favors extended to certain of the new entrepreneurs, was ultimately financed by taxes collected from the rural population. Although funds spent on promoting industry were only a small portion of the government's total outlay they still represented the largest single accumulation of capital in the country. Without the gathering of government powers into the hands of the leaders at Tokyo in the first place, this reallocation of resources would not have been possible.

"Civilization and Enlightenment"

The rest of the population did not sit idly by as the government plunged headlong in its efforts to transform Japan into a Western-style modern nation state. A popular craze for the paraphernalia of Western "civilization" swept through many areas, especially the large cities like Tokyo, where both foreign goods and government Westernization were most visible. The sudden opening of Japan, as the scholar Nishi Amane remarked in 1874, was like "the overturning of a bottle"—Western clothing, architecture, food, fashion, even haircuts spilled out into Japan in indiscriminate, often bizarre, ways.[8] The new yen for Western things was satirized by Kanagaki Robun in 1871. The typical man of the day, he said, was the "beef-eater," a Westernized swell with long flowing cologne-scented hair, calico underwear peeping from under his kimono, a gingham umbrella at his side, and a cheap Western pocket watch ostentatiously consulted from time to time. Sitting in a new-style restaurant, he gobbled down a plate of beef (long proscribed by Buddhist practice), telling his neighbor how fortunate it was that "even people like ourselves can now eat beef, thanks to the fact Japan is becoming a truly civilized country."[9]

This fad for Western material goods, which has not really stopped since, was the vulgar version of an attempt to bring about a cultural revolution through the importation of Western ideas and values. Since the 1850s the number of Japanese, usually samurai, sent abroad by bakufu or domain governments to study in the West had grown slowly but steadily. There were also many, coming out of the rangaku tradition, who avidly learned about the West through books without leaving Japan. In contrast to earlier Dutch scholars, who were mainly interested in Western science and technology—medicine, anatomy, astronomy, navigation, and the like—this new group of Western experts was more interested in the society, laws, institutions, and philosophy of the West. Many had been attached to the Institute for Investigation of Foreign Books (*Bansho shirabesho*) established by the bakufu in 1855 as a translation office *cum* Western studies center. The new Western experts emerged as a new intellectual elite in the 1860s and 1870s, replacing the old-style Confucian scholars as the critics and arbiters of social ideas. Through their translations and other writings detailed knowledge of the Western world diffused to the educated classes. Fukuzawa Yukichi's *Conditions in the West*

(*Seiyō jijo*), an encyclopedic compendium describing everything from Western tax systems and lunatic asylums to table manners, sold 150,000 copies in its first edition (1866). Nishi Amane summarized the whole corpus of Western scholarly knowledge, from history and theology through mathematics and physics, in his *Links of All Sciences* (*Hyakugaku renkan*). Others made translations of Samuel Smiles' *Self-help,* a Victorian paean to the virtues of ambition and hard work, or John Stuart Mills' *On Liberty,* the bible of English liberalism.

This effort at bringing new knowledge to Japan was no mere intellectual pastime. Men like Fukuzawa and Nishi, no less than the leaders of the new government, were much concerned with the building of Japan as a "rich and powerful country." But in contrast to those who saw the adoption of Western technology as the main path to national strength, they felt Japan could become a truly strong modern state only if she underwent a revolution in ideas or a revolution in values. Trained in the didactic tradition of Confucian learning, they saw study and morality as inextricably linked with statecraft. At the same time they saw the civilization of the West as more than just a useful tool for political purposes. In their eyes the West represented not simply wealth and power, but a higher form of civilization, which had advanced farther on the ladder of human progress than Japan. Accepting the optimistic notion of Western writers like Buckle, Guizot, and Spencer that mankind was marching ever upward and onward toward increasing prosperity and happiness, they saw Japan as weak because it seemed enmired in "superstition, irrationality, ignorance, and backwardness." The goals of the Westernophile translator-intellectuals was the enlightenment (*keimō*) of the Japanese mind. "Schools, industries, armies, and navies are all the mere external forms of civilization," wrote Fukuzawa.

> They are not difficult to produce; all that is needed is the money to pay for them. Yet there remains something immaterial, something that cannot be seen or heard, bought or sold, lent or borrowed (that) pervades the whole nation and (whose) influence is so strong that without it none of the . . . external forms would be of the slightest use. This supremely important thing is . . . the spirit of civilization.[10]

The primary role of the enlightenment intellectuals was iconoclastic. In order to promote the spirit of civilization they felt they had to destroy so-called backward and uncivilized ways and customs.

They were particularly hostile toward the metaphysics and morality of Buddhism and Confucianism. As Nishi Amane pointed out, these older systems of belief stressed basically negative virtues—gentleness, weakness, modesty, deference, frugality, self-abnegation, and obedience—which not only suppressed men's normal instincts and desires but also kept the country weak and backward. Similarly, Confucian learning with its emphasis on hierarchical values in family, marriage, and politics came under their withering attack. Fukuzawa ridiculed the dutiful son who had dowsed himself with rice wine and slept naked by his parents' bed to keep the mosquitoes from biting them. It would have been simpler, he said, to buy mosquito netting.

If there was general agreement among the new intellectuals on what was wrong with the old Japan, there was less certainty about what constituted the spirit of civilization. A minority saw it in Christianity. "The industry, patience, and perseverance displayed in (Western) arts, inventions, and machinery," wrote Nakamura Keiu, "all have their origin in the faith, hope, and charity of their religion."[11] For him, Western strength and wealth were "the outward leaf and blossom" of Christianity. Western missionaries, who argued in the same fashion, applauded these sentiments, but most of the enlightenment intellectuals felt rather that the spirit of civilization lay rather in secular values of the West: materialism, scientific rationality, and personal individualism. "If we would look for the origins of Western civilization," said Fukuzawa, "it comes down to one thing: doubt." In countries like Japan men never questioned the principle underlying nature and society but relied on uncritical acceptance of authority. They lacked a spirit of personal independence, initiative, and responsibility. "To defend our country against the foreigners," said Fukuzawa, "we must fill the whole country with the spirit of independence, so that noble and humble, high and low, clever and stupid alike will make the fate of the country their own responsibility and will play their part as citizens."[12]

The ideas of the enlightenment thinkers were those of the liberal, middle-class, capitalist nations of Western Europe and North America. But for all their alien and radical character, these ideas enjoyed a tremendous vogue. Their impact was enormous on educated Japanese who came of age in the 1870s. Many enlightenment intellectuals founded their own schools, the most famous being Fukuzawa's Keio Academy (later Keiō University). Even more important, the government shared their belief that the new knowledge from the West and the spirit of independence could liberate Japan from the bondage of ignorance and make it strong, and in 1872, in advance of many European countries, the government adopted a compulsory elementary school system. The Education Code, echoing Fukuzawa's ideas, boldly proclaimed that "henceforth, universally, without any distinction of class or sex, in no village shall there be a house without learning, and in no house an individual without learning . . ."[13] The philosophy behind the new educational system was to promote the spirit of self-reliance or independence touted by the enlightenment intellectuals, whose writings and translations emphasizing natural rights and self-help were often used as textbooks. Local schools were relatively autonomous, and education was to be geared to make "free and independent individuals." The long-run goal was national strength, to be sure, but it was to be achieved only indirectly by developing the character, talents, and minds of the population.

6

Protest and Dissent

Despite their initial caution the leaders of the new imperial government had wrought a major social revolution by the mid 1870s. To some degree they were social revolutionaries in spite of themselves. They jettisoned old institutions less from ideological fervor or commitment to a blueprint for social change than from a gradual realization that these institutions were liabilities both politically and financially. Nevertheless the country was swept up in the turmoil and confusion that comes in the wake of all revolutionary change. Even though many post-Restoration reforms were slow to take hold, by the 1870s the shock waves of change from Tokyo had traveled to the farthest reaches of the country. Many elements in the population reacted violently. Disgruntled members of the Restoration coalition left the government in protest, cosseting personal grievances and resentments against their erstwhile comrades; massive changes resulting from centralization created a reservoir of discontent in the countryside; and the ruthless firmness of the government in carrying out its new policies awoke resentment of "official tyranny." The 1870s were marked not only by a breakthrough to modernity but also by vocal antigovernment criticism, sometimes coupled with outbursts of political violence, making the decade a troubled one.

Peasant Riots and Samurai Rebellions

In the early 1870s the most obtrusive response to the government's reform program was of a nostalgic, conservative, and counter-revolutionary kind. Not surprisingly, much of this conservative opposition came from the peasant population, whose folkways and village traditions were unsettled by government policies. Peasant disturbances, common during the last century of Tokugawa rule, reached a new peak in the years around the Restoration. During the first decade of the Meiji period over two hundred disturbances were recorded, reflecting a much higher rate of frequency than before the Restoration. In 1869–1870 alone, there were forty-two incidents. To be sure, many of these disturbances were of a kind most characteristic of the early nineteenth century—outbursts of violence by the mass of the poorer and middle peasants against village officials or rich peasants. Basically these were manifestations of class conflicts within the village, often centered on the demand for the reduction of rents or taxes and set off by high prices, the dishonesty or unfairness of village officials, or the hoarding of rice by rich peasants. They reflected both the effects of long-run commercialization of agriculture and the unsettled conditions created by civil war and political change.

During the 1870s, however, another pattern of peasant disturbances became important—disorders sparked by the government's reform programs. Sometimes they were provoked by the alteration of village boundaries in the establishment of new local administrative apparatus, by overzealous tax collectors sent out by the new government into old bakufu territories, or by the destruction of the old domain system. (In 1871, for example, the peasants of Fukuyama rose in protest over the replacement of their daimyo by a new prefectural governor appointed by Tokyo.) Many risings were also prompted by the onslaught of newfangled reforms of long standing customs. Peasants rose to protest the abolition of the old class distinctions, the emancipation of the *eta* or pariah class traditionally regarded as polluted, the destruction of Buddhist temples as part of the campaign to establish Shintō as the state religion, the legalization of beef-eating, or the outlawing of traditional coiffures for men. The substitution of the Western solar calendar for the traditional lunar calendar in 1873 likewise provoked trouble in many areas. Villagers, whose whole yearly cycle of agricultural work and community festivals was tied to the old calendar, felt the world was turned topsy-turvy by "Jesus Christ's New Year." Many of the customs regarded as absurd or ignorant by government officials or enlightenment intellectuals were the warp and woof of the peasants' daily life.

The oppressive new burdens placed on the population as the result of modernizing reforms also awoke peasant protest. The obligation to pay taxes in cash instead of rice, unfair land value assessments, and the inflexibility of the new tax laws were resented by many. So was the new compulsory elementary education system that took youth away from work on the family land. The new conscription law excited suspicion and bewilderment. In some areas rumors spread that the young men called up for military service were going to be mutilated for some dire purpose or to be sold to the foreigners. The personal costs of modernization were resented by those who bore the burden most directly.

Peasant protest against new government policies often united the villagers into communal political action. Internal class tensions were overwhelmed by a sense of threat from the outside, and rich peasants as well as poor were united by the village leadership to make their resentments known. Since peasant discontent was often diffuse these village coalitions often broke down, and wealthier villagers found their storehouses ransacked as retribution for the central government's misdeeds. But often new political alignments were forged within the village too. In either case the government usually moved swiftly and harshly to put down the local disturbances. Since unarmed peasants were no match for government police and troops, suppressing them was not difficult. Initially, therefore, village unrest neither worried the government nor made much of an impact on the country as a whole.

Far more alarming was the emergence of antigovernment sentiment and antigovernment movements among the ex-samurai class, many of whom felt the new government had betrayed the original goals of the Restoration. Some samurai activists, especially in the domains that had toppled the bakufu, had expected the fall of the Tokugawa to signal the final expulsion of the foreigners. They were shocked when it did not. A number of prominent pro-Westernizing officials, such as Ōmura Masajirō, an advocate of conscription, were felled by the swords of reactionary assassins in the first years after Restoration. In 1869–1870 dissident elements in Chōshū attacked local government officials, setting off local disorders that lasted some months. As the pace of change accelerated, discontent deepened. One resentful ex-samurai voiced the feelings of many in 1874, when he memorialized the emperor:

> In the reforms . . . introduced since the Revolution, has the method been in accord with that of a well-governed country? Or have things been managed as in a country of disorder? . . . If the latter has been our practice let it at once be reformed, and let us return to the institutions of our ancestors. What need have we to imitate the customs of foreign countries 10,000 *ri* [leagues] away?[1]

There is little doubt such feelings were widespread.

By the mid 1870s the steady erosion of the social status and economic security of the former samurai class made clear that the government intended to sacrifice the interests of the class to the interests of the nation. Some discontents who had gone along with some degree of Westernization now began to turn against the government. The crisis over the Korean invasion plan in 1873 pushed many ex-samurai leaders toward open revolt. A number of samurai rebellions, such as the Saga revolt of 1874, involved leaders who had quit the government on the Korean issue. Some personal jealousy and rivalry doubtless spurred these leaders, but equally important was the feeling expressed by Maebara Issei, who led a rebellion in late 1876 at Hagi, the old castle town of Chōshū, following the final abolition of the former samurai rights to receive stipends and bear swords. "What on earth have one million samurai done wrong?" he asked bitterly. "If the government rides herd on the samurai with this attitude in mind, then for certain it will foment great troubles in the realm."[2] Other revolts in Kumamoto and Akizuki confirmed his point.

The most serious revolt of all came in January 1877 when an army of former samurai under the leadership of Saigō Takamori set out from Kagoshima to overthrow the imperial government at Tokyo. Sentiments of localism had remained strong in the domain (renamed Kagoshima prefecture) ever since the Restoration. Because of the special role the domain had played in overthrowing the bakufu it had managed to retain much of its autonomy, refusing even to forward tax money to Tokyo and still operating under the lunar calendar. After Saigō had left the government he used his government pension to help finance a number of paramilitary local academies to train former samurai in military arts and classical Confucian learning.

Kagoshima remained a citadel of all the institutions the government was eagerly demolishing—traditional learning, samurai privilege, and local autonomy. Concerned by this, government leaders decided to confiscate arms at the arsenal in Kagoshima. In response, fearing that government leaders were also planning to assassinate Saigo, members of the local academies rose in revolt. In July 1877 a force of 15,000 samurai under Saigō set out from Kagoshima to march on the capital.

The Satsuma rebellion was the last serious internal threat to the new government. It taught both the government and its critics some important lessons. The Satsuma rebels had hoped their bold initiative would spark a wave of response among other resentful samurai. But the legion of sympathizers that the Satsuma army hoped would join its ranks as it marched toward Tokyo never materialized. Complaining about the government was one thing, but open sedition was another. At the same time, though the new conscript soldiers sent out by the government to suppress the rebellion proved no better as individual fighting men than their opponents, the government army was vastly superior in number, much better equipped, and much better supported than Saigō's forces. The benefits of modernization, at least for the government, were demonstrated clearly. The government army harried the rebels through Kyushu until in September 1877 Saigō, realizing the hopelessness of his cause, committed *seppuku* on the battlefield. The possibility of counterrevolution through violence was foreclosed with his death.

"Liberty and Popular Rights"

In contrast to the peasant riots and samurai rebellions in the early and mid-1870s, a more peaceful form of political protest, relying on political agitation, local organization, journalistic attacks, and direct petition to the central government, gathered strength in the late 1870s. This was the popular rights movement begun in 1874 by Itagaki Taisuke, Etō Shimpei, and Gotō Shōjirō, shortly after their resignation from the government over the Korea question. Unlike Saigō, who simply returned to his province, these men instead urged radical political reforms to end the "tyranny" of the increasingly narrow group controlling the government. In early 1874, under the influence of ideas disseminated by the translations of the enlightenment intellectuals, they issued a public manifesto calling for the establishment of a national council chamber elected by the "people." By broadening the base of political decisions, they said, the assembly would "arouse in our people the spirit of enterprise and . . . enable them to comprehend the duty of participating in the burdens of the empire."[3] Not surprisingly this petition was rejected. In 1874 Itagaki and his followers organized the Risshisha, a local political association in Tosa, to agitate for a national assembly, lower taxes, and revision of the unequal treaties. Adopting the new and untraditional tactics of rousing public opinion, they began to spread the doctrines of "natural rights" or "inherent rights of all men" to support their demands for greater public involvement in government.

In its initial stages, the popular rights movement was neither particularly democratic nor even very popular. It was recruited and led mainly by former samurai, many from Itagaki's old domain of Tosa (now Kōchi). The Risshisha aimed as much at helping local samurai in Tosa adjust to changing economic conditions as it did at arousing their political consciousness. The movement was also permeated by vestigial samurai attitudes. The former samurai had little confidence in the wisdom of the common people or in their ability to participate in politics. When they spoke of the "people," they had in mind the ex-samurai class and the well-to-do peasants who had formed the village elite in pre-Restoration times. Moreover, many members of the movement, despite their talk of natural rights and public opinion, had a strong penchant for violence. Ueki Emori, one of the leading Aikokusha propagandists, wrote that liberty had to be bought with "fresh blood" and proclaimed the right of the people to revolt against a tyrannical government.[4] A number of Itagaki's followers were less committed to the new tactics of agitation than to resisting the government by force, and indeed urged him to join Saigō's revolt in 1877.

The popular rights movement began to change in character with the death of Saigō, whose tactics of violence had proven a dead end. A number of political hot-heads in the movement were arrested by the government for seditious activities. More important, the movement began to gather into its ranks men of all social classes, well-to-do peasant landlord-entrepreneurs, some government officials, journalists, school teachers, poorer peasants and even some common laborers. The broadening of the movement, particularly among the well-to-do peasantry, took place against a period of relative prosperity in the countryside. In the late 1870s, especially after the Satsuma rebellion, rising rice prices and declining currency values produced tremendous windfall profits for the rural landowning classes. In Tokugawa times, when taxes were collected as part of the harvest, landholders had to share their prosperity with the government. But now that taxes were assessed in fixed money payments inflation reduced the financial value of taxes and increased the economic value of the harvest. The result was a rise in land values, a rash of land speculation, and the burgeoning of new local businesses and enterprises, all of which meant good times in the countryside. The new prosperity strengthened the confidence of the local rural well-to-do and generated leisure time and capital that could be diverted into politics.

The politicization of the well-to-do peasants was further accelerated by the organization of prefectural assemblies in 1878. The assemblies were intended to draw the support of the more prosperous and stable rural elements behind the government. The right to vote for representatives to the local assemblies was restricted to local well-to-do propertied elements who bore the heaviest tax burden and might wish some say in how the government spent their money. Far from being friendly to the government at Tokyo, however, many members of this class harbored considerable hostility toward it. There was in fact a strong populist mood that had taken shape in the countryside. The government seemed to be drawing off the wealth of the rural areas without giving anything in return. Many of the local governors and prefectural officials sent out by the central government were outsiders, arrogant and insensitive to local interests, concerned mainly with building up the power of the central government, and enforcing its writ. This volatile combination of circumstances often led to clashes between government officials and the local assemblies, which became training schools for opposition politics.

The spread of new ideas, especially the writings and translations of the enlightenment intellectuals, also made many converts to the broadened popular rights movement. In antigovernment newspapers not only did the traditional attitudes of docility and submissiveness to authority come under attack but the spirit of self-help and independence was linked with political protest. "[Nature] endows men with freedom," wrote Ueki in his *Discourse on Freedom and Popular Rights* (*Minken jiyūron,* 1879). "If people do not take this natural endowment it is both a great sin against nature and a great disgrace to themselves. Disgrace does not merely reside in taking things which should not be taken, but in not taking things *which should be taken!*"[5] The message was clear: the people should take into their hands some measure of government power. Popular rights journalists and agitators spoke of a "constitution based on contract with the people" and even of "popular sovereignty." The meaning of *people* began to broaden in concept as well as in fact.

From the fall of 1877 members of the Aikokusha, a popular rights organization started by Itagaki, embarked on a campaign to generate broad support for its demands for a national assembly. Speakers and organizers staged rallies all over the country. In response local political associations drawing membership from the old commoner class sprang up all over Japan to debate and discuss politics in the new style. Local newspapers were started to voice the demands of the movement. The agitation snowballed until finally in 1880 representatives of these local associations met at Osaka to organize a League for the Establishment of a National Assembly. A central headquarters was set up in Tokyo, the rest of the country was divided into twelve districts for the purpose of propaganda and agitation, and a movement was begun to petition the government for a representative assembly and a constitution. During the year pressure group tactics produced at least fifty-five such petitions as well as a host of private constitutional drafts, and a corporal in the imperial guard even tried to commit suicide in front of the palace to shame the government into action.

To be sure, much of the activity of the popular rights movement took place against a background of indifference or confusion among the mass of the rural population, but that it took place at all was a radical departure from traditional politics. In pre-Restoration times, even well-to-do peasants rarely had concerned themselves with events beyond the village or domain boundaries. The emergence of the popular rights movement with a national organization cutting across local provincialism represented a broadening of political consciousness. It also marked the awakening of a new kind of nationalist sentiment. Although its methods were radically different from the government's, it nonetheless had the same goals—creating a strong and unified Japan that was of one mind through the establishment of a national assembly. The popular rights movement represented the kind of awakening of the people that even the government felt necessary to make Japan powerful.

Toward Constitutional Government

The authorities in Tokyo put the popular rights movement in a somewhat different perspective, however. In Tokugawa Japan there was no conception of a loyal opposition, and failure to obey constituted authorities, like all acts of insubordination, was regarded as a threat not merely to those in office but to the very regime itself. Opposition was equated with disloyalty, and those who formed factions outside the government were thought to be acting in pursuit of selfish ends rather than the public good. Against the background of earlier violent antigovernment outbreaks the popular rights movement was therefore regarded with considerable apprehension by the government leaders. As Yamagata Aritomo noted in a letter to Itō Hirobumi in 1879, "Every day we wait, the evil poison will spread more and more over the provinces, penetrate into the minds of the young, and inevitably produce unfathomable evils."[6] To blot up the "evil poison," the government was quick to resort to the tactics of repression. A series of laws, beginning with libel and slander laws promulgated in 1875, gave the government considerable discretionary powers to censor the press, disband political rallies, and clamp down on political agitation of all kinds. Police supervision of the movement was so intense that some antigovernment newspapers employed "jail editors," nominally in charge of the paper, but in fact hired to suffer imprisonment if the paper infringed the libel laws. At the same time, however, it should be pointed out that the government's repressive activities were far less harsh than those of the traditional regime, which had usually punished dissent, particularly popular dissent, with death.

Although alarmed at talk of natural rights or popular sovereignty, many government leaders were not opposed in principle to establishing either a national constitution or some sort of national assembly. In 1875, on Ōkubo Toshimichi's initiative, the government had set up a bureau to investigate the drafting of a constitution and in 1878 it also established the prefectural assembly system. Constitutionalism appealed to the government leaders because all of the advanced Western powers were constitutional nations, and they felt that the establishment of a constitutional order as a sign of progress in Japan would perhaps help to make possible concession by the foreigners on the treaty revision question. At the same time it was clear from the Western example that a constitutional government was compatible with internal order. Indeed, as Kido Kōin had noted on his return from Europe in 1873, a constitutional system might buttress national power by setting "the weal of the entire country on a firm basis."[7] By the late 1870s the main question for most government leaders was not *whether* to establish a constitution and national assembly but *what kind* should be established and *when*. It was on these latter questions that they differed with their opposition in the popular rights movement.

The rising strength of the popular rights movement finally forced the government to come to grips with these issues. As Iwakura Tomomi noted, the problem was whether Japan should follow the English model of parliamentary government and responsible cabinets or the German model of a strong monarchy and executive and a weak assembly. In response to a request for their opinions on the matter in 1880–1881, the majority of the government's leaders expressed preference for the latter model. Not only had Germany emerged as the leading continental European power in the 1870s, but like Japan it was a newly unified nation, woven together from a welter of smaller principalities and enjoying a strong monarchical tradition. The one exception was Ōkuma Shigenobu, who in March 1881 proposed that Japan adopt an English-style responsible cabinet system. He urged that a national assembly should be established by 1883, that the cabinet be responsible to the national assembly, and that political parties should control the government. Ōkuma's memorial, written with the aid of young graduates from Fukuzawa's Keiō Academy whom Ōkuma had brought into the government, startled the other leaders by its radicalism. It also brought to a head resentment of Ōkuma's emergence as one of the top contenders for the mantle of leadership left by Ōkubo Toshimichi's death in 1878. The other top leaders, nearly of all them Satsuma and Chōshū men, closed ranks against Ōkuma, forcing him out of office in the fall of 1881.

The ouster of Ōkuma in 1881, like the earlier split in the government over the Korean question, narrowed the inner circle of government. A small number of men from Satsuma and Chōshū consolidated their hold on power. The crisis of 1881 also forced the oligarchs to defuse the public clamor for popular rights by having the emperor announce his intention to establish both a constitution and a national assembly by 1890. But the imperial edict also included a warning that "those who may advocate sudden and violent changes ... disturbing the peace of the realm" would fall under imperial displeasure.[8] Opposition was to be tolerated only just barely.

Nonetheless the opposition popular rights movement continued undaunted, though it aspired to greater respectability and better organization than during its earlier phase. In late 1881 the followers of Itagaki formed the Jiyūtō (Liberal Party) under his leadership and in early 1882 the Kaishintō (Progressive Party) formed around Ōkuma and a number of junior officials who had resigned when he left the government. Both groups styled themselves as political parties, but in fact they really functioned as pressure-group organizations, engaged in a continuing intellectual and propaganda war with the government. The Kaishintō continued to argue for a moderate British-style constitutional system, stressing the need for caution and moderation and drawing its support from urban intellectuals, journalists, and businessmen. The Jiyūtō continued to display the radical streak characteristic of the early popular rights movement, committing itself to the notion of popular sovereignty, a national constitutional convention, and greater decentralization of government. In 1882 the government felt constrained to form a party of its own, the Teiseitō (Imperial Party), a claque of progovernment journalists who engaged propagandists from the other two parties in a heated newspaper debate over the locus and character of national sovereignty.

Since political initiative on the constitutional questions had shifted into the hands of the government, neither the Kaishintō nor the Jiyūtō flourished. Their leaders began to see the futility of putting public pressure on a government little inclined to heed it, and the popular base on which the parties rested began to show signs of fracture. Many of the local well-to-do landowners in the local assemblies began to realize that they could use their influence there not simply to fight the government but to extract from it concessions beneficial to their own interests. Gradually the acrimonious clashes of the early prefectural assembly sessions were replaced by bargaining and political horse-trading. Local assembly members managed to lighten their tax burdens or persuaded prefectural governors to use tax moneys to build roads or make other local improvements in their districts in return for support. At the same time, as the result of a new deflationary policy adopted by the government (see page

107), economic conditions in the countryside began to worsen, creating unrest than in various places exploded into political violence and reducing the ability of local elements to support the movement financially. The Kaishinto, drawing support from among educated and well-to-do elements in Tokyo, was not much affected by these developments, but the Jiyūtō found itself divided by internal disputes. It finally disbanded in late 1884, leaving many of its followers despairing and disillusioned.

The long-run significance of the popular rights movement was not that it forced the government to agree to a constitutional system or that it established a potent and stable national organization. Rather it was important because it established a new tradition of legitimate political dissent. Even though the advocates of popular rights were excluded from power memories of the movement lived on. Many veterans of the movement went on to become professional party politicians after the opening of the Diet in the 1890s, continuing there the struggle begun a decade earlier against the government oligarchy. The charges of official tyranny originally raised by the movement also lingered on, haunting the oligarchs as they constructed new constitutional order. These charges also became the property of conservative critics, who began to play an increasingly important role in politics.

Conservative Countercurrents

The unsettled political atmosphere of the 1870s led many educated Japanese to fear that the government reform programs might be doing as much damage as good. They had no quarrel with the government's goals of centralization, military self-strengthening, and industrialization, but they were disturbed by the influx of radical new ideas, often with government encouragement. The spread of popular rights ideas—natural rights, the legitimacy of rebellion and protest, and equality of people—seemed to be undermining respect for constituted authority. Nostalgic for the virtues of discipline, obedience, and order so central to pre-Restoration attitudes, a new group of conservative intellectuals began to call for a return to the values and morality of the old society. They were aware it was not possible to turn back the clock completely but they felt that the goals of national wealth and power would be served by revitalizing traditional ethical attitudes.

A strong undercurrent of cultural anti-Westernism buoyed up the

conservative movement. As Motoda Eifu, the emperor's personal
advisor, complained in 1878, "Efforts are being made to convert
Japanese into facsimiles of Europeans and Americans." He severely
criticized the use of Western-inspired textbooks in government
schools and argued that the new government educational system
spread idle theories that made students into troublemakers and malcontents. In a long memorial on the educational system he urged that
instruction in the schools be founded upon "the Imperial ancestral
precepts, benevolence, duty, loyalty, and filial piety" and that Confucianism be revived as the cornerstone of ethical instruction.[9]
Similar views were expressed by Nishimura Shigeki, a prominent
member of the enlightenment movement of the early 1870s. He was
not a diehard defender of Confucianism like Motoda, since he realized the inadequacies of Confucian metaphysical theories and felt
that as a system of thought it was too oriented toward the past. But
like Motoda he hoped that a selective revival of Confucian morality,
especially the virtues of loyalty and filial piety, might help to mobilize the country spiritually and buttress popular patriotism.

The cry for a revival of Confucian-style moral education, however,
was merely one aspect of the conservative intellectual reaction of the
late 1870s. More important was the discovery by many intellectual
leaders that the West had more to offer intellectually than the virtues of Anglo-American liberalism propagated by the popular rights
movement. Just as a man like Iwakura preferred Prussian-style constitutionalism to British-style parliamentarism, so did many political
critics and commentators turn their attention to German political
thought, which they found more congenial to the government's
program of national self-strengthening. Particularly striking was the
case of Katō Hiroyuki, an early advocate of natural rights theory,
who began to discover more pessimistic continental social and political theories in the late 1870s. Under their influence he came to the
conclusion that people were not naturally endowed with rights but
won them by political struggle. He also came to feel that human
progress was not an inevitable historical trend but the result of a
hard and brutal struggle among people in which the strong triumphed
over the weak by sheer force. Consequently, he concluded, Japan
should not be so concerned with the rights of the people as with its
own rights as a sovereign state, and its people should concentrate on
preserving it in the "international struggle for survival" rather than in
theorizing about liberty and equality.

The retreat from an earlier attachment to the values of liberal individualism even affected men like Fukuzawa Yukichi, who was also influenced by the doctrines of national rights. Although he continued to believe that a "spirit of independence" was a good way to build national strength he qualified it by a growing concern that the country develop its military and international strength as well. In 1882 he remarked,

> The one object of my life is to extend Japan's national power. Compared with the considerations of the country's strength, the matter of internal government and into whose hands it falls is of no importance at all. Even if the government be autocratic in name and form, I shall be satisfied if it is strong enough to strengthen the country.[10]

Like many others he still admired the Western nations as being the vanguard of civilization and he wished Japan to join their ranks, but at the same time his zeal for intellectual and political reform was muted by a growing pessimism and concern over Japan's future in the international world struggle.

The emergence of a new conservatism in the late 1870s and early 1880s, even among those who once had led the enlightenment movement, was as important in the long run as the spread of popular rights ideas against which it was reacting. If the popular rights movement laid the groundwork for continuing opposition to the bureaucratic centralism of the Meiji leadership, the conservative reaction provided intellectual justification for the increasingly statist policies of the government. Neither movement won a decisive victory over the other but both had to be accommodated in the political and social order that was to emerge in the 1880s.

7

The Turn Toward Stability

In contrast to the confusion, uncertainty, and experimentation of the early 1870s, Japan entered a period of retrenchment, increasing conservatism, and return to stability by the beginning of the 1880s. The change in atmosphere resulted in large measure from the consolidation of the nation's leadership. In place of the loose and volatile coalition of daimyo, court nobles, and samurai who had come to power in 1868 there had emerged a tightly knit oligarchy, purged of dissenters, confident in its control of the state, and possessed of a much clearer vision of what the new Japan should be. Its members, all former Satsuma and Chōshū men, were less interested in radical innovation and institutional change than in consolidation of gains already made. Reacting in part against the unforeseen consequences of their policies they had grown concerned that Japan had moved too far in too short a time, perhaps pushing ahead too carelessly and without forethought. At the same time, although not fearful of violent popular revolution, they were concerned over the long-run effects of both popular rights ideas and enlightenment thought in the popular mind. Consequently the oligarchs began to consolidate their regime with the goal of maintaining long-run political stability without sacrificing progress toward national wealth and strength and equality with the West. Indeed it is perhaps artificial to separate these twin goals since both reinforced one another. In the end, by the late 1880s, they had created an institutional and constitutional structure that was to last for the next two generations.

Retrenchment and Deflation

Perhaps the most pressing problem faced by the government in 1880, aside from the rising demand for a constitution and national assembly, was the prospect of imminent financial crisis. Despite the institution of the land tax system and the commutation of samurai stipends the government had continued to operate in the red during most of the 1870s. Interest payments on samurai bonds still ate up a large portion of the government's revenues and the suppression of the Satsuma rebellion in 1877–1878, though very profitable politically, had cost the government an enormous amount. Inflation, which doubled the price of rice between 1877 and 1880, had resulted in rural prosperity but it cost the government dearly by reducing the purchasing power of its tax revenues. To make matters even worse, since Japan was buying much more abroad than it sold, gold and silver bullion were flowing out of the country, further increasing inflationary pressures and undermining the government's financial position. By 1880 only about 5 percent of the government's paper currency was backed by metal and public confidence in the government's credit was plummeting. The dimensions of the financial crisis, increasingly clear to the government, were the cause of much anxiety in official circles.

Before his ouster from the government Ōkuma Shigenobu had proposed to float a large loan in London to tide over the crisis but most of the other government leaders were agreed that it was unwise to borrow abroad. Iwakura Tomomi commented he would just as soon sell Kyushu and Shikoku to the foreigners as borrow from them.[1] Given this determination not to rely on foreign help the only alternative for the government was to embark on a policy of retrenchment. The main architect of this new policy was Matsukata Masayoshi, who became minister of finance in 1881. A student of current Western doctrines on financial orthodoxy, Matsukata believed that the only way to establish the government's credit and fiscal reliability was to balance the budget, keep expenditures within the limits of revenues, and establish a sound currency backed by specie. The main thrust of his policy was budgetary reform. Since government factories were operating at a loss, the government enterprise policy was abandoned and except for certain strategic arsenals and shipyards most of the government's factories were sold off to private capitalists. A tight clamp was put on new spending, new consumer taxes were raised on tobacco and sake, and the quantity of money was decreased by 20 percent between 1881 and 1885. Furthermore, as a means of cutting expenses a number of government expenditures were shifted to prefectural governments and higher local taxes were raised to pay them. As a result of this belt tightening prices fell rapidly—the rice price by 50 percent—between 1881 and 1885 and the government now enjoyed the same kind of windfall that landlords had a few years before.

At the same time Matsukata began to build a sound central banking system in order to create an atmosphere of economic confidence and stability needed for increased business activity. The national banking system established in 1876 proved to be a disaster, for not only were the new banks poorly managed but they issued their own private bank notes with an abandon that much exacerbated inflation. In 1885 Matsukata established the Bank of Japan, a central government bank that issued bank notes backed by specie in order to redeem the unsound inconvertible paper money earlier issued by both government and private banks. By soaking up much of the inflated paper money the government created a sound national currency in which both business and public had confidence. The Bank of Japan also became the center of a whole system of specialized semigovernment banks (such as the Yokohama Specie Bank, the Hypothec Bank, and the Agricultural and Industrial Bank) backed in part by government capital and placed under close official supervision. These financial institutions were established to promote long-term investment in industry, agriculture, and foreign trade.

The main positive effect of Matsukata's policies was to smooth the way for increased private initiative in the development of the modern sector of the economy. Inflation was checked, confidence was restored in the government's credit, and there was new machinery to provide backing for large entrepreneurial ventures. Businessmen and merchants could now turn to the government-connected banks for capital without having to build up their own financial resources. Similarly, as a result of the decision to establish a firm currency, interest rates began to fall after 1885. Since this lowered the cost of investment entrepreneurs were encouraged to start new ventures. As a result, by the late 1880s a modest boom occurred in the infant industrial sector of the economy, especially in railroads and cotton textiles where certain private firms managed to show substantial profits, prompting a surge of investment. Private railroad track expanded from 63 to 898 miles between 1883 and 1890, and the number of cotton spindles in operation doubled between 1886 and 1890.

If the "Matsukata deflation," as it is sometimes called, made businessmen and investors happy, it was enormously unpopular with much of the rural population. The drop in rice prices brought farm incomes tumbling down. Local weather conditions also brought a series of bad harvests throughout much of the country between 1881 and 1884, so that many peasant cultivators found themselves driven to the wall. Larger landholders tried to tide over the situation by collecting rents willy-nilly, calling in loans, and foreclosing mortgages ruthlessly. Many peasant families went down the path to debt, foreclosure, and tenancy. As a result, between 1883 and 1891 the number of peasant cultivator families dropped from 39 percent to 33 percent of the total farm family population, and even the number of landholders paying sufficient taxes to qualify for suffrage in prefectural assemblies dropped by one third. Hardship in the countryside, especially among the poorer peasants, was the price paid for economic stability.

Not surprisingly, the result was a new wave of unrest in the countryside. Local risings, often highly organized, occurred in the less prosperous areas in the northern and northwestern sections of Honshu. Major disturbances occurred in Fukushima (1882), Kabasan, Chichibu, and Iida (all in 1884). Often these were led by members of the well-to-do landlord class, still resentful of the central government or inspired by popular rights ideas, but they generated widespread support among the hard-pressed poorer peasants harassed by debt and the prospect of tenancy. In Chichibu, for example, the local rebels called for better terms for repaying debts, reduction of consumer taxes, closing of schools for three years, revision of the conscription law, and reduction of village expenses. All these demands directly or indirectly reflected their straitened economic circumstances. Although these local disturbances were put down handily by government troops and local police they revealed the resentment against the government that continued to smolder in the countryside.

The Bureaucratic State

While Matsukata put government finances aright other oligarchic leaders were hard at work constructing a new political structure. There was an informal division of labor between the two more aggressive leaders, Yamagata Aritomo and Itō Hirobumi. While Yamagata aided by Ōyama Iwao and Katsura Tarō consolidated the military command structure and developed a local government system, Itō together with Inoue Kaoru set down to work on the establishment of new central institutions and the drafting of the constitution. Caution, moderation, and gradualism were their watchwords. As a result of their Confucian education they were inclined to think of good government as elitist government—rule by the "wise and able" who were loyal to the emperor and ready to put public duty above private gain or personal ambition. As a result of their political experience they were convinced that their opponents were irresponsible extremists or ambitious opportunists and the mass of the people were still not ready for political responsibility. Consequently their ultimate goal was a strong centralized bureaucratic state, run by "men of talent" with little popular control or interference.

The basic assumption of the oligarchs was that the state structure would be monarchical, centering on the imperial institution. They had already decided that the constitution was to be imperially granted, and they opted to bring most of the new organs of state into being by imperial decree. But the imperial institution itself needed strengthening. Despite his frequent progresses through the country in the 1870s the emperor remained a remote and little-known figure to much of the populace. One foreign resident was distressed to find in 1880 that people hung out flags on the emperor's birthday only when prompted to by the police. Equally important, the imperial family continued to remain relatively impecunious, dependent on the government for most of its expenditures. To build the dignity of the throne and to assure its financial independence from outside political pressure the government began to turn over to the imperial family government-owned land, especially forest land originally confiscated from the Tokugawa. It also diverted into the imperial household large amounts of cash, private company stocks, and government bank bonds. By 1889 the imperial family held 3,650,000 *chō* of land (as opposed to 600 *chō* in 1880) and ¥ 7,880,000 in stocks, an amount roughly equal in value to the government's budget that year. The administration of this enormous fortune was in the hands of the Imperial Household Ministry, an independent body created in 1885 and staffed by officials appointed by the emperor. Some of the imperial income went to charitable enterprises but it was also used on occasion as a slush fund for the government and tapped for both political and governmental purposes.

The imperial court was a self-contained financial and administrative citadel, immune from outside political leverage, but the oligarchs also felt the need to establish a new aristocracy as the "living ramparts" of this citadel. In July 1884 a new hereditary peerage system was created, giving new titles to former court noble families and the heads of former daimyo houses, including the Tokugawa. More to the point, the new peerage included "mature statesmen, men of merit, and erudite scholars," honored for their service to the state rather than their family pedigree. This service aristocracy included the oligarchs themselves, most of whom came from relatively humble positions in the samurai class, and even men like Itagaki Taisuke, Gotō Shojirō, and Ōkuma Shigñobu, who had helped build the post-Restoration regime despite their later dissidence. Having done so much good for Japan, the oligarchs felt they should do well themselves.

In practical terms the strengthened imperial institution and the new peerage were of secondary importance, since both were set above and apart from the actual administration of state affairs. The task of making policy and executing laws was to be in the hands of a professional bureaucracy and a professional officer corps.

The civilian side of the state structure centered on the cabinet created in 1885 to replace the old and rather unwieldy grand council that had functioned as the highest executive body since the early 1870s. The cabinet was the central decision-making body. It was headed by a premier, appointed by and legally responsible to the emperor, and consisted of nine other ministers (foreign affairs, home affairs, justice, finance, army, navy, education, agriculture and commerce, and transportation). At first the premier had the right to appoint and supervise his ministers, but these strong executive powers were eventually eliminated in 1889. The importance of the cabinet was indicated by the appointment of Itō as the first premier and by the monopolization of the other portfolios by other central fig-

ures in the oligarchy. Indeed, this oligarchic monopoly over the
cabinet continued through the 1890s.

The civil bureaucracy that executed the policies of the cabinet also
took shape in the 1880s. In the hectic early years of Meiji the lower
ranks of officialdom had been recruited rather haphazardly. Fellow
provincials, personal followers, and promising young men possessed
of the new knowledge were pulled into the government as need
required, though often they proved to be inept or incompetent time-
servers. In the early 1870s the government had attempted to set up
training academies, often attached to particular government bureaus,
to train specialists to work for the burgeoning state. But by the late
1880s, after some experimentation, it was finally decided to set up a
rational system of recruitment by civil service examination. In 1887
regulations established a new civil service, divided into "higher civil
servants" who were to occupy key executive positions in government
ministries, and "ordinary civil servants" who were to take care of
routine paper work and detail. The higher civil service became the
new bureaucratic elite. To assure it recruited the brightest and best
of the population, the government offered enormous salaries to
officials, just as earlier it had offered them to foreign advisors. It also
turned the new Imperial University in Tokyo (founded in 1888),
especially its Faculty of Law, into the main training ground for
fledgling bureaucrats by exempting graduates of the institution from
the need to compete in examinations. Naturally this favored the
university's graduates, who dominated the middling ranks of the
bureaucracy by the late 1890s. Most important of all, the professional civil servants were expected to be technicians and experts. All
but the highest posts (bureau chief and vice minister) were closed to
free patronage appointments, assuring that the bureaucracy would be
kept chaste of extrabureaucratic political pressure.

Parallel to the cabinet-civil service side of the state structure was
the relatively autonomous military high command and officer corps.
In the wake of the Satsuma rebellion, army leaders, especially Yamagata Aritomo, had decided to separate the command structure of the
military from military administration. In 1878 an army general staff
following the German model was created with full responsibility for
strategic planning and command control over military forces, and the
principles embodied in the reform were later reiterated in the general
staff regulations of 1889. The army and navy chiefs of staff, like the

premier, were appointed directly by the emperor and responsible to him alone, giving the high commands the same right of direct access to the throne as the head of the civil government. The military bureaucracy and the officer corps were not under control of the cabinet and the chief of staff had the power to send troops into the field unchecked by any civilian authority except the emperor. The war minister in the cabinet was not in control of the army, merely its representative in the cabinet.

The original intention behind the separation of military and civil policy-making was to keep decisions on defense and strategy above or outside of politics in the hands of professional military men. Like the civil bureaucracy the officer corps was supposed to be technical and not political in character. The army leaders were particularly anxious to keep the army from being subverted by the government's opponents. They had been alarmed in 1878 when members of the imperial guard had planned an incursion into the palace grounds and assassination of leading officials in protest over pay cuts after the Satsuma rebellion. A series of official admonitions were issued culminating in the issuance of the Imperial Precepts for Soldiers and Sailors of 1882, which enjoined military men to "neither be led astray . . . by popular opinions nor meddle in politics, but with single heart fulfill your essential duty of loyalty."[2] In fact, however, the separation of military policy from civil policy, as well as the isolation of the army from politics, was easier said than done, particularly in the area of foreign policy and budget-making, where the military's interests were intimately involved. Consequently the army involved itself in politics when convenient but retreated behind its right of direct access to fend off outside political pressure, using it as a legal rampart from which it could again later sally forth at will. As long as the oligarchy remained unified, in control of both the army and civil hierarchy, disputes could be resolved informally, but in the long run the independence of the military was to give it much political influence.

The 1880s saw not only the rationalization of the state structure and the formation of a bureaucracy to run it but also the greater penetration of central government into local communities. In the decade and a half after the Restoration local towns and villages had retained a large degree of autonomy, despite the dispatch of new prefectural officials from Tokyo. Town or village assemblies raised

The Turn Toward Stability / 113

local taxes to be spent locally, and town mayors or village chiefs were publicly elected, albeit by a highly restricted suffrage. If not quite as independent as the Tokugawa village, local communities in the 1870s still had much say in the management of their own affairs. Beginning in 1884 this local autonomy was gradually stripped away in the name of administrative centralization and convenience. Village heads and town mayors were appointed instead of elected. Town assemblies were headed by an appointed mayor and the central government assumed greater power over the expenditures of local tax revenues. Towns and villages were converted into the bottom rung of an administrative ladder that ran up through the prefectural governors to the Home Minister. The Tokugawa tradition of local self-control came to an end and men looked to Tokyo for both favors and influence. At the same time the merging of many older natural communities into newly created village administrative units meant that the local village community was no longer a political entity. Local self-government was created from above, placing the mass of the rural population under direct control while shutting out all but the more aggressive and well-to-do from political participation.

The Meiji Constitution

By the late 1880s all the main elements of the new constitutional order had been created with the exception of the promised national assembly. This was not accidental, since the oligarchs had wished to assure the firm existence of a bureaucratic state structure before venturing into the uncertain waters of constitutional politics. Unlike the American constitution the Japanese constitution did not create new institutions; it merely set in place institutions already in existence. The work of drafting began in the summer of 1887 under the personal direction of Itō Hirobumi aided by Inoue Kaoru, Kaneko Kentarō, and Itō Miyōji. Since the constitution was to be the gift of the emperor to his subjects there was no need to submit it to a constitutional convention. But to assure it enjoyed the support of the oligarchy it was submitted to a privy council established in 1888 on the model of the English system. The privy council's twelve members, headed by Itō, were nearly all members of the Sat-Chō oligarchy, and conducted their deliberations in such elaborate secrecy that the councillors were required to return their draft documents at the end of each meeting. As a result the provisions of the constitution were unknown to the public until its final promulgation by the emperor on February 11, 1889.

In keeping with the original intentions of the oligarchs the constitution concentrated most powers in the hands of the emperor. The preamble unequivocally stated that the emperor had inherited "the right of sovereignty of the State" from his ancestors and would bequeath it to his heirs. Other provisions gave the emperor the right to appoint all the top officials of state, as well as the power to legislate, to convoke a national diet, to alter the organization of the bureaucracy, to declare war and make peace, to conclude treaties, to confer ranks and honors, and so forth. But in fact it was clearly understood by the oligarchs—and established by precedent—that the emperor would not exercise any of these powers on his own personal initiative. Having overthrown what they regarded as a despotic regime, the oligarchs were not anxious to create a new one. Although neither democratic nor liberal in outlook, the oligarchs—particularly Itō—understood the rationale behind limited government. As Itō noted in 1888,

> The spirit behind the establishment of constitutional government is first to impose restrictions on the powers of the monarch, and second to secure the rights of subjects. . . . In whatever country, when you do not protect the rights of subjects and do not limit the power of the monarch, you have a despotic government, in which the rights of the ruler have become as unlimited as the duties of the subjects.[3]

The emperor might have been the keystone of the state, but he was firmly held in place by the pillars of constitutional law.

Not only were the powers of the emperor limited by being defined but the various organs of state created in the 1880s were woven into a complicated fabric of checks and balances. The emperor could appoint and remove ministers at will, but his decrees had to be countersigned by his ministers to take effect; the premier had no appointive control over his ministers, but he could suspend or reprimand them; the cabinet was granted considerable executive powers, but had to share them with the privy council, the imperial household ministry, and the military high command. Far from creating an absolutist system, the constitutional framework provided much scope for political conflict and competition. Except for the perpetuation of the imperial authority the political future of the country was open-ended.

The main new element introduced by the constitution was the establishment of an elective national assembly, the Diet. The last of the new state organs to be created, the Diet was regarded as the most peripheral by the oligarchs. Some government leaders, Mori Arinori, for example, wanted it to be merely a sounding board for the cabinet, able to debate legislation but not able to enact any. But Itō felt that consent of the governed was an essential element of constitutional government, particularly on budget matters. His views won out and the constitution gave the Diet not only the power to debate and approve the annual budget, but also to enact legislation of its own, confirm or reject imperial ordinances issued when the Diet was out of session, and petition or memorialize the throne. Given the general distrust of the oligarchs for the opposition outside the government these were rather considerable concessions.

Every effort was made to assure that the actions of the Diet would be moderate, however. For one thing, the Diet was bicameral. In order to check the "rash impulses" of a popularly elected house of representatives the constitution provided also for a house of peers dominated by the newly created hereditary aristocracy, whose consent was required on both the budget and other legislation. At the same time the Diet session was limited to three months a year, hardly sufficient time to allow it to dominate the business of government, and the House of Representatives could be prorogued or dissolved at the order of the emperor. To assure that only sound, stable, and respectable social elements would be elected to the House of Representatives, suffrage was limited to those who paid over fifteen yen in direct national taxes, a limitation that excluded all but 400,000 (or about 1 percent) of the population in 1890. Similar restrictions were placed on candidates for Diet seats as well. Moreover, since the ballot was open, not secret, it is clear that the oligarchs hoped to exclude "extremist" or "radical" elements from the start.

Nevertheless, the initial public reaction to the constitution was highly favorable. To be sure, long-time critics such as Ōkuma, Itagaki, and other veterans of the popular rights movement found much in it wanting, but they were no less proud than others that Japan had become the first Oriental nation to adopt a constitutional system.

The constitution was the capstone of the long effort to achieve political parity with the Western powers. Moreover, though the constitution in operation still had to be tested, its promulgation signaled an advance beyond the oligarchic domination of politics characterizing the first two Meiji decades. The oligarchs still occupied the political high ground but their wall of political exclusiveness had now been breached.

Education and Indoctrination

In the long run the political consequences of new educational policies adopted in the 1880s were no less than the consequences of constitutional consolidation. Neither were they less reflective of the general caution and conservatism that dominated the thinking of the oligarchs. The spread of liberal ideas and radical doctrines accompanying the rise of the popular rights movement had brought about a rethinking of the educational goals adopted in the early 1870s. Government leaders began to feel that the development of autonomous, independent, and self-reliant citizens for the new Japan was less important than restoring the social discipline and order of the old Japan. The facile liberal notion that education could make people free was abandoned in favor of the more traditional notion that education could make them docile. On the one hand, the Ministry of Education began to purge the schools of radical influences. In 1881 teachers were admonished not to engage in "stubborn or extreme talk"[4] about politics and religion, and along with students were forbidden to attend political meetings or join political associations. The intent was to purge the schools of antigovernment teachers. In 1881, for example, the governor of Kōchi prefecture, heart of the popular rights movement, fired all teachers suspected of being activists in the movement. At the same time the central government authorities also began to assert greater control over the content of the curriculum. Schools were no longer allowed to choose their own textbooks and the government in 1883 issued a list of authorized textbooks, eliminating most liberal or radical works regarded as dangerous.

But if the government authorities were averse to having the schools used by opponents to radicalize the young, they had no qualms about turning them to political purposes of their own—the inculcation of the virtues of obedience, patriotism, loyalty, and filial piety.

Older ethical traditions were mobilized for the service of the new state. Conservative scholars like Nishimura Shigeki and Motoda Eifu, who felt Confucianism should provide the best moral guide for the young, began to exercise much influence on the Ministry of Education. The old habits of submissiveness condemned by Fukuzawa and others were now converted into civic virtues. The primary school ethics primer authorized in 1883 admonished pupils to doff their hats and bow low before the emperor, to treat government officials with respect, and to refrain from insulting policemen, "who protect us all and help us at times of hardship and disaster."[5] The new spirit of education was summed up by Mori Arinori, Minister of Education in the late 1880s, when he commented, "What is to be done is not for the sake of the pupils, but for the sake of country."[6]

The attempt to turn the elementary school system into an instrument for a kind of civil religion culminated in 1890 with the issuance of the Imperial Rescript on Education, a basic statement of the moral and political attitudes defined as correct by the government. The document, however, was produced only after a long struggle within the government.

Men like Motoda Eifu wanted to make Confucianism the official faith of the country while Itō and Inoue Kaoru opposed any attempt to establish an official orthodoxy on the grounds that morality was a matter of private conscience and that education, like the army, should be kept free of politics. The result was an uneasy compromise, a document which stressed traditional Confucian virtues such as loyalty (*chū*) and filial piety (*kō*), as well as the more modern ideas of respect for the constitution and devotion to the state. But in the long run educational authorities tended to stress the conservative traditionalist virtues in formulating policy.

The inculcation of loyalty to the emperor and to a lesser extent obedience to the state became a central function of the school system from 1890 onward. The Imperial Rescript became a talisman of respect, solemnly intoned like a Buddhist sutra at school ceremonies on national holidays. Probably few children understood the difficult and archaic language of the document, but as they stood with heads bowed in respect they knew it dealt with grave and important matters. Similarly, the emperor's "august photograph," placed in every school, was revered in the same concrete way. There were occasionally cases of school principals who after failing to rescue the portrait from fires committed ritual suicide to atone for their negligence. By the end of the 1890s the emperor was still an awesomely distant and exaltedly high figure for most graduates of the school system but at the same time he was also a more personal leader than he had been for earlier generations who were barely aware of his existence.

The physical veneration of the emperor was reinforced by the diffusion in ethics, reading, and history courses of the idea that Japan possessed a special national polity (*kokutai*). Scholars like Inoue Tetsujirō and Hozumi Yatsuka, both professors at the Imperial University, produced moral tracts and educational materials stressing the uniqueness of the Japanese people, who had enjoyed the imperial rule in an unbroken line for generations. This remarkable continuity was attributed in part to the divine origins of the dynasty, whose holy ancestors had "deeply and firmly implanted virtue" both in the monarch and in the common people. At the same time it was said to spring from the natural and spontaneous unity between the emperor and the subjects, knitted together in a kind of family state. In a very literal way the emperor was described as the father of the subjects, and they as the emperor's children. Filial piety, or respect for one's parents, was a paradigm for loyalty to the monarch, the state, and superiors in general, and the concept of political loyalty was reinforced by respect for the family head. The whole of Japanese society was depicted as a great family, stretching from the father-figure emperor at the top through to the individual family below, weaving around individuals a strong and unlimited sense of obligation to all above them, whether father, teacher, official, or employer. Stress was also laid on willingness to sacrifice oneself for the good of all. Elementary history textbooks were filled with stories about historical exemplars of these virtues, such as Kusonoki Masashige, making concrete the models on which subjects were to shape themselves.

The net effect of these educational policies was twofold. On the one hand it presented to the mass of the people a model of behavior based on the traditional elite ethic. It turned the class virtues of the samurai into a national ethic for the commoners. At the same time, by associating these virtues with the emperor and with the national polity, it made them specifically Japanese virtues, not shared with the rest of the world. Loyalty and filial piety were not virtues that all people should practice, as many had thought in Tokugawa times, but were rather particular virtues of the Japanese people. The notion of the family state strengthened not only obedience to constituted authority but also a sense of national identity. Drawing as it did on social values and attitudes deeply imbedded in Japanese culture, the official morality was doubtless easier to propagate than some foreign faith such as Christianity or secular liberalism. But at the same time it was highly selective in its use of traditional virtues and slighted the ideas of cooperation, moral responsibilities of superiors, and the virtue of achievement, which were equally part of the traditional morality.

The values implanted by the educational system were not necessarily compatible with the other institutional reforms of the 1880s. To be sure, they meshed well enough with the needs of a highly centralized bureaucratic state, mobilizing popular support behind it. But they did not fit so well with either the burgeoning capitalistic economy or popular participation in the political process through elections and the Diet. Although the oligarchs aimed for long-run stability these contradictions were to produce new social stresses and tensions ultimately disruptive of the institutional structure. The conservatism of the 1880s was to produce as many unforeseen results as the radical policies of the 1870s.

8

The Rise of
Imperialism

During the early years of the Meiji era the new imperial government had found itself relatively free from foreign pressure. The last venture in Western gunboat diplomacy came in 1865 with the dispatch of a joint fleet to Osaka Bay in order to force the opening of Hyōgō (later Kobe) and the negotiation of a new commercial treaty. But by 1868 the foreign powers had gotten most of the concessions they were after and Japan ceased to be much of a problem in their eyes. Most of the issues that arose after the Restoration were minor ones easily resolved by negotiation—the residence rights of foreigners, the currency to be used in foreign trade, the status of Christianity, and the like. Since the bakufu had drained off the wrath of the foreigners as well as the hostility of domestic xenophobes, the new imperial government did not bear the stigma of having been pusillanimous toward the barbarians, nor of having been obstructive of their demands. Doubtless this clean slate on foreign policy issues helps to account for the survival of the government in its early years. No foreign wars or outside interventions threatened the existence of the new regime. Dealings with the foreigners, however, especially on the question of treaty revision, were never very far from the minds of the new leaders. In a sense most of their domestic reforms and innovations were diplomacy carried on by other means. Even more important, there were already in the early 1870s first signs of an impulse to engage in an aggressive, expansionist policy abroad. With the abandonment of isolation Japan began a slow but steady 180-degree turn toward expansion.

The Expansionist Impulse

The transition to an imperialist foreign policy did not come suddenly. During the early 1870s the foreign policy of the imperial government was marked by restraint, prudence, and caution. The tone was set by the decision in late 1873 not to invade Korea as chastisement for alleged diplomatic insults toward the Japanese. The peace party within the government, whose position was most persuasively argued by Ōkubo Toshimichi, was not opposed to an aggressive foreign policy in principle but as a practical matter.[1] They felt that "hasty ventures" abroad had to take second place to internal consolidation. Consequently, although the government tried its best to avoid foreign conflicts that might jeopardize the task of building national wealth and strength, it pursued a foreign policy that blended an astute use of Western-style diplomacy and international law with a willingness to make a display of force in defense of Japan's rights. Aggressive pursuit of Japan's interests was combined with a strong sense of restraint and a continuing awareness that Japan was weak in comparison to the Western powers.

Most of this early foreign policy revolved around the question of defining Japan's boundaries. To the north, where the much-distrusted Russians made claim to certain islands north of the newly developing Hokkaido, the government resorted primarily to negotiation. In 1875 after lengthy diplomatic interchange the Japanese signed a treaty with the Russians trading their claims on the island of Sakhalin for Russian recognition of the Kurile Islands as Japanese territory. To the south, where there was no European power to deal with, the government showed more willingness to indulge in saber-rattling. In the spring of 1874, partly as a sop to the war party, the government dispatched a punitive expedition under the leadership of Saigō Tsugumichi (Takamori's brother) to chastise Taiwanese aborigines for attacks made on fishermen from the Ryukyu Islands. The Ch'ing government, which claimed suzerainty over Taiwan, finally agreed to pay an indemnity to the families of the fishermen, thereby establishing its own claims on Taiwan but also tacitly recognizing Japanese claims over the Ryukyus.

This attempt to define national boundaries in disputed areas was natural enough but in 1875 the government showed a willingness to make even bolder moves in her relations with the outside world. In more-or-less conscious imitation of the Western example the government decided to open Korea just as earlier the Americans had opened Japan. Traditionally Korea had been a vassal state of the Ch'ing dynasty, regularly sending tribute missions to Peking, but otherwise remaining a "hermit kingdom" closed to all intercourse with the outside world, just as Japan had been down to 1854. Using an attack on the crew of a Japanese surveying vessel as an excuse, the Japanese dispatched a gunboat expedition to Korea to demand the establishment of normal diplomatic and trade relations. No more willing to risk war than the bakufu had been, the Korea court finally agreed to negotiations. The Treaty of Kangwha, signed in January 1876, recognized Korea as an independent sovereignty, provided for the exchange of diplomatic representatives, opened a number of ports to trade, and gave the Japanese certain extraterritorial rights in the new treaty ports. Ironically, the Japanese imposed on the Koreans the same kind of unequal treaty system that they sought to shed themselves.

The international context of early Meiji diplomacy had been one of relative calm in East Asia. By the early 1880s, however, a new wave of Western aggressiveness began to trouble the area. With the consolidation of national boundaries in Europe, the achievement of an international balance of power on the continent, the advance of industrialization, and the perfection of a technology for long-distance communication by steam vessels and telegraph, the European powers engaged in intensified competition for colonies, naval bases, and spheres of influence in the world outside Europe. Everywhere signs of this "new imperialism" were evident. The Russians and English struggled for influence in Central Asia on the western borders of China, the French began to penetrate the Indochina peninsula, Germany began to show an increased interest in China and the South Pacific, and the United States was developing strong interests in Hawaii. Although these developments were motivated primarily by rivalries among the Westerners, to many Japanese they seemed to represent a clear and present danger to the peace of East Asia.

This new turn of events in the 1880s, coupled with a growing confi-

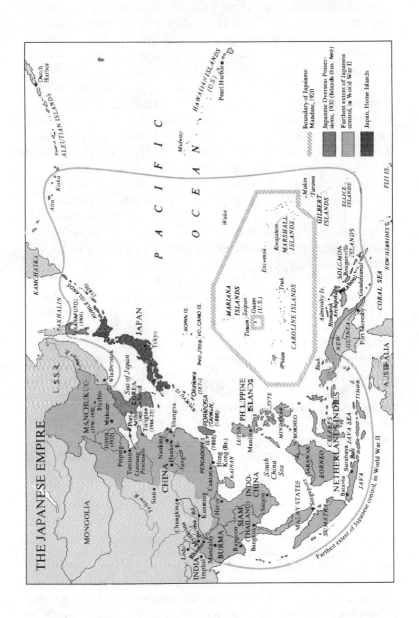

THE JAPANESE EMPIRE

Boundary of Japanese Mandate, 1920

Japanese Overseas Possessions, 1930 (Islands thus, *Iwo*)

Farthest extent of Japanese control, in World War II

Japan, Home Islands

MONGOLIA

U.S.S.R.

KAMCHATKA

SAKHALIN

KARAFUTO (1905)

KURILE ISLANDS (1875)

ALEUTIAN ISLANDS

Attu

Kiska

Dutch Harbor

MANCHUKUO (1931-1932)

Harbin

JEHOL (1932)

Mukden

Peiping

Tientsin

Port Arthur (1905)

Liaotung Peninsula

Tsingtao (1914-23)

Vladivostok

Sea of Japan

KOREA (1910)

JAPAN

Tokyo

Okinawa (1879)

RYUKYUS

HAWAIIAN ISLANDS (U.S.)

Pearl Harbor

Midway

P A C I F I C   O C E A N

Wake

Amur R.

Sungari R.

CHINA

Nanking

Hankow

Shanghai

Yangtze R.

Yellow R.

Chungking

Kunming

Hanoi

Siam R.

BONIN IS.

Iwo Jima

VO. CANO IS.

MARIANA ISLANDS

Saipan

Tinian

Guam (U.S.)

Yap

Palau

Eniwetok

CAROLINE ISLANDS

Truk

Kwajalein

MARSHALL ISLANDS

Makin

Tarawa

GILBERT ISLANDS

ELLICE ISLANDS

FIJI IS.

Farthest extent of Japanese control, in World War II

PESCADORES IS.

FORMOSA (TAIWAN) (1895)

Hong Kong (Br.)

Canton

HAINAN

South China Sea

PHILIPPINE ISLANDS

LUZON

Manila

MINDANAO

LEYTE

Admiralty Is.

Bismarck Archipelago

Bougainville

SOLOMON ISLANDS

Buka

Guadalcanal

NEW GUINEA

Port Moresby

NEW HEBRIDES

CORAL SEA

BURMA

Mandalay

Bhamo

Ledo

Imphal

INDIA

Rangoon

Burma Rd.

Ledo Rd.

SIAM (THAILAND)

Bangkok

Saigon

INDO-CHINA

MALAY STATES

Singapore

SARAWAK

BORNEO

CELEBES

NETHERLANDS INDIES

Batavia

Surabaya

Bali

JAVA SEA

JAVA

SUMATRA

TIMOR

AUSTRALIA

dence in Japan's own military and economic progress, led many Japanese to feel the need for a more positive and aggressive foreign policy than the government had pursued in the preceding decade. Of the advocates of a strong foreign policy perhaps the most vociferous were among the government's opposition. On the one hand there was much talk of a need for expansion among a handful of displaced former samurai who had difficulty in adjusting to the stability of post-Restoration society. In 1881 a number of these men, many of them former supporters of Saigō Takamori, formed the *Genyōsha,* a chauvinist society dedicated to defending the honor of the nation and promoting reverence to the emperor. On the other hand members of the popular rights movement and the political parties that grew out of it found foreign policy a convenient stick with which to beat the government. Public debate on foreign policy issues, infused with strong antigovernment sentiment, focused on the government's failure to revise the treaties as well as on Japan's relations with China and Korea, both easy targets for the renewed advance of Western power into the East.

Arguments in favor of an expansionist Asian policy ranged from the opportunistic to the idealistic. At one extreme was a man like Sugita Teiichi, a popular rights activist who returned from a tour of China in 1884 convinced that the Chinese were too "narrow-minded and obstinate" to protect their own independence. Since he felt it likely that the Westerners, competing for profit and power, were about to make a feast of China, he urged that Japan also be a "guest at the table."[2] Such notions, reinforced by the growing currency of Social Darwinist ideas, were common among those who saw international politics as a struggle for the survival of the fittest. On the other hand there were some who felt that Japan's new strength brought with it a responsibility to help her neighbors "civilize" themselves. Fukuzawa Yukichi, for example, suggested that Japan offer both military and cultural protection to the Chinese and Koreans, defending them from Western power while introducing them to Western civilization. Impelled by such sentiments Ōi Kentarō, a radical who styled himself a "Japanese Lafayette," gave financial and other support to Korean reformers bent on overthrowing reactionary elements at the Korean court. Finally there were a handful of men like Arao Kiyoshi who held that economic expansion and the promotion of Japanese trade with China would meet the threat of Western commercial domination in East Asia.

Many critics of the government's relatively moderate foreign policy were long on vision but short on a sense of possibilities. Nevertheless government leaders were not impervious to their criticisms nor were they entirely unsympathetic with their goals. For the most part however, the primary concern of the oligarchics was less a sense of Japan's mission in Asia than an acute sensitivity to national security. Economic development and institution-building at home continued to be the main focus of their efforts to build national wealth and power, but new strategic doctrines began to influence their thinking too. Colonies, naval bases, and spheres of influence abroad seemed as necessary to maintain national independence as a strong army and navy. Major Jacob Meckel, a German advisor to the army, told military leaders that the security of Japan depended on maintaining Korea, "a dagger pointed at the heart of Japan," independent from control by any other power. This soon became a basic axiom of the government, as well as the General Staff, which in 1887 began preparing contingency plans for a war with China to secure the independence of Korea. At the same time the navy was coming under the influence of the doctrines of the American Admiral Mahan, an advocate of naval expansion. Many naval officers felt that trade and commerce backed by a strong navy and merchant marine and an ability to control the seas neighboring Japan were both essential to national progress and national security. The leadership's new perspective on foreign policy was summed up in 1890 by Yamagata Aritomo, who argued that the way to national independence and defense lay in protecting not simply Japan's home territories ("the line of sovereignty") but also an outer perimeter of adjacent territory ("a line of interest") strategically necessary for Japan.[3] There was little danger that the foreigners would encroach on the Japanese "line of sovereignty," but there was much danger that they might get a foothold within the "line of interest." Hence there was a growing desire to assure Japanese ascendency in these adjacent territories.

The nascent imperialist mentality of the government leadership was therefore a kind of reactive imperialism roused by a renewed sense of outside threat and colored by Western imperialist doctrine. Strategic and political considerations were more important than a concern for economic advantage. The idea of building a Japanese colonial empire in order to secure raw materials, new markets, or overseas investment opportunities was peripheral to their thought. In the early 1890s Japan had little need of an economic empire. Her own modern industries were still in their infancy, just beginning to find capital and markets at home, and her existing economic interests in Asia were marginal. Only a quarter of her trade went there, in contrast to the much greater volume of trade with advanced countries of Europe and North America. The "line of interest" was primarily strategic rather than economic.

Korea and the Sino-Japanese War

The Korean peninsula was the main focus of Japan's initial expansionist impulse. After the "opening" of Korea by Japanese gunboats in 1876 the Japanese began to gain a strong economic and political foothold there. Japanese traders moved into the new treaty ports of Pusan, Wonsan, and Inchon selling cotton textiles and other manufactures and exporting rice and other foodstuffs back to Japan. At the same time certain members of the Korean aristocracy began to look to the rapidly modernizing Japan as a model for reforming their own country. The Korean king, much influenced by the members of the Min family, began to turn directly to Japan for advice and assistance. In 1880 a group of Korean officials, like the Iwakura mission to the West, went to Japan to observe conditions there, and the following year the government invited a number of Japanese army officers to train a modern military force for Korea. Far from seeing Japan as a potential aggressor, reformist elements in Korea saw her as a nation that had successfully repelled Western aggression.

But just as the arrival of Perry had provoked the formation of an expulsionist party in Japan, so the sudden influx of the Japanese, bearing new ideas and new goods, roused a conservative opposition in Korea. Far from regarding the Japanese as a model to be followed, Korean conservatives felt that there they were "Oriental renegades" who had betrayed their heritage. In July 1882 the conservative forces used a rising of Korean soldiers against their Japanese advisors to recoup their declining fortunes. Rebel forces attacked the residence of the Min family, killing many of its leaders, set fire to the Japanese legation, and forced Queen Min to flee from the palace. The rising restored to influence the virulently antiforeign regent, who had opposed opening the country, but the main advantage really came to the Chinese. Anxious to re-establish its declining influence in Korea, the Ch'ing government dispatched a force of 5,000 to "assist" the Korean court. The Chinese troops restored to power the

Min family, who promptly abolished all the Japanese reforms and re-
established tributary relations with Peking. Chinese advisors or
pro-Chinese foreign advisors were installed in every department of
the government, and normal commercial relations were established
with the Westerners in order to undercut the Japanese economic
position. The Japanese found they could do little more in the face of
these new Chinese initiatives than demand an indemnity and an
apology from the Korean court. In 1884 pro-Japanese elements led
by Kim Ok-kyun and Pak Yŏng-hyo attempted a countercoup to oust
the Chinese. They had financial backing from private sources in
Japan as well as unofficial collusion with the Japanese minister to
Korea. The coup aimed at instituting a Meiji-style program of reform
and modernization but it was quickly put down with the help of
Chinese troops, who forced the reformers and the Japanese minister
to flee the country.

The disturbances of 1882 and 1884 both had caused minor war
scares in Japan but the government, still pursuing a policy of caution,
chose to follow the path of diplomatic detente. The Chinese, then
fighting the French in Indochina, were not anxious for war either.
In 1885 Itō Hirobumi and Li Hung-chang negotiated the Tientsin
Convention, which provided for a withdrawal of both Chinese and
Japanese troops and military advisors from Korea and an agreement
for each to give prior notice to the other in the event grave disturbances required a new dispatch of troops. Since the pro-Chinese
faction remained in control of the Korean court, however, the influence of the Chinese continued to grow. The Chinese resident in
Korea, Yüan Shih-kai, pressed forward to convert Korea from a tra-
ditional-style tribute state into a modern style protectorate, subservient to Chinese interests and relying heavily on China for aid.
Japan's political influence declined and so did her trade.

The Japanese government might not have been so concerned about
Chinese domination of Korea had China itself been strong, but as the
disintegration of Chinese influence in Indochina made clear, China
was basically weak. A backward and weak Korea under the control
of an equally backward and weak China seemed to invite the seizure
of Korea by one of the Western powers. There was every evidence
that this was a distinct possibility. In 1885 Korea had already become
a pawn in the more general Anglo-Russian rivalry in Asia. The Korean
king, playing the double game so characteristic of Korean policy in
this period, had proposed a secret treaty to the Russians in order to

counterbalance the influence of the Chinese. To frighten the Russians off the English dispatched a gunboat fleet to occupy the island of Komun at the entrance of the Korean Straits and withdrew only in 1887 when the Russians agreed not to occupy any Korean territory. But there remained the possibility that the Russians, anxious to have a warm-water port in Korea, still harbored ambitions there. Such anxieties in the minds of the oligarchs grew even more intense when the Russians announced their intention to build a trans-Siberian railroad to link her maritime eastern provinces with European Russia.

By the early 1890s "the independence of Korea" had become an urgent concern. The term, however, was an ambiguous one. For the Japanese army it meant a Korea free from Chinese rule and firmly under Japanese political domination. For many civilian politicians and opinion leaders outside the government it meant a Korea free of reactionary Chinese influence, open to guidance by a progressive Japan, dedicated to freeing the Korean people from the thrall of ignorance and a "backward and despotic government." For the leaders of the Japanese government it meant both, since in their eyes Japanese political control over Korea and internal reform within Korea were inextricably linked. On the whole it is probably also fair to say that those elements within Korea most committed to national self-strengthening and national independence regarded the Japanese as their most likely savior.

The stage was finally set for a clash between Japan and China over the Korean question by two incidents. One was the murder of Kim Ok-kiun by Chinese and Korean agents in Shanghai in early 1894. When the news reached Japan the press portrayed Kim as a martyr to the cause of progress and condemned the incident as an example of Chinese perfidy and Korean backwardness. A growing war fever was further fueled by the dispatch of a brigade size force of 4,000 Chinese troops to help in suppressing the Tonghak rising, an antigovernment, antiforeign rebellion. In accordance with the Tientsin convention the Japanese government responded with plans to dispatch troops of its own. Within the government there was a difference of opinion of what role Japanese forces should play. Prime Minister Itō, together with most of his ministers, saw the move as an attempt to maintain a balance of power in Korea, against Chinese pressure. But the Mutsu Munemitsu, the foreign minister, and Kawakami Sōroku, deputy Chief of Staff, saw the move as an opportunity to oust the Chinese from Korea and place the country under firm Japanese influence. At first the government tried to reduce the crisis by proposing to the Chinese a plan for turning Korea into a joint protectorate but when the Chinese, already well entrenched and quite belligerent toward the "dwarf barbarians," rejected the proposal the government finally opted for war. In late July 1894 Japanese troops seized the Korean king and forced him to sign an agreement authorizing the Japanese to expel the Chinese. On August 1 war was finally and formally declared.

The Sino-Japanese War of 1894–1895 was vindication of all the government's efforts to build up national wealth and strength. Although most foreign observers, and the Chinese themselves, were convinced that the tiny Japanese island kingdom was no match for the great Chinese empire, the well-trained, well-equipped, and well-disciplined Japanese army and navy forces swept the Chinese before them like a juggernaut. Within six months the Chinese, whose military was riddled with corruption and incompetence, were forced to admit defeat. As one Japanese journalist ungraciously noted, the war proved the Ch'ing empire was not a "sleeping giant" but a "sleeping pig." The peace terms exacted by the Japanese in the wake of victory were harsh. By the Treaty of Shimonoseki, signed in April 1895, the Chinese (1) recognized the independence of Korea, (2) ceded to Japan the territories of Taiwan and the Pescadores Islands, giving her bases to protect her southern flanks, (3) ceded control over the Liaotung peninsula, which commanded sea approaches to the capital of Peking, (4) agreed to pay an indemnity of 364 million yen, and (5) agreed to a commercial treaty that gave Japan the same extraterritorial rights and most favored status that the European powers enjoyed. All in all the terms placed Japan in the ranks of the imperialist camp by any conventional standard of the day. They also reflected the primarily strategic impulse that prompted Japan's decision for war.

The Russo-Japanese War

Although the Americans and the English, on the whole, reacted favorably to the emergence of Japan as a new international force the continental Europeans were not so ready to admit the Japanese to the club. Indeed, much alarmed at the Japanese victory, they took steps to curb the country's gains. In May 1895 Russia, backed by

France and Germany, advised Japan to relinquish her new rights over the Liaotung peninsula. Since war with the Europeans or unsuccessful mediation were the only likely alternatives, the Japanese government decided to give in peacefully and returned the peninsula to the Chinese. This "Triple Intervention" was a serious blow to Japanese pride for it robbed the Japanese of what they felt had been rightfully won on the triumphant battlefield. To add insult to injury the Russians secured a ninety-nine-year lease on the Liaotung peninsula in 1898, making it obvious that they kept Japan out in order that Russia could get in. All this assured the growth of strong anti-Russian sentiments in the late 1890s. In army contingency planning Russia replaced China as the chief hypothetical enemy and the cabinet proposed a crash program of naval and military expansion in preparation for a possible war. Aroused by a determination to "suffer privation to achieve revenge" (*gasshin shotan*), the Diet in 1896 authorized an increase of the army by six divisions and a naval construction program to add four new battleships, sixteen cruisers, and twenty-three destroyers to the Japanese fleet.

The main practical bone of contention with the Russians continued to be Korea. The war of 1894–1895 had made Korea independent of Chinese suzerainty but it also opened the way for Russia to supplant China as Japan's chief competitor there. An enthusiasm for reform and political bungling by the Japanese had a good deal to do with this new turn of events. In July 1894 the Japanese had forced the Korean court to undertake a massive program of political and social reform—the establishment of legal equality for all classes, the institution of modern legal procedures, the prohibition of slavery, child marriage, and joint responsibility of families for criminal acts of their members, and the like. These reforms were not mere window dressing, but reflected the exasperation of the Japanese at the wanton backwardness of the Korean ruling class. The radical character of the reforms, to say nothing of their Japanese sponsorship, once again produced a conservative reaction within Korea. Encouraged by the sight of Japan buckling under Russian pressure in the wake of the war the Korean conservatives once again began to move against pro-Japanese reform elements. Instead of bending with the wind the Japanese government dispatched as minister to Korea a blunt and simple-minded general, Miura Gorō, who apparently on his own initiative arranged the murder of Queen Min, now center of the anti-Japanese faction. When the Korean king, as the result of Japanese pressure, ordered all Koreans to cut off their topknots (worn as a mark of filial piety), open rebellion broke out in many areas against the Japanese and their allies in the Korean government. Taking advantage of the absence of royal troops from Seoul the Korean king fled to the Russian legation for protection in February 1896 and remained there for a year.

The escape of the king marked the end of postwar Japanese supremacy in Seoul and once again the Japanese had lost out to the forces of inertia and conservatism within the country. But this time Korean conservatism was allied with the Russians rather than the Chinese. The Russians, as it turned out, proved as inept as the Japanese and were unable to use their advantage as effectively as the Chinese had. Finally, in recognition of the diplomatic standoff, the two powers signed the Nishi-Rosen agreement of March 1898 which created Korea as a joint protectorate, committing both sides not to assist Korea in military or financial matters without prior consultation and agreement. The Russians also agreed to recognize the paramount economic interest of Japan in Korea but this was cold comfort to the oligarchs who were less concerned with economic privileges than with securing their strategic "line of advantage."

Tension between the two countries rose once again in the wake of the Boxer Rebellion of 1899–1900, which the Russians used as an excuse to send a large army in to southern Manchuria. After the rebellion was over the Russians stayed on and began to press the Chinese for an agreement to make Manchuria a Russian protectorate. These new Russian territorial designs alarmed the Japanese leaders for if Manchuria became a Russian preserve Russian forces would stand on the Korea borders, ready for a sudden penetration, and this was clearly intolerable. For all the urgency with which they had pursued rearmament the oligarchs were reluctant to resort to force. Rather they attempted once more to solve the problem through diplomacy. But counsels within the government were divided. Itō Hirobumi, together with Inoue Kaoru, wanted to make a deal with the Russians, trading recognition of Russian paramount interest in Manchuria in return for recognition of Japan's paramount interest in Korea. A policy of "trading Manchuria for Korea" (*Man-Kan kōkan*) was imperialist diplomacy in the best fashion, but the majority of the senior leadership, as well as younger men such as Katsura Tarō, who became premier in 1901, thought that the Russians were not to be trusted. They proposed instead to outflank Russia by an alliance with England, Russia's chief diplomatic rival in Asia. In January 1902 an Anglo-Japanese treaty was signed, committing each country to come to the defense of the other if it were engaged with more than one opponent. In effect, the Anglo-Japanese alliance warned Russia's allies against being involved in the event Russia went to war with Japan. With Japan's diplomatic flanks now secured, the Katsura government began to negotiate with the Russians for a settlement of mutual differences through a variety of Manchuria-Korea exchange proposals. But the Russians remained adamant. Although the oligarchs continued to hesitate their lieutenants, including Katsura and Komura Jūtarō, favored a decision to use force, and the press, still nourishing the affront of 1895, raised a hue and cry for hostilities. When it appeared that little more could be expected from negotiations the Japanese government finally declared war in February 1904.

Although the army leadership had been relatively confident it could beat China in 1894 war with Russia was more of a gamble. Not only was the Russian government protected by the vast expanse of the Siberia subcontinent but she possessed an enormous army garrisoned in European Russia. If these forces were brought to bear on the fighting, Japan would almost surely face defeat. On the other hand the Japanese enjoyed the initial advantages of surprise, proximity to the scene of the fighting, and a temporary superiority in the number of troops immediately available for combat. Consequently the Japanese strategy was to use these advantages in a short quick war, winning decisive land victories at the outset to bring the Russians to the negotiating table. The war went according to plan at first, but land operations became bogged down in General Nogi's long and bloody seige of Port Arthur, which finally fell only in January 1905. The Japanese army was unable to follow up this belated success by destroying the Russian forces, which instead managed to retreat to defensive positions in central Manchuria.

By the spring of 1905 the strains of war were beginning to tell in Japan. Manpower reserves had dwindled, munitions were in short supply, and the burden of financing the war was beginning to strain the government's resources, already committed to heavy borrowing in New York and London money markets. The Japanese land offensive in Manchuria had bogged down near Mukden, and it was clear, as Yamagata Aritomo pointed out, that the Russians were not likely to sue for peace short of a Japanese assault on Moscow—obviously an impossibility. Fortuitously, in late May a Japanese fleet under Admiral Tōgō won a major naval victory in the Straits of Tsushima, all but destroying a vast but incredibly inept Russian fleet that had sailed around Africa from the Baltic Sea to support the Russian land effort. Since a military stalemate had been reached, both sides agreed to accept the good offices of Theodore Roosevelt as broker for peace negotiations.

The Treaty of Portsmouth concluded in September 1905 rounded out Japan's territorial empire. The Russians ceded to Japan the southern half of Sakhalin, their leasehold on the Liaotung Peninsula (called the Kwantung peninsula in Japanese), and the South Manchurian Railway line built by the Russians between Port Arthur and Mukden. The Japanese now had a firm foothold on the Asian mainland. At the same time the Russians recognized Japan's paramount political, military, and economic interests in Korea. The United States had already done so through the Taft-Katsura memorandum of 1905 and other European powers followed suit. In contrast to 1895, when Western powers had intervened to prevent Japan from becoming overly influential, they now gave full recognition to her new international position. Equally important, the diplomatic consolidation of the victory over Russia placed the Korean dagger safely in Japanese hands.

Popular Imperialism

The price of empire was high. The extraordinary military expenses for the war amounted to ¥ 1.9 billion, or about seven times the regular budget of 1904. Every form of taxation was increased to help defray the costs and the public was also committed to pay interest on the public bond issues and foreign loans raised to finance the war. The human cost was also great. About 1,080,000 were mobilized for action, and of these, over a third (370,000) were casualties, killed, wounded, or struck down by disease at the front. Yet in spite of these hardships public enthusiasm for the war was enormous. Peasant families pitched in to help neighbors whose menfolk had been mobilized; middle-class housewives celebrated the fall of Port Arthur with hairdos modeled on the "203-meter hill," from which General Nogi's guns had bombarded the city; politicians in the Diet eagerly voted the staggering appropriations necessary to keep the war going.

A handful of socialists attempted to stage an antiwar movement, but they were hardly noticed by the majority of the population, who were if anything more imperialistic than their leaders.

Popular imperialist sentiment had been on the rise since the days of the Sino-Japanese War. It was fed by understandable pride in Japan's triumph over China, by revanchist sentiments toward Russia, and, perhaps most important of all, by a feeling that Japan was finally achieving a place of equality with the Westerners. The military triumph of 1895 naturally gave impetus to a widespread feeling that Japan had truly joined the ranks of the "civilized" nations. As Ōkuma Shigenobu put it, Japan was no longer a "Japan for herself alone," absorbed in her own domestic concerns, she had become a "Japan for the world."[4] But at the same time self-doubt had persisted. Commenting bitterly on foreign apprehensions over Japan's policy toward Russia, Itō Miyoji told a German friend in 1904, "Of course, what is really wrong with us is that we have yellow skins. If our skins were as white as yours, the whole world would rejoice at our calling a halt to Russia's inexorable aggression."[5] The capitulation of the Russians, however, resulted in a resurgence of national self-confidence and a renewed sense of national achievement.

The disparity between popular chauvinism and official caution became evident when the terms of the Portsmouth Treaty were made public in September 1905. The failure of the government to secure greater concessions from the Russians, especially an indemnity to defray war costs, infuriated much of the public. Knowing only of the steady string of victories against the Russians, and ignorant of how tightly pressed the government had been in the last months of the war, they were angered at the "leniency" of the "humiliating terms" of the treaty. An antitreaty movement erupted throughout the country, reaching its high point in a major riot at Hibiya Park in Tokyo. To be sure, some of this popular discontent was exacerbated by the high wartime taxation and inflation, but it is perhaps significant that the first major flare-up of public disorder since the popular rights movement was inspired not by domestic concerns but by a foreign policy issue.

Even after the antitreaty movement died down there remained a vast reservoir of popular imperialist sentiment. On the one hand popular memories of wartime sacrifice lived on, and so did the illusion that the Japanese army was invincible. Every village had its monument to the fallen war dead; veterans of Manchurian campaigns spun tales for village youth; and schoolbooks celebrated the glorious deeds of General Nogi and Admiral Tōgō. On the other hand among the more educated the idea that Japan had a national mission or national destiny to pursue on the world stage became commonplace. For some, like Okakura Tenshin, the nation's mission was defined in purely cultural terms. Japan, he said, could become a spokesman for the "spiritual East" to the "materialist West."[6] For others, the national mission meant Japan should work for a "harmonization of East and West," both in ideas and politics. But for most the victory of 1905 meant Japan was now in a position as never before to protect the "backward" nations of Asia and help them toward independence and self-government. For better or worse, many now felt that Japan could rightly aspire to a role of leadership in Asia, a sentiment that was to animate the popular imagination for the next four decades.

9

The Beginnings of Industrialization

Turning points are hard to discern in social and economic history, but somewhere between 1885 and 1895 Japan reached what economists call the take-off stage of modern industrial growth. The happy statistics of rising factory production began to show a sharp upward turn, manufacturing companies mushroomed, and brick factory chimneys began to pierce city skylines. In some parts of the country the screech of the morning whistle even shattered the calm of the countryside. All of this was made possible by the early efforts of the government to increase production and promote industry. The government factories of the 1870s had produced a core labor force of skilled factory workers, technicians, and managers able to run a modern-style factory without foreign help; the establishment of the joint-stock company principle made it possible for native entrepreneurs to raise the huge sums of capital needed to finance the importation of Western technology and machinery; and social capital created by modernization of transportation and communication facilities provided a context for economic growth. These developments coupled with the growth in population and the spread of literacy, laid the groundwork for an industrial revolution carried out by private initiative. By the turn of the century Japan was already establishing itself as the first non-Western industrial capitalist economy, just as it was establishing itself as the first non-Western imperialist power.

The Changing Countryside

The ease with which Japan made its transition to economic modernity was aided by the resilience of the rural economy, which continued to make a major contribution to the nation's prosperity. During the first three decades of the Meiji period agricultural growth was constant. Some of this growth came in response to foreign economic demand for agricultural products. Tea and silk, both produced in the countryside, were the main staples of Japan's export trade down to the 1890s, and many other rural products also found their way abroad. These export products earned Japan foreign exchange to buy the raw materials and machinery needed from the outside world to build up the modern sector of the economy. Without these exports the country might have faced a persistent foreign deficit, long-term inflation, and continuing instability—most of which it avoided. At the same time these rural by-products put extra cash and buying power in the hands of the rural population, creating the domestic demand needed to sustain long-term economic growth.

Even more important, the early years of Meiji also saw a continuing growth in food production. With the population growing by leaps and bounds—from 33.1 million in 1872 to 41 million in 1892, and to 52.1 million in 1912—increased food production was necessary to protect Japan from the race with famine so common in late-developing countries during the initial stages of modern economic growth. Economic historians are not agreed on just how fast agriculture grew, however. Some say as little as one percent a year after 1868, while others estimate as high as 2.4 percent. But all are agreed that food supplies grew at a rate exceeding the average annual population growth (about one-half percent per year), making it possible to feed the increasing number of Japanese born every year with enough left over to finance both the government's modernization efforts and investment in the modern sector of the economy.

The expansion of agricultural production was not achieved by the kind of social reorganization of production that occurred in the West during the agricultural revolution of the eighteenth and nineteenth centuries. Land holding remained fragmented and the main production unit continued to be the peasant farmer family. Neither was agricultural growth achieved by a massive importation of foreign farming techniques. In the 1870s the government had brought in foreign agricultural experts from England and the United States, the two most advanced agricultural countries in the West, and these experts had recommended that the Japanese peasants turn themselves into good Western-style dirt farmers, raising cabbages, potatoes, and corn, and hitching horses to the family plow. Here and there, enterprising well-to-do peasants planted apple orchards or grazed cows on marginal lands too difficult to turn into rice paddies, but this foreign advice more usually met with considerable cultural resistance. Only in the newly settled area of Hokkaido was Western-style agriculture adopted on a large scale. Elsewhere, the peasants continued to raise rice, a crop better suited than Western cereals to sustain as dense a population as Japan's on as limited a land base.

Most agricultural improvement during the Meiji period came rather from the diffusion of the best existing agricultural technology—higher-yielding strains of rice, more intensive use of fertilizer, and improved irrigation techniques. All these more efficient farming techniques had been known during the Tokugawa period but barriers to communication and population movement had hindered their spread from local areas where they were used to areas where they were not. When the government realized that its experiment with foreign-style agriculture was a failure it shifted to a policy of making the best traditional techniques more widely available. Beginning in the late 1870s the government organized local farmers' meetings and local agricultural fairs where seasoned and successful model peasant farmers told their fellows how to increase crop yields. Their advice found a ready audience among a rural population long accustomed to the notion of agricultural improvement and used to producing more than was needed for consumption.

In the aggregate, increased agricultural surpluses contributed to general prosperity and agricultural growth but since the social structure of the villages remained unchanged agricultural growth was accompanied by the continuing concentration of land ownership. The tenancy rate continued to climb, perhaps even faster than it had during Tokugawa times. Aggressive and well-to-do peasants, through direct purchase or foreclosure of mortgages, continued to acquire land from their less fortunate or foresighted neighbors. If they had more land than they could farm by themselves they leased it out to tenants, often the former owners. Small-scale tenancy made more social and economic sense than the development of large-scale farms worked by hired hands, and the labor-intensive character of wet-rice agriculture made it more efficient to farm the land in small-scale units than in large ones.

The existence of a rural population surplus also tended to keep rents high. Many peasants who lost their land were reluctant to leave their ancestral villages. It was easier to remain in the community of their birth, with all its emotional ties and psychological security, than to risk embarking on the uncertainties of life in the cities. For all these reasons, tenancy grew steadily. According to some estimates about 30 percent of the land was farmed by full-time or part-time tenants in the early 1870s but by 1908 the proportion had risen to 45 percent. The trend was not really checked until the 1920s when falling rice prices and land values made landlordism less and less profitable.

The term "landlordism" perhaps conjures up visions of rapacious exploitation, rank-renting, and dispossession of inefficient tenants, but this probably misrepresents the general situation. Although tenants usually held their land at the will of the landlord, village custom and opinion served as a powerful check against arbitrary dispossession. The tie between the landlord and the tenant was not usually embodied in a legal contract, enforceable in the courts, but rather rested on an informal mutual understanding between both parties. The most general tenancy pattern was that of sharecropping, whereby the landlord collected a portion of the harvest in kind rather than a money rent. This meant that in bad years the landlord and the tenant shared the loss, but in good years they could share the gain. Consequently the old patterns of village solidarity tended to triumph over any incipient growth of class sentiments among the tenant population.

Equally important, the landlords, by and large, were peasants themselves. They lived in the villages where they held land and often farmed plots of their own. They were very different from the Junkers in Germany, the landed aristocracy in England, or the plantation owners of the antebellum American South who controlled vast estates and lived in grand manor houses. There were some absentee landlords: tradesmen who held land as an investment, or heirs of well-to-do peasants who moved to the city after inheriting their patrimony. But more typical were the village landlords, peasant farmers who had more land than they and their families could work themselves, or village members with some other source of income—as village official, school teacher, doctor, priest, or shopkeeper—who rented out land inherited or purchased for investment. The majority of the landlord class therefore lived a life not radically different from their tenants, either culturally or economically.

A minority of the village landlords were affluent gentlemen landowners who "wore white *tabi* (socks)," instead of dirt-stained *geta*. With more substantial means and leisure than their neighbors, they tended to dominate village leadership. They made the biggest contributions to local shrines or temples, found jobs for the sons of the less affluent villagers, arranged marriages for their neighbors, and dominated deliberations on village affairs. It is also this minority that tended to have the most interest in national politics since only they paid sufficient taxes to obtain the right to vote. As the pillars of village society most of them tended to stand behind the traditional collectivist morality of harmony, cooperation, conformity, and respect for authority. Like most of their neighbors, they rarely progressed beyond the elementary or middle school education, and consequently retained a highly provincial and parochial outlook, distrustful of the city and confident that they enjoyed an older, slower, and better way of life than their city cousins. Fairly typical was one large landlord who, when he formed a mutual savings society for his tenants, made them pledge to "preserve our station in life, show humility and proper respect for others, be industrious and frugal, and so live up to the deeds of our ancestors and bring their work to fruition."[1] The large, more well-to-do landlords thus tended to constitute a bulwark of social and sometimes political conservatism.

At the same time, however, it was from the families of modestly affluent rural landholding class that the urban middle class tended to come. Within the villages it was only they who had sufficient means to send their sons, or at least one of them, off to the city for an education. By contrast, even when elementary education was all but universal in the early 1900s, poorer peasants often found any kind of education a luxury. They needed the help of all their children to make ends meet. Among the children of the well-to-do villagers it was usually younger sons, who did not inherit the family land or side-business, that went off to middle school, and then perhaps the university. School expenses were a kind of substitute for the family patrimony to help them get established. Once out of the village they usually did not return. "An educated child," as a popular saying had it, "turns up his nose at the privy back home." But it was easier to escape the village than the village outlook on life, and beneath a surface attachment to new ideas and customs acquired through education there remained a residue of village morality.

The Industrial Revolution

Just as agriculture continued to grow during the early years of Meiji, so did traditional small-scale industry. The early Meiji fad for foreign goods paradoxically had created new opportunities for cottage industry. Umbrellas, kerosene lamps, clocks, iron pots, and the like could be made as easily in small workshops as in large factories simply by substituting manpower for machinery and capital investment. Matches, for example, could be dipped and packaged with the same kind of painstaking hand labor that earlier had gone into the production of paper fans and lanterns. At the same time the consumption habits of most Japanese continued to be traditional. They wore homespun tunics or handmade kimonos not frock-coats and bustles, they ate with chopsticks and rice bowls not forks and Western-style dinnerware, and they lived in wooden dwellings with straw mat floors not cozy wooden bungalows with brick chimneys. Consequently all the old trades from carpentry to mat-making continued to flourish, and with the expansion of population and effective demand their total output grew as well. As in the past, small workshop production was an important source of by-employment and income for both peasant families in the countryside and for poorer families in the city.

By the late 1880s, however, modern productive techniques had begun to take hold and grow with dramatic rapidity. The government, of course, continued to operate arsenals, shipyards, and other strategic industries even after the sell-off of many government factories and mines in the early 1880s, but new private initiatives were being made in the development of light industry oriented toward the consumer. Not surprisingly, the most dramatic breakthroughs occurred in the textile industry, typically a leader in early industrial development. The foundations for a modern textile industry were laid in 1882 with the founding of the Osaka Spinning Company by Shibusawa Eiichi, who formed the new company by gathering capital from private investors through the sale of stock. Using these funds, Shibusawa hired a staff of Japanese technicians and managers, bought the most advanced cotton-spinning machinery available in the West (more advanced even than that used by the Lancashire mills of England), and in a daring move installed electric lighting, making possible the operation of the company's plant day and night. Although an enormous investment was needed to start operations, the new company was soon returning a substantial profit. Other private entrepreneurs, encouraged by Shibusawa's success in producing domestic cotton goods competitive in price with foreign-produced, soon followed his example. By the late 1880s a small boom in the cotton industry was underway, and during the following decade, Japanese mills not only supplied most domestic needs, but had begun to produce for the export market as well.

With such pace-setting firms as the Osaka Spinning Company leading the way, together with the business conditions improving as a result of Matsukata's financial policies, breakthroughs in private industry occurred in other fields as well—railways, mining, ceramics, cement, paper, and even beer. By the time of the Sino-Japanese War a self-sustained industrial revolution was clearly underway. Factory production more than doubled between 1890 and 1900, and doubled again by 1914. In 1894 there were only 1,400 factories in the country employing more than ten workers, but by 1902 there were 7,821; similarly the number of private companies jumped from around 4,500 in 1894 to 8,612 in 1902.

The expansion of the industrial sector also owed much to the emergence of Japan as an imperialist power—rather than vice versa. Since the Sino-Japanese War had been fought with ordnance, munitions, and warships purchased abroad, the government felt an urgent need to make the country self-sufficient in military hardware, especially in anticipation of possible hostilities with Russia. Increased postwar military budgets boosted the production of Japanese-made armaments and naval vessels and the Diet also authorized subsidies for expansion of the civilian merchant fleet, useful in wartime for troop transport. The ¥ 364 million war indemnity received from China in 1895 was also a substantial windfall for the economy. Using funds from the indemnity, which amounted to nearly one third of Japan's gross national product, the government expanded national railway, telegraph, and telephone networks. These funds also made possible the founding of a domestic iron and steel industry. In 1901 the government, with authorization from the Diet, completed construction of the Yawata steel works, which used coal from mines in northern Kyushu and iron ore imported from the Hanyehping mines in China. As a result Japan was no longer so heavily dependent on the outside world for its iron and steel, over 90 percent of which it had still imported in 1896.

Once begun, the process of industrial growth was largely a bootstrap operation. Most investment came from domestic sources mobilized not only through the joint stock technique but also through specialized government banks. Private banks also began to assume a central role in the financing of industry. In contrast to Japan's neighbors, China and India, foreign capital played hardly any role in the development of native industries. Foreign loans did not begin on any large scale until 1900 and even then the government rather than private industry was the biggest borrower. At the same time most manufacturing production was for domestic markets rather than foreign trade. Export items accounted for three percent of the GNP in 1880, and this had increased to only 13 percent by 1913. Moreover, foreign trade grew because Japan was more and more able to produce economic surpluses, not because she needed exports to sustain growth. To be sure, fluctuations in foreign demand had important short-run effects on the business atmosphere, influencing both boom and recession in certain industries, but the fundamental factor behind Japanese industrial growth continued to be internal demand.

From the beginning the new industrial sector of the economy showed a strong trend toward the concentration of control over markets, resources, and capital in the hands of a small number of firms. In large measure this oligopolistic trend resulted from the economies of scale characteristic of modern industry, and the difficulties of importing foreign technology in small chunks. It also resulted from the desire of the Japanese to compete effectively with foreign firms, whose greater resources, capital, and experience made their products highly competitive in the Japanese market. Cut-throat competition among Japanese firms made little sense in the face of foreign competition and the government, ever mindful of the need for strong domestic capitalism, encouraged the tendency toward combination from the 1880s onward. As a result, cartels, industry-wide trusts, and the creation of financial combines were the most characteristic form of business organization in the modern sector.

Cartels and trusts were created by pacts or agreements among firms engaged in the same kind of business to set production quotas, to make joint purchases of raw materials, to fix prices, or to cooperate in the marketing of goods. Often cartels were organized during periods of economic recession, when firms tried to weather hard times by cooperating with their rivals rather than underselling them. They made their first appearance with the organization of manufacturers' associations in the paper (1880) and cotton spinning (1882) industries, but their number multiplied particularly in the years following the Russo-Japanese War. Often they were dominated by one or two companies with more powerful assets than the others. Not surprisingly, such firms frequently were linked with *zaibatsu* or "financial combines."

The zaibatsu were business empires founded by the aggressive pioneering entrepreneurs of the 1870s and 1880s like Iwasaki Yatarō and Yasuda Zenjirō, who had enjoyed close government patronage or who had taken over government-owned enterprises. By the 1890s the larger and more powerful zaibatsu—the Mitsubishi, the Mitsui, and the Sumitomo—began to build up conglomeratelike firms, usually centering on a zaibatsu bank, but also including trading companies, manufacturing firms, and service industries such as insurance and shipping companies. Smaller zaibatsu tended to specialize in banking (like the Yasuda interests) or rested on dominant control in a particular industry (like the Furukawa in coppermining). But all zaibatsu were interested in the maximization of profit and the minimization of business risk through a combination of capital, resources, technology, and human talent.

It would be a mistake to assume that the industrial revolution of the 1890s marked an immediately decisive change in the overall character of the Japanese economy. According to one recent estimate private factory output still accounted for less than 6 percent of the total national product and even if the government factories are included the proportion was probably under 10 percent. Most industrial plants, moreover, remained fairly small in size. For example, the Oji Paper Mill, which in 1897 produced one third of all the country's supply of Western-style paper, employed a labor force of only 363 workers. Even by 1909 only a little over a thousand factories in Japan employed as many as one hundred workers and only fifty-eight had as many as a thousand. Industrial capitalism had made headway mainly in the cities, and it was only there that its social implications and consequences were becoming conspicuous.

For all the rapid growth in the modern industrial sector, the economy and the society still remained predominantly agricultural in character. In 1902 whereas only 14 percent of the employed labor force worked in manufacturing, 67 percent worked in agriculture, fishing, or forestry.

The Meiji Business Class

By the turn of the century the most notable social consequence of industrial growth was the emergence of a new business class, whose social position rested neither on pedigree, land, or official position, but on success in the once-scorned profession of making money. Recognition of the new position of the business plutocracy came after the Sino-Japanese War, when Mitsui Hachiroemon, head of the Mitsui zaibatsu, was granted the rank of baron in recognition for the services of his firm to the country. Soon other business leaders, like Shibusawa Eiichi, were to join him in the peerage. Equally significant was the enormous wealth of the new business class. In 1901, according to one newspaper estimate, there were only 440 individual Japanese with personal fortunes over ¥ 500,000. The overwhelming majority—about three-quarters of them—were bankers, merchants, financiers, manufacturers, and company officials. The two richest men in the country were probably Iwasaki Hisaya and Iwasaki Yanosuke, heirs of the formidable founder of the Mitsubishi zaibatsu. Times had clearly changed since Tokugawa days, when merchants and traders were placed at the bottom of the Confucian hierarchy of classes.

The Meiji businessman, however, did not like to think of himself as a latter-day descendant of the old merchant-*chōnin* class. In fact, many Meiji business leaders came from the other traditional social classes, including a disproportionately high number of former samurai or children of former samurai. Despite their involvement in profit-making, many Meiji businessmen were engrained with older antimercantile attitudes and needed to justify their activities to themselves as well as to the larger society. In the 1870s, for example, Shibusawa had coined a new term, *jitsugyōka* or "man of affairs," to distinguish the new business entrepreneurs from the old chōnin or townsman class. What set the businessmen apart, as most business leaders were wont to reiterate, was that they, like government officials, were working for service to the state or national profit rather than mere personal gain. One early pioneer in foreign trade, Morimura Ichizaemon, proclaimed grandly, "I state positively that the secret to success in business is the determination to work for the sake of society and mankind as well as for the future of the nation, even if it means sacrificing oneself."[2] When businessmen were in a particularly fervent mood of self-congratulation, they likened themselves to modern-day samurai, rallying stockholders instead of vassals, and plunging into the fray armed with abacus and balance sheets instead of horse and sword.

Though the motives of most Meiji businessmen were a canny mixture of acquisitiveness and patriotism there can be little doubt that many of them felt they were participating in the national quest for wealth and power. Certainly few of them were committed to the classic liberal doctrines of free competition and government noninvolvement in the economy. Quite the contrary, when government economic activity promised to have general advantages for the country the business community actively supported it. In the early 1890s Premier Matsukata proposed a bill authorizing the nationalization of private railway lines through government purchase. A few business leaders objected on the grounds that government operation might give primacy to military-strategic rather than economic goals in the formulation of railroad construction and other policies. But there was general agreement among the larger business community that railroad nationalization was perfectly natural and even desirable, since only the government commanded the sums of capital necessary for railroad development. The bill failed in the Diet but when a similar law finally passed in 1906 there was no major outcry except from the Mitsubishi interests, which had invested heavily in private railway construction. Generally speaking, the business community regarded the government as an ally rather than as an adversary. They realized that the government shared the same goals as they and that officials felt what was good for business was good for the country.

The rising social position and economic importance of the business community was parallelled by a growth in their political importance and influence. Since the government was dependent on the banking community for the sale of public bonds and the raising of war loans after 1900, cabinet leaders and ministers frequently consulted with the heads of large private banking interests—Yasuda, Mitsui,

Mitsubishi, Sumitomo, and Daiichi. On the eve of the Russo-Japanese War Premier Katsura summoned leaders of the financial community to his official residence, urging them to give their whole-hearted political and financial support to the conflict with Russia. During the postwar years it became a regular practice for the finance minister to brief assembled leaders of the business community on the new annual budget and in 1912 a professional banker, Yamamoto Tatsuo, was appointed to head the ministry, a practice followed with some frequency afterward.

Businessmen also began to organize themselves to put pressure on the Diet, whose political role and weight increased during the 1890s. In 1898, for example, a number of business organizations in Tokyo systematically lobbied in the Diet to forestall tax increases on personal incomes and business activities. After the Russo-Japanese War the National League of Chambers of Commerce, led by the businessman Nakano Buei, mounted a national campaign to oppose continued armament expenditure, to eliminate consumer taxes, and to balance the budget. In 1908 there was even an attempt to form a businessman's party in the Diet, and some business leaders urged the business community to put up their own candidates for election.

Ties between businessmen and government officials or Diet politicians rested on a tradition of government-merchant cooperation already established in Tokugawa times "special favors for special services," as Professor Tiedemann has put it.[3] At the crassest level of practice this involved bribing of government officials or Diet members to secure special favors. In the famous "sugar scandal case" of 1909 executives of the faltering Japan Sugar Refining Company paid ¥ 600,000 in bribes to certain Diet members (twenty-three of whom were later convicted) to vote for nationalization of the sugar industry and in 1913 a number of civil bureaucrats and ranking naval officers were caught accepting large bribes from the Siemens interests in Germany. No doubt many other cases of bribery or misuse of personal connections by businessmen never came to light. But generally speaking, most larger business firms, especially the zaibatsu, could prosper without corrupting officials or politicians and were less interested in specific favors than in maintaining a political atmosphere generally congenial to business interests. On the whole, businessmen tended to be mainly interested in economic policy—the stability of the national finances, tax legislation, labor legislation, customs policy, and the like. As one top Mitsubishi official noted in his memoirs, "All we wanted was fair government"—meaning fair to businessmen, of course.[4]

The New Middle Class

If business leaders had come to share the heights of social prestige and political importance with the old aristocracy and the *arriviste* oligarchy, the middle echelons of society were slowly being populated with a new middle class—company executives, middle-level bureaucrats, journalists, professors, and professional men. This new class owed its position not to personal wealth or inherited status but to the new society's need for men with technical and managerial skills. It was recruited from ambitious youths imbued with the spirit of self-improvement and success so prevalent in the 1870s and 1880s, a period when government ethics texts dwelt on the achievement of diverse figures like Napoleon, Benjamin Franklin, and Toyotomi Hideyoshi, who rose from humble origins to positions of public eminence as a result of hard work, diligence, and devotion to the public good. It was a class inspired by the ringing phrase of one foreign teacher—"Boys, be ambitious!"

As the "society of talent" (in Fukuzawa's phrase) took shape in the early Meiji decades the shadowy outlines of the middle class emerged from the ranks of the ex-samurai class. At first, it was they who provided most middle-level bureaucrats, scholars, journalists and other professionals, and it was their sons who accounted for most of the students in the new government-sponsored and privately founded institutions of higher learning at Tokyo. But by the 1880s the new educational system played an increasing role in recruiting talent. Since university graduates were guaranteed a good position and rapid advancement, the universities began to attract ambitious youth from all over the country and from every social class, including the families of well-to-do peasants and affluent urban shopkeepers.

By the turn of the century the prospects of most ambitious young men came to depend less on status or patronage than on the ability of their parents to provide them with an education. The result was a growing mania for education and the blossoming of self-help magazines like *Seikō* (*"Success"*) which, in its editor's words, aimed at the "man of character who helps himself and respects himself."

The typical candidate for middle class status, as Ronald Dore has described him, was

> the lad from the country inspired by articles in the magazines on 'How to Live in Tokyo on 6.50 Yen a Month,' making his way through the university on a diet of rice, dried fish, and bean curd . . . sustained through it by hopes of glittering rewards to follow, of honor in his native village, of the gratifying glow of virtue fulfilled in which he would kneel at [his ancestors' shrine] and tell them that he had made—or restored—the family fortune.[5]

At first the main opportunities for access to middle class status were in government service. The prestige and respectability traditionally attached to official rank and position persisted—so much so that in the Meiji period the government bureaucrat was often addressed as "Your Excellency, Mr. Official" (*Kannin-sama*). There were also ample material rewards for government service. According to a government report in 1884 officials as a group, second only to Buddhist priests, enjoyed the highest living standards in the country. Many were able to buy houses or villas once owned by the bakufu's direct retainers, especially in the more bucolic Yamanote ("mountainside") section of Tokyo, where the great mansions of the daimyo had been concentrated. But as industrial growth accelerated, opportunities for employment in business expanded as well, and a growing number of university graduates were attracted to careers as company officials.

In contrast to the old middle class of shopkeepers and tradesmen, the new middle class was basically bureaucratic in character. Salaries depended not only on proficiency or accomplishment in work, but also on seniority. Once a fresh graduate had found a post he was also assured of life-time employment. Most large business firms, inspired by a tradition of employer paternalism and by the model of the new civil service, encouraged loyalty to the firms by the promise of job security and fringe benefits such as company housing and free medical care. The middle class, whether in business or government service, was therefore innocent of the insecurity that plagued small entrepreneurs and even better-off landlords, who remained at the mercy of fire, flood, famine, and the market.

Since the university was the threshold for entry into the middle class, ties formed there, or at the national preparatory schools, often became the basis for old-boy networks in both government and business. Just as the government bureaucracy recruited mainly from the Law Faculty at Teidai, most companies took their new men from a particular school or university. The more prestigious the company the more it tried to recruit from one of the "better" universities, whether public (like Teidai) or private (like Waseda and Keiō). Within most government or business offices, there emerged "old school cliques" (*gakubatsu*), intimate and informal groups who worked to promote the advancement of their old school friends or classmates. Such cliquism often led to favoritism and worked against talented young men without the right connections but at the same time it also cut across rigidity and red tape by making it possible to do things outside channels through contacts with old friends.

The Industrial Workers

If the growth of the government and the economy required a new middle class to perform managerial functions, it also needed a new industrial work force to man factories and machines. Since there had been no floating industrial population in Tokugawa times this new working class had to be built from scratch. Conditions varied from industry to industry, but generally speaking it consisted of three main groups: unskilled female workers in the textile industry, skilled male workers in heavy industry, and the semiskilled workers in small-scale enterprise. Since the textile industry was the largest employer of factory labor until the end of the First World War, over half the new labor force came from the first group, and only in the 1920s did the proportion of skilled or semiskilled male workers become predominant.

In the early days of industrialization, since the cost of machinery and capital were relatively high compared to the cost of labor, most factory owners tried to minimize the size of their wage bill while maximizing the output of their workers. In order to compete with Western goods the textile industry in particular required large numbers of cheap, docile, unskilled factory workers. Not surprisingly, a plentiful supply could be found in the almost inexhaustible number of young peasant women in the villages. Many cotton mills, in fact, located in the provincial towns to be near this source of cheap labor. Since the local supply was rarely sufficient factory owners sent recruiting agents to lure farm girls to work with glowing promises of good food, excitement of life away from the village, and money to spend on clothes or save for a dowry. Often recruiters enticed the reluctant with presents or advanced loans to their parents. Such efforts were most successful in poorer rural areas, where peasant families needed extra income. For example, Niigata prefecture, an area of hostile climate and low yields in northeastern Honshu, was a well known recruiting ground for factory women as well as for prostitutes, who likewise needed little skill but sound bodies. Factory women from such areas were often little better than indentured workers, forced into the textile mills because of family poverty.

Some factory owners were relatively conscientious, exploiting the cheapness of female labor, but otherwise living up to their promises. Frequently, however, this was not the case. "Free lodging" in company dormitories was designed to assure punctuality and reduce absenteeism. Work was tedious and hours were long. At a time when factories ran eight or nine hours a day in England and perhaps ten in the United States, textile mills in Japan were kept going an average of twenty-two hours a day, with night shifts made possible by electric lights in the factories. Wages were low and often were used to pay off loans to parents or sequestered for some other reason. Under these circumstances factory women often hated their prisonlike existence, and some studies estimate that perhaps half of them fled their jobs in the first six months. Mill owners retaliated by posting guards at factory gates, and sometimes even at nearby railway stations to trap escapees.

The blatant exploitation of cheap female labor was less possible in heavy industry, which required a different kind of working force. Those needed to run shipyards, arsenals, iron foundries, and the like had to be skilled, and, given the social standards of the day, they had to be men. In the initial stages of heavy industry growth, factory owners relied on straw bosses or labor gang leaders (called *oyabun*) who would contract the service of young workers under their control to employers. The straw boss, often a man who had learned his craft in one of the government pilot plant operations, trained his followers as mechanics, carpenters, smiths, or whatever and also served as their foreman in the factory. He paid his gang wages from money given him by the company and pocketed the rest. He also supplied food, clothing, and housing for his charges. With the advance of mechanization, the use of new and complicated machinery, and the rationalization of factory operation, this haphazard system of recruiting proved less and less satisfactory to employers. The skills needed by workers were very different from the craft skills the oyabun taught his men and often they had to be trained to run a specific piece of machinery in a specific plant. The oyabun, moreover, was a free agent. When another company made a higher bid for the services of his labor gang he had no hesitation about pulling them off the job and moving them to the new factory. Factory managers consequently began to look for ways of creating a stable, reliable work force trained in the special needs of their plant and not subject to the whims of a straw boss.

The result was a new pattern of employment that eventually spread to most industries requiring high level technology and skilled labor. At first some large concerns set up in-factory training programs, such as the school established at the Mitsubishi Nagasaki shipyards in 1899 to train young workers. Other companies hired young workers and paid their tuition to public technical schools. In order to keep such skilled workers, who were in relatively short supply, many companies also began to extend to them the same benefits of lifetime employment, seniority raises, and company welfare programs offered to middle-class employees. Skilled workers who enjoyed these privileges repaid their employers with a strong sense of loyalty. Since most were migrants from the countryside, the skilled workers were willing to cooperate with their bosses as readily as their peasant fathers cooperated with the rest of the village. The company easily became a substitute for village or family as a buffer against the uncertainties, loneliness, and isolation that otherwise awaited them in the city or factory town.

Industrial paternalism, although it developed for sound practical reasons, found ideas in the traditional value system to sustain it. Many business leaders described their enterprises as families, where workers and employers were bound by the same mutual affection that held parent and child together. In 1898 the Tokyo Chamber of Commerce noted, "In our country, relations between employers and employees are just like those within a family. . . they are enveloped in a mist of affectionate feeling."[6] Less dewy-eyed businessmen, however, argued that better working conditions were simply good company policy. Shoda Heigorō, a leading Mitsubishi executive, noted that workers produced more when employers took good care of them. In any case, as the result of paternalism, the skilled male worker in heavy industry constituted a kind of labor aristocracy, sharing some measure of security with the middle classes, and set off from the vast majority of workers who did not.

The remainder of the new working class was made up of semi-skilled or unskilled workers. It is difficult to generalize about their condition since it was quite varied. At one extreme were those little better than day laborers, working irregularly, hired and fired at will by employers in temporary need of their services, and barely able to scrape together a living. At the other extreme were workers employed in small-scale enterprises or in the construction trades. They were paid less generously than workers in large-scale modern factories, their living standards tended to be lower, and they bore the brunt of recessions and hard times more quickly and more severely. When the economy was in a slump, the differences between wages in small-scale enterprise and in larger-scale enterprise widened, and when the economy was on the upswing, the difference narrowed. But to some degree workers in small-scale industry were protected from the vagaries of the labor market by close personal ties to their employers, which afforded some psychic advantages if not necessarily material ones.

10

The Rise of Party Government

The constitution of 1889 established a framework for national politics but it created as many problems as it solved. On many points the constitution was ambiguous, and nowhere was it more ambiguous than on the question of recruiting governmental leadership. In the 1890s this presented no particular problem. The oligarchs, nearly all still in their early fifties, were capable of providing firm and vigorous leadership. They were all elevated to the extraconstitutional status of *genrō* or "elder statesmen," with the informal function of advising the emperor on the appointment of cabinets. Their opinions also carried decisive weight on major questions of policy. But by the late 1890s many had become impatient with continued oligarchic rule, feeling that the genro had outlived their usefulness to the nation. Many thought they should step aside to make way for new and younger leaders. It was less clear who would take their place. On the one hand there was a younger group of ranking bureaucrats, protégés and lieutenants of the oligarchs, who had helped in building up the new political and social order in the 1870s and 1880s. On the other hand, there were the opposition politicians outside the government and bureaucracy, who organized themselves into political parties in the Diet. Both groups aspired to national leadership and both groups felt they had legitimate claims to it, but the clash between their competing views was not easily resolved.

The result was the onset of a new kind of political conflict, centering on the national Diet and the struggle of the political parties to achieve power. It was only after nearly three decades of experimentation and maneuver that they finally succeeded in doing so.

The Struggle Against Clique Government

The first years of constitutional government were marked by almost constant clash between the cabinet and the lower house of the Diet. From the outset the oligarchs had made clear that they did not intend to share power with their old foes or with the popular representatives elected to the newly established national assembly. All the oligarchs, including Itō Hirobumi, the author of the constitution, stood behind the principle of "transcendental cabinets" (*chōzen naikaku*). By this they meant nonpartisan cabinets responsible to the emperor and not to the Diet. As genro, advising the emperor, they were fully capable of barring outsiders from the government. Indeed, they made sure that control of the government would not slip from their hands. Down until 1901 all the premiers were drawn from the ranks of the oligarchy and so were most key ministerial posts. The only junior figures admitted to the cabinet were senior bureaucrats, like Katsura Tarō or Saionji Kimmochi, who enjoyed the special trust of one or the other of the oligarchic leaders. In popular parlance this cosy political cronyism was known as *hanbatsu seiji* or "clique government."

Opposition to clique government soon found its most ardent champions in the vigorous newly opened lower house of the Diet. There was enormous competition for seats in the House of Representatives during the first election of 1890, with an average of three to six hopeful candidates standing for elections in each constituency. Since a Diet seat was an official post and therefore a mark of status, many men sought election simply for prestige. (As one candidate freely admitted, "Were I to receive only one vote . . . I should want this for my family tree."[1]) But the election also returned many former popular rights movement activists who longed to oust the oligarchs from power. When the first session of the Diet convened, new political parties called "popular parties" (*mintō*)—organized themselves around antigovernment leaders of the 1870s and 1880s, Ōkuma Shigenobu and Itagaki Taisuke. With memories of official harassment still fresh in their minds the popular parties were determined to fight for constitutional government against the entrenched oligarchic cliques. Not surprisingly, during the early sessions they chose the tactics of head-on clash and confrontation with the government.

The parties discovered rather quickly that despite all the restrictions the constitution placed on the Diet they still had a considerable amount of leverage against the government. For one thing, the Diet offered a forum to attack the oligarchic leadership free from police harassment and unhindered by press or libel laws. (Indeed, so outspoken were some Diet members, that Yamagata had attacks of dyspepsia when obliged to address it as Premier.) Similarly, the parties discovered they could use the Diet's right of appeal to the emperor by calling for the impeachment of ministers. Even though these impeachment resolutions had no legal force they were profoundly embarrassing to the government. Most important of all, the constitution also gave the Diet power to debate and approve the budget. The cabinet could use the previous year's budget if new appropriations were not approved, but the steadily rising cost of government due to inflation and increasing expenditure left the cabinet vulnerable to Diet pressure on financial matters. During the first years of the Diet fights over the budget were chronic and bitter, and the government was forced either to give in to the parties or dissolve the House of Representatives and call new elections.

The oligarchs were divided on how best to deal with the recalcitrant Diet. Yamagata Aritomo, chief of the hardliners, advocated firm resistance to party demands and urged the use of state power to destroy their electoral base. In 1892 his protégé Home Minister Shinagawa Yajirō ordered prefectural governors to use every means at their disposal to defeat antigovernment candidates. Open interference by the police and the use of progovernment strong-arm men (*soshi*) were so widespread that twenty-five were left dead and 388 wounded in the wake of the polling. But still the antigovernment parties retained a Diet majority. The futility of fighting the parties by electoral interference became clear to men like Itō Hirobumi. He proposed instead that the oligarchs should form a national party recruited from those in the Diet who were loyal and sympathetic to the emperor. He had come to feel that transcendental cabinets were politically impractical and that more positive efforts should be made to educate the people for responsible participation in politics. He was not able to put his ideas in practice in the early 1890s but he was ready to retreat from a policy of governmental intransigence.

A similar trend emerged within the parties as well. Many party leaders began to urge a shift from the tactics of confrontation to the tactics of compromise. Attacks on the oligarchs might satisfy a taste for political revenge but they were not likely to achieve the long-run goal of constitutional government. As one party leader put it, it was better to outflank the oligarchs than to plunge in headlong charges against their ranks. The outbreak of war with China in 1894–1895 brought a temporary truce between the government and the parties, who willingly cooperated with the oligarchs in the interests of national unity at a time of crisis. Once the war was over a new attempt was made to resolve party-oligarchic conflict through political compromise. In 1895 the Jiyutō under the leadership of Itagaki agreed to support the Itō cabinet in order to facilitate the passage of increased military appropriations in response to the Tripartite Intervention. This was the first of a series of party-oligarchic alliances in the late 1890s. It was followed by cooperation between Matsukata and the Shimpotō in 1897 and a second but unsuccessful attempt at cooperation between Itō and the Jiyutō in 1898.

The party-cabinet alliances of the late 1890s have sometimes been criticized as a sell-out by the political parties but it would be equally fair to describe them as a political sell-out by the oligarchs. Both sides had had to make concessions. If the parties gave up their forthright opposition to clique government, the oligarchs were forced to abandon the idea of transcendental cabinets. At the same time the parties used their new political leverage to secure the execution of policies they favored, the appointment of party leaders to the cabinet, and the opening of the upper ranks of the bureaucracy to party men. Distasteful as this was to men like Yamagata and Katsura it was the only way of preventing government from coming to a standstill. The parties had established themselves as a formidable element in the political process. Indeed, by 1898 the pressures for the establishment for constitutional government had become so strong that the genro finally decided to turn the cabinet over to Ōkuma and Itagaki, whose followers banded together to form the Kenseitō, a party commanding an absolute majority in the Diet.

This experiment in constitutional government proved short-lived since the coalition of Diet members on which it rested soon fell to squabbling among themselves, jealously competing for official posts and unable to agree on basic policies. When civil service officials in certain ministries refused to cooperate with party-linked ministers the cabinet soon collapsed. Yamagata, wooing one faction of the splintered Kenseitō with the offer of another party-oligarchic alliance, took power again in 1899, and moving to blunt the effects of increased party power, issued a series of ordinances designed to protect both the civil bureaucracy and the military high command from party influence. All posts in the civil bureaucracy, from vice minister on down, were closed to patronage appointment (and therefore party influence), and the ministers of war and navy were to be filled by generals or admirals on active service, giving the military services veto power over the formation of cabinets. To make sure his work was not undone, Yamagata also enlarged the powers of the Privy Council (of which he soon became president) to include approval of any further changes in civil service and military personnel regulations. Surrounded by a clique of close personal protégés, including Katsura Tarō and Ōura Kemmu, he set his face against further expansion of party power.

In contrast to Yamagata's intransigence, Itō Hirobumi tried to take advantage of the expanding weight of the parties, a trend he regarded as ineluctable and even desirable by the turn of the century. In 1900, with the help of Inoue Kaoru and Saionji Kimmochi, he finally organized the Seiyūkai, the kind of national party he had first mooted in the early 1890s. As he told a friend, with such a party backing him in the Diet he would no longer have to rely on "mercenaries" but would have a "standing army" of his own, loyal to his leadership and ready to support his policies. The new party, however, proved less tractable to Itō's will than he had hoped. Its members, mainly experienced Diet politicians, were delighted to have a prestigious figure like Itō as their leader but little inclined to follow his dictates docilely. Faced with political opposition even within his own party, Itō resigned its presidency, turning the formal reins of leadership over to Saionji Kimmochi. His departure from the scene hurt the party temporarily, but it was soon to emerge as the central force in the Diet—and a main contender for national political power.

The Rise of the Seiyūkai and the Expansion of Party Power

The further expansion of party power rested on the success of the Seiyūkai in converting party-cabinet alliances from a temporary expedient to a permanent strategy. The man mainly responsible was Hara Kei, an astute ex-official who rose rapidly in the Seiyūkai after joining its ranks in 1900. Compared to the veterans of the popular rights movement in the party Hara was a newcomer to Diet politics but he was no less committed to the achievement of constitutional government. He realized, moreover, that this would have to come about through behind-the-scenes maneuvering and salami tactics rather than heroic confrontations on the floor of the Diet.

Opportunities for a new relationship with the cabinet came after Itō's resignation from power in 1901. The oligarchs withdrew from the forefront of politics, leaving responsibility for the government in the hands of Yamagata's chief lieutenant, Katsura Tarō. Katsura managed to get through his first several Diets by striking temporary bargains with shifting coalitions in the Diet, but on the eve of the Russo-Japanese War Katsura felt the need to assure himself of firm Diet support for the massive budget increases. In December 1904 he met with Hara, who promised the Seiyūkai's wartime support in return for assurances that at the war's end Katsura would resign in favor of Saionji, the Seiyukai president. A man of his word, Katsura lived up to his pledge and between 1906 and 1912 the premiership passed back and forth between Katsura and Saionji, with the Seiyūkai supporting both in the Diet.

The working relationship between Hara and Katsura established the Seiyūkai as a semipermanent government party. The inclusion of Seiyūkai leaders in the cabinet on a regular basis, moreover, opened the way for the penetration of the party's influence into the bureaucratic structure. When Hara became Home Minister under the first Saionji cabinet he worked assiduously to win over key civil service officials under his jurisdiction. His task was facilitated by the emergence of younger officials who had worked their way to top positions through the civil service system and who were not beholden to oligarchs' patronage as Katsura and other older bureaucrats were. Hara succeeded in creating a group of pro-Seiyūkai officials in the Home Ministry in Tokyo and he also used his powers of promotion and transfer over prefectural governorships to create a body of loyal followers among them as well. The prefectural governors were particularly crucial to the expansion of political party power since they had enormous local political influence—supervising the administration of national elections, controlling local official appointments, and making a host of decisions affecting the local economy. A prefecture under the control of a pro Seiyūkai governor was more likely than not to return a pro-Seiyūkai majority at election time and its prefectural assembly was more likely than not to be dominated by Seiyūkai partisans. Naturally Hara did his best to expand the number of pro-Seiyūkai governors.

Some historians have suggested that Hara and his party paid too much attention to making friends in high places and striking compromises with top bureaucrats and far too little time cultivating popular support. But it is clear that the party could not have struck compromises with men like Katsura or created partisans in the bureaucracy had it not enjoyed support at the rice roots level as well. Indeed, one of Hara's principal goals was to build an absolute majority for his party, a task he accomplished between 1908 and 1915. Of course, to politicians of the day building a popular base did not mean the creation of mass support or mass political organizations. Down to the 1920s the right to vote was restricted by tax-paying qualifications, and this meant that the electorate consisted only of the moderately affluent elements in society—large landlords, prosperous peasant farmers, provincial entrepreneurs, urban property owners, and, of course, the leaders of the business world. Expanding the popular base of party support therefore meant catering to the interests and aspirations of this group.

Party politicians had long since learned that one sure way to rally electoral support was to protect and advance the economic interests of key social groups. This was a lesson learned from experience in the prefectural assemblies during the 1880s, where local politicians and landlords first learned the tactics of political horse-trading and log-rolling. The party politicians in the Diet were well aware that furthering local economic interests was a good way to build electoral support. During the 1890s they were careful to build strength in rural constituencies by resisting increases in the land tax, fighting to shift the tax burden to urban elements, and by pressing for cut-backs in the civil budget. Their slogan was "Relief of the popular burden" (*minryoku kyūyō*). By the end of the 1890s party pressure had helped to reduce the land tax from 60 percent of government revenues in 1890 to around 35 percent, mainly by raising personal, business, customs, and consumption taxes. The emergence of vocal business interests, the need to strike compromises with the oligarchs, and the growing expenditure on military budget forced a retreat from these policies, but the parties' politicans had learned the usefulness of the tax issue in appealing to the electorate.

What the Seiyūkai did in the early 1900s was to make pork barrel politics routine. After the defeat of Russia in 1905 the party proclaimed its attachment to a "positive policy" in government spending, promising to divert tax money from military to civilian purposes, especially for local economic development. It began to use its influence to increase appropriations for local railroad construction, new roads and schools, bridges and telegraph lines, local harbor development, and expansion of irrigation works, promising local farmers and business to work for these in return for votes. Wakatsuki Reijirō, a leading Finance Ministry official, complained, "We are not building railroad lines where they must be built, but we are building them through little mountain villages with small populations. Here no one supports the Seiyūkai, so we don't build railroad lines, and there they do support the Seiyūkai, so we construct them. That's how the railroads are being used for the expansion of party power."[2] By the 1910s there were few Diet members, in the Seiyūkai or not, who did not attempt to exploit local demands for government funds or cater to local economic groups. Even more blatantly, many resorted to the tactic of buying votes directly, through the distribution of bribe money to voters, sometimes relying on local prefectural assembly members and sometimes on election brokers who made a profession out of electoral corruption.

The experience of the 1890s and early 1900s also led the Seiyūkai to look to the newly flourishing business class for support. As one Diet leader had noted in 1898, "If you do not have the confidence of the businessmen you cannot manage state affairs smoothly."[3] Significantly, Itō Hirobumi, when he founded the Seiyūkai, took great pains to extend invitations to leading industrialists like Shibusawa as well as to leaders of business organizations like the local Chambers of Commerce. Close ties with businessmen were advantageous not simply because of their social and economic influence but because businessmen were an important source of political funds. Hara himself relied on political contributions from Furukawa Ichibei, the copper magnate, but other large entrepreneurs and zaibatsu concerns also gave freely to the Seiyūkai and other parties in the Diet. Smaller businessmen often patronized individual politicians either by giving them direct monetary support or by offering them sinecures on the boards of directors of their companies.

The expansion of Seiyūkai power, and party power in general, therefore rested not simply on strategic ties with the suboligarchic bureaucracy. Rather it rested on a complex web of local and national interest groups woven together by increasing party influence over national policy. The cost of this kind of expansion in political power was a decline in the crusading zeal, the obstreperous tactics, and the rhetorical heroics of the popular parties of the early Diets. But the willingness of the Seiyūkai leaders and other party politicians to work for special interests was prompted by a conviction that there was no other way to build a base for party rule. As Hara himself once told a fellow politician, "If you don't give men official position or money, they won't be moved."[4] There were elements of political cynicism in such a view, but by the same token men like Hara were simply adapting their political tactics to the acquisitive society created by the oligarchs.

"Normal Constitutional Government"

The final achievement of constitutional government might have come more quickly had the Seiyūkai continued to dominate the Diet unchallenged. The political situation was complicated, however, by the emergence of a two-party system in the Diet. The expansion of Seiyūkai during the early 1900s naturally aroused the hostility of other politicians who found themselves sinking into impotence while the Seiyūkai piled up majorities. Some were indignant at the Seiyūkai's willingness to strike bargains with the leaders of clique government, but others were moved by the more palpable disappointment that they might be missing out on a good thing. The result was the emergence of merger movements in the Diet aimed at creating a second large political party able to compete with the Seiyūkai for votes, funds and influence. The principle of constitutional government was one motive behind these movements but the more immediate concern was a yearning for power.

The anti-Seiyūkai movements, however, were unable to achieve their goal until the political crisis of 1912–1913. This crisis was precipitated in 1912 when the army, under the influence of the Yamagata faction, decided to bring down the second Saionji cabinet, which had refused to expand the military budget. Utilizing the regulations devised by Yamagata in 1900 the War Minister resigned and the army high command refused to provide a replacement. Public indignation at this power play was exacerbated when the genro, reasserting a prerogative that had fallen into abeyance after the Russo-Japanese War, nominated Katsura as Saionji's replacement. In itself this was not unusual, but Katsura, despite his longstanding accommodation with Hara, remained a potent symbol of clique government and the public still saw him as a minion of the Yamagata faction. In December 1912 a coalition of journalists, politicians, and businessmen under the leadership of two popular rights movement veterans, Inukai Tsuyoshi and Ōzaki Yukio, organized a nationwide "movement to protect constitutional government." The goals of the movement were to destroy clique government by replacing Katsura with a party cabinet based in the Diet. Katsura might have weathered the flurry of demonstrations and rallies that spread over the country if he had sought the help of the Seiyūkai, as in the past. Instead he decided to weather the storm by forming a political party of his own, the Dōshikai, just as Itō had organized the Seiyūkai earlier. Since the new party drew into its ranks many anti-Seiyūkai leaders Hara decided to cast his lot with the popular movement. Without the votes of the Seiyūkai's absolute majority in the Diet, Katsura was forced to step down from power after three months in office.

The fall of Katsura did not bring about the establishment of party rule, as many in the popular movement had hoped it would. The Seiyūkai, pursuing its strategy of compromise, offered its backing to Premier Yamamoto Gonnohyoe, who was neither a party man nor a Diet member but a ranking admiral and a nominee of the genro. However, the 1912–1913 crisis did alter the political landscape in other significant ways. For one thing, it showed how easily a political party could determine the fate of a cabinet and how weakened clique government had become since the 1890s. Indeed, Hara even utilized his return to power to open certain key bureaucratic posts to party patronage and to end the requirement that service ministers be general officers on active duty. Equally important, however, is the fact that although Katsura died in 1913 his political party managed to survive. Led by Katō Kōmei, an ex-diplomat married to an Iwasaki heiress, and a group of former Finance Ministry officials, the new party soon emerged as a potent rival to the Seiyukai. Its policies and programs at first were not radically different from those of the Seiyūkai but it did provide an alternative Diet base for the formation of cabinets. When the Yamamoto cabinet fell as the result of political scandals in 1914, the oligarchs, hopeful of finally breaking the Seiyūkai majority, en-

couraged his successor, Ōkuma Shigenobu, to rely on the support
of the Dōshikai. In 1915, when the Ōkuma government called new
elections, the Seiyūkai found itself challenged by the same combination of government pressure and money power that earlier
it had used against its opposition, and when the returns came in the
party suffered heavy losses.

If the genrō had hoped Katō Kōmei and his party would prove any
more docile than the Seiyūkai their hopes were soon shattered. An
ardent Anglophile, and a longtime opponent of oligarchic interference in diplomatic affairs, Katō proved to be an independent spirit
even less inclined to compromise than Hara. He was a firm believer
in the sort of stable middle-class parliamentary democracy he had
observed while a diplomat in England. When the Ōkuma fell from
power in 1916, the oligarchs decided to revert to clique government, nominating as Premier another Yamagata protégé, Terauchi
Masatake. This reflected continuing distrust of the parties, especially
on the part of Yamagata, who still regarded them as private cabals,
more concerned with their own partisan interests than with the
national good. Such sentiments, justified or not, collided with hard
political reality, however. The personal cliques of men like Yamagata
were showing increased signs of fracture. Even loyal followers like
Terauchi were impatient at the continued interference of the
oligarchs in daily deliberations of government and the lower echelons of the civil bureaucracy were no longer amenable to control
from behind the scenes. Many young bureaucrats, convinced that
the political parties represented the wave of the future, were eager
to climb on the party bandwagon, hoping to advance to ministerial
posts by party membership rather than by currying favor with the
genro or their protégés.

Under these circumstances the genro were finally forced to accept
open party rule in 1918. When ill health and the outbreak of nationwide rioting over the inflation of rice prices brought an end to
Terauchi's cabinet the genro decided to nominate Hara Kei as his
successor. The immediate reasons were threefold: first, none of the
oligarch's immediate protégés were willing to take the job; second,
Hara led the majority party in the Diet; and third, there was a danger that if a party premier were not finally appointed both major
parties would organize resistance to the government in the Diet. The
decision, however, was not intended to establish a permanent precedent nor did it signify that the genrō were ready to relinquish their

informal right. Indeed, Yamagata secretly hoped the Seiyūkai leadership would make such a botch of things that the country would welcome a return to bureaucratic cabinets.

No such luck was in store. After Hara's untimely death by assassination in 1920, the genro tried to reinstate transcendental government by nominating three nonparty cabinets between 1922 and 1924 under Katō Tomosaburo, Yamamoto Gonnohyoe, and Kiyoura Kiyotaka. The party leaders in the Diet, however, decided to join hands in a coalition to force the genro to return to party rule. In 1924, in response to the appointment of a cabinet of peers under Kiyoura, Katō Kōmei (Kenseikai), Takahashi Korekiyo (Seiyūkai), and Inukai Tsuyoshi (Kakushin Club) organized a second "movement to protect constitutional government." Unlike the 1912–1913 movement it was neither a popular manifestation nor one that generated much public enthusiasm, but the coalition parties supporting it were able to make considerable gains in the 1924 election. Collectively they had enough Diet strength to overturn the Kiyoura cabinet. The deaths of Yamagata in 1922 and Matsukata in 1923 had removed the last of the oligarchs from the political scene and the only remaining genro was Saionji Kimmochi, the former Seiyūkai president. In the face of pressure by the new "movement to protect constitutional government," Saionji, a mildly liberal man willing to shift with the trends of the times, finally agreed to the appointment of Katō Kōmei to head a three-party coalition government.

The appointment of the Katō cabinet ushered in a new period of constitutional practice. From 1924 to 1932 control of the cabinet passed back and forth between the leaders of the two major Diet parties, the Seiyūkai and the Kenseikai (renamed the Minseitō in 1927). Many observers concluded that finally, after more than three decades of struggle, "normal constitutional government" had come to stay, and that the main path to political power and influence lay through the portals of the Diet. In 1924 even Tanaka Giichi, a top ranking general former Chief of Staff and a close protégé of Yamagata, was confident enough in the future of the parties to accept the presidency of the Seiyūkai. Indeed, nearly all the party premiers of the 1920s were former bureaucrats or financial leaders. Other less prominent bureaucrats, including many former prefectural governors, also continued to retire from official service to enter party politics. Among the wider public there was also a strong recognition that the political balance had shifted in favor of the parties.

When a local school principal wanted extra funds from the Ministry of Education or a town mayor needed a government subsidy to cover a tax deficit, he was likely to turn to a local party leader or Diet member to intercede on his behalf with the bureaucracy. The partisanization of the civil service, so very much feared by Yamagata, seemed well under way.

Ironically the political position of party cabinets, like that of clique government earlier, rested on the continued need for compromise. The Privy Council, the House of Peers, and the military high commands still remained relatively independent power centers, able to obstruct or delay party policies as earlier the parties had obstructed or delayed the programs of nonparty cabinets. The parties might have circumvented these other power centers by embarking on a program of constitutional revision or legislative reform, but both were extremely difficult in practice. For example, in 1925, when Premier Katō Kōmei attempted slight alterations in the powers and composition of the House of Peers, the upper house held the rest of the cabinet's legislative program in hostage until the proposed reform measure was considerably diluted. Consequently party premiers, rather than pursuing institutional reform, instead opted to find allies among the nonparty power centers or to play one nonparty faction off against another. With the oligarchs gone as a unifying element in the political world such maneuverings were unavoidable but the party leaders were no more at a disadvantage than the peers, the military, or the bureaucracy. Thus the continuing existence of party cabinets rested neither on law nor precedent but on pragmatic political working arrangements. As long as party cabinets proved capable of handling the nation's problems there was no reason to abandon party rule. Only a major national crisis was likely to shake it.

Democracy, Socialism, and Dissent

The final triumph of the political parties was not greeted with undiluted public enthusiasm. Many regarded the emergence of party cabinets as a triumph neither for popular government nor for good government. Indeed, complaints about the abuse of party power and about party corruption had been common grist for journalistic mills ever since the turn of the century. By the 1920s the press referred to the political parties not as "popular parties" (*mintō*) but as "entrenched parties" (*kisei seitō*). There was widespread disillusionment with the political parties particularly among the middle-class intellectual community. This reflected the feeling that the parties and their leaders had been tainted in their drive for power. They seemed more interested in raising funds, buying votes, and behind-the-scenes maneuverings than they were in giving expression to the aspirations of the people. As one reform-minded Diet member noted in 1923, "It is a grave fact for the future of parliamentary government in our country that we can discern a trend toward loss of confidence in parliamentary politics . . . even among the educated classes who believe in constitutional government."[5]

Much of the public indignation aroused during the "movement to protect constitutional government" in 1912–1913 had been fed by distrust of the parties. When the movement failed to achieve concrete results pessimism only deepened. After the outbreak of World War I discontent with the political parties burgeoned into a general demand for political reform. The standard bearer of the movement was Yoshino Sakuzō, a professor in the Law Faculty at Tokyo Imperial University, who called for the establishment of more democratic government. For too long, he said, popular interests had been sacrificed to the pursuit of national power or the private gain of vested interest groups, and the time had come for greater popular control over government and greater government responsiveness to popular needs and demands. The popularity of Yoshino's ideas lay in his argument that democracy, or *minponshugi* (literally, "people-as-the-base-ism"), was compatible with both the Meiji constitutional structure and the doctrine of imperial sovereignty. Other middle-class intellecturals, inspired by the slogans of Wilsonian democracy given wide publicity in the national press, joined Yoshino in his plea for democratic reform.

This new style of political criticism gained momentum in August 1918 when massive rice riots, sparked by sharp increases in rice prices and rumors of rice hoarding, swept over the country. The riots began with a small incident involving a few fishermen's wives in Toyama prefecture, but disturbances soon spread along the main roads and highways especially in western Japan. For nearly two weeks mobs of ordinary folk—farmers, workers, fishermen, shop clerks, and housewives—took to the streets, breaking into the shops of rice merchants and attacking the homes of the well-to-do. The government estimated that over 700,000 persons participated in 36 cities, 129 towns, and 145 villages. Even major cities like Osaka were affected. Most newspapers were sympathetic to the rioters, and their coverage of the disturbances may have contributed to the rapid spread of disorder. Although the rioting subsided as quickly as it had broken out, it was not difficult to draw an object lesson from the outbreak. There seemed to be enormous discontent among the common people who were less and less willing to accept their condition in life docilely. As one leading liberal newspaper pointed out, "the people are not asking, 'What will become of the country?'; they have risen to cry out, 'What will become of us?' "

If these domestic events helped to accelerate the diffuse urge toward democratic reform so did the victory of the Western democracies in World War I. The collapse of the German empire, the model on which the Meiji oligarchs had built the Japanese state, seemed to mark the final defeat of the forces of militarism and autocracy in the world. The establishment of constitutional republics in Germany, Austria, and Hungary, as well as in Tsarist Russia, suggested that the wave of the future lay with government based on popular consent. Not surprisingly the gospel of democratic reform spread quickly. It stirred the imagination not only of middle-class intellectuals but also of university students and educated younger workers. In late 1918 and early 1919 small political associations and study groups sprang up all over the country, just as earlier they had in the 1870s. Their brave new rhetoric called for "democracy," "emancipation," and "reconstruction," and their pamphlets and programs urged everything from women's rights to the lightening of the people's tax burden.

The movement for democratic reform soon focused on concrete issues—the abolition of tax qualifications on the right to vote and the establishment of universal manhood suffrage. Many felt universal suffrage was the key to the democratization of Japan since it would make the Diet less dependent on the corrupting influence of special interests and more responsive to popular needs and aspirations. From the beginning of 1919 suffragist rallies and demonstrations were staged in Tokyo and other major cities. In contrast to earlier popular movements including the rice riots the suffrage movement was marked by a high degree of political consciousness, disciplined organization, and a concerted effort to appeal directly and peacefully to the government. Blue-coated laborers even walked the halls of the Diet, buttonholing legislators and presenting peaceful petitions for suffrage reform. A new style of political action had begun to take shape and so had a new rhetoric of popular rights, extended now from the stable propertied elements in society to the propertyless classes who were equally affected by the decisions of the government.

The reaction of the political parties to the suffrage movement was mixed. The Kenseikai, together with a number of smaller factions in the Diet, hesitantly decided to introduce a universal suffrage bill in the 1920 Diet largely in response to the popular movement. The Seiyūkai majority, under the leadership of Hara, was fearful of the effects an expanded electorate might have not only on its own power but also on the stability of politics in the long run. As if to confirm the most pessimistic appraisals of party politicians, the government party voted the bill down; and a surge of public indignation of the sort once reserved for the leaders of clique government was now directed against Hara. More important the defeat of the suffrage bill, coupled with other events, paved the way for political radicalization of the reform movement.

Since the Diet was apparently impervious to popular pressure, interest in simple political reform began to wane; and more sweeping solutions to Japan's assorted political and social ills attracted attention. The early 1920s saw a sudden surge in the appeal of doctrines of socialism which laid the blame for the nation's problems on the capitalist social and economic system. A small socialist movement had taken shape in the late Meiji period, but it had been subjected to a rigorous suppression in 1911 when a number of its leaders were executed for allegedly plotting the assassination of the Meiji emperor. After 1917 inspiring reports of the socialist reconstruction in the Soviet Union, coupled with clear evidence of new discontent among the working class in Japan, gave the movement a new lease on life. To be sure, there was considerable confusion as to just what *socialism* meant for an immense variety of translated books of radical "ism's" were tumbling into the country—guild socialism, anarcho-syndicalism, theories of class revolution, and even national or state socialism. The newly emerging left wing was united in a desire for more equitable distribution of political power and wealth in Japanese society, but its members were uncertain whether these might best be achieved by parliamentary action, organization of coopera-tives, worker agitation, general strikes, or even revolutionary violence.

To party politicians and government officials the more visible and militant elements seemed to seize leadership of the new left wing at first. The staging of a May Day demonstration and the formation of a Socialist League in 1920, the ascendancy of anarchosyndicalist leaders in the working class movement in 1921, and the formation of a clandestine Communist Party in 1922 were alarming developments. They seemed to mark a retreat of the new left wing from politics in the parliamentary framework. The police seized every opportunity to put down the movement by force. In the confusion created by the Tokyo earthquake of 1923 a number of leading radical intellectuals and labor leaders were killed in cold blood by zealous policemen, and police harassment and surveillance of dissident groups were routine. However, many responsible political leaders both in and outside the parties felt it was better to provide "proper guidance for popular thought." They argued that an extension of the suffrage would curtail the spread of radicalism and mollify a popular discontent that might otherwise be vulnerable to "dangerous thoughts." In late 1923 the short-lived Yamamoto cabinet promised to bring a suffrage bill to the Diet, and in 1925, as a result of the efforts of Premier Katō Kōmei, universal suffrage became the law of the land. The country had taken "a leap in the dark" (as Katō put it) by creating a mass electorate.

The passage of the universal suffrage law marked an important turning point in the politics of the 1920s. On the one hand, it encouraged many left wing leaders to return to the path of moderation and parliamentary action. Optimistic that the newly enfranchised masses would seek out new leaders, they organized a proletarian party movement, aimed at capturing the new voters by representing the interests of the propertyless. The original goal was a single unified mass party, but both ideological sectarianism and personal factionalism frustrated efforts to create one. Instead there emerged a confusing welter of small parties. By the late 1920s there were roughly three main groupings on the left: non-Marxist social democrats committed to parliamentary action and moderate social reform; revisionist Marxists, hoping for proletarian revolution, but willing to achieve it by legal means; and finally revolutionary Marxists, who organized a parliamentary group as a tactical maneuver. Beside this legal left, there was also a small but influential and active Japanese Communist Party, which worked through a variety of front organizations, supplied with guidance and funds from the Soviet Union, and aimed at the creation of a revolutionary working class.

At the same time, however, the organization of the proletarian party movement was paralleled by the creation of new machinery for the control of political radicalism. From 1919 onward alarmist elements in both the political parties and the civil bureaucracy urged the passage of repressive legislation to deal with the spread of "dangerous thoughts" at home and to curb the intrusion of "subversive elements" from outside Japan. In 1925, moved by a desire to counter the possible dire effects of universal suffrage and the resumption of diplomatic relations with the Soviet Union, the Diet passed a Peace Preservation Law by a nearly unanimous vote. The new law outlawed political organizations advocating change in the *kokutai* and attacking the system of private property, both of which were presumed to be part of the program of more extreme radical elements. The law was first used to crack down on student Marxist study groups in elite higher schools and universities, but in May 1928 it was also invoked to carry out a major round-up of Communists. The government also created a new special bureau within the Home Ministry to deal with the control of "dangerous thoughts" and to study methods used abroad to counter Communist activities.

Although the party governments of the 1920s were severe in their repression of the Communist Party and other Marxist extremist groups, they tolerated the activities of the more moderate legal left. Leaders of the parties realized that the new proletarian parties constituted no immediate political challenge either to the established social order or to their own political power. This became apparent when the first universal suffrage election was held in 1928. The proletarian parties managed to win only five percent of the popular vote and to capture only eight seats in the Diet. Split into small factions, lacking financial resources or political experience, and distrusted by the rural population, the left parties were simply not able to compete with the entrenched parties at election time. Although left-wing candidates continued to make slight gains in the early 1930s, the Diet remained in firm control of the Seiyukai and the Minseitō, who continued to run up overwhelming electoral majorities by relying on their customary use of pork barrel, vote-buying, and personal influence of local political bosses.

The political parties did not emerge unscathed from their encounter with the left, however. Distrust of Diet politics deepened among the intellectual community as the notions of class struggle, radical reform, and the identification of party rule with "bourgeois domination" became commonplace. Declining confidence in party rule was accelerated by the outbreak of fistfights and brawls on the Diet floor and by reports of political scandal. The *Asahi shimbun,* a major spokesman for the liberal intellectual point of view, concluded in 1926 that the Diet was like a bullring and its members like whores running after money and patrons.[6] This middle-class disaffection was all the more ominous since the parties were also under attack from the right. The parties' competition for power and the pursuit of special interests ran counter to the traditional values of selflessness, harmony, and loyalty. One right-wing ideologue[7] fumed against the very electoral process as being basically un-Japanese:

> The candidate must speak of himself as if he were the best person in the world and has to beg votes from people as a begger would do or otherwise he has to buy votes like a mean merchant. Is this really a thing for a gentleman to do? . . . Thoughtful Japanese would prefer not to join in politics, and the Diet becomes a gathering place for scoundrels.

Since the mass of the population, especially those in the countryside, still clung to traditional values and learned them in the schools as well, many doubtless shared these feelings. Consequently despite their continuing electoral success and their control over the central levers of power, the political parties did not command a popular respect commensurate with their influence and authority.

11

Economic Growth and Social Change

The years of party ascendancy saw the maturation of the modern sector of the economy. Between 1912 and 1932 there were technical advances in every field, from agriculture to heavy industry. Real national income per capita more than doubled and living standards rose. The capital at Tokyo, still a mildly exotic port of call for foreign tourists at the turn of the century, took on the aspects of a modern metropolis, its downtown streets clogged with trolleys and lined with the new modern office buildings. The visible signs of economic growth and prosperity were evident everywhere. But the prosperity of the 1910s and 1920s brought with it a new set of problems. Despite overall economic improvement the mass of the population became more susceptible to the vagaries of the business cycle with its periodic booms and busts. The influence of world economic conditions began to have a dramatic impact not felt during the Meiji period. It was also becoming evident that the benefits of industrialization and economic growth were not evenly distributed within Japanese society. If some Japanese prospered complacently others found themselves faced with new insecurities and hardship. Consequently, by the late 1920s the country was on the brink of a major economic and social crisis, generated in no small way by the way in which prosperity had been achieved.

Boom, Bust, and Stagnation

In the wake of the conflict with Russia Japan had been plagued with a large public debt, rising prices, a fall-off in exports, and a steadily unfavorable balance of trade. The outbreak of World War I, however, reversed the country's economic fortunes dramatically. Save for the occupation of the German concession on the Shantung peninsula in China and the capture of German island naval bases in the Southwest Pacific the Japanese engaged in no major military operations and consequently did not have to devote economic resources to military expenditure. More important, the war created new opportunities for Japanese trade. The Allied powers, unable to meet their own wartime needs, turned to Japan for supplies of munitions and other manufactures. Under the pressures of war British and European businessmen also were compelled to withdraw from the markets of India, the Dutch East Indies, and China. To fill up the slack, Japanese exports began to move into these areas, supplying them with cotton yarn, textiles and other goods to replace European-made products. In China the Japanese exported capital as well, investing in cotton spinning mills in Shanghai, Tsingtao, and Tientsin to take advantage of cheap Chinese labor.

The combined effect of these developments was a tremendous wartime boom between 1914 and 1919. The GNP rose by more than a third during these years and the output of the mining and manufacturing rose by nearly a half. Much of this advance came in light industries producing for the export trade, such as textiles, but there was tremendous growth in other fields too. The Japanese merchant fleet doubled in size to handle the expanded volume of trade; heavy industry grew to meet the need for producer capital goods such as iron, steel, coal, and heavy machinery; the growing use of hydroelectric power as a substitute for steam power spawned the sudden growth of the electrical goods industry; and finally, rising employment and rising wages created new effective demand for consumer goods and foodstuffs. The business community was swept by a mood of exhilarating optimism. Profits were so great that some companies even declared annual dividends of 100 percent on the par value of their stock. Since a rapid inflation accompanied the war boom much of the profit and prosperity was fictitious, but business confidence remained high.

The postwar period was a different matter. With the return of the

Western world to normality the Americans and the Europeans moved to regain their old position in world trade. This had a depressant effect on the Japanese economy, which once again began to face foreign trade deficits. Part of the reason lay in the relatively high price level of Japanese goods, severely inflated by the boom, and part of the reason also lay in the low value of Japanese export staples, especially cotton textiles, relative to the unprocessed raw materials, semimanufactures, and advanced technology Japan continued to import from the West. The result was the onset of a postwar recession, in full swing by 1920. During the decade that followed growth continued to lag and the GNP expanded at only half the rate it had during the war years.

The collapse of the boom left many Japanese business firms overcapitalized and plagued with chronic financial difficulties. To finance wartime industrial expansion many firms borrowed heavily at inflated wartime prices. With the onset of recession, prices fell and many firms found themselves saddled with debt burdens they could not hope to redeem from reduced profits. To further aggravate the situation many firms were still so imbued with the boom psychology that they continued to pay their stock holders dividends even though profits were falling or even nonexistent. Bankers nevertheless continued to extend loans to risky clients, not simply out of friendship but because many banks held stocks in companies to which they had loaned money and would suffer loss by their collapses. Much bank credit went to pay dividends and interest rather than to retire loans or to build new productive capacity. With the halt thus leading the blind it is not surprising that although serious banking crises weeded out some of the shakiest firms in 1920 and 1922, many more managed to keep afloat by taking on more debt. A new shock to the economy came with the Tokyo earthquake in 1923 which destroyed large sections of the capital and the industrial complex around it. The government extended new credits to business as a relief measure, but much of this money was simply used to buoy up debt-ridden and overextended companies.

By the mid-1920s the general state of the economy was of great concern to government and financial circles. Prices remained high, foreign trade deficits continued to grow, and foreign exchange reserves dwindled. In hindsight a number of economists, echoing the sentiments expressed by many financial leaders at the time, have suggested that general prosperity and faster growth could have been

spurred had the government adopted a policy of tight money and deflation aimed at bringing prices down and making Japan more competitive in world markets. But like the governments of most advanced
industrial countries in the 1920s, and unlike the toughminded
Matsukata in the 1880s, party cabinets and financial bureaucrats
temporized and dithered, pursuing no consistent policy. There
was little agreement between the parties about the best course of
action. While the Kenseikai-Minseitō stood for retrenchment,
balanced budgets, and fiscal conservatism, the Seiyūkai generally
advocated a reflationary free-spending policy. With each change in
cabinet national fiscal policy swung from one pole to another.
Equally importantly even those party leaders committed to retrenchment and deflation were careful not to tread on the toes of political
supporters. Budget-cutting efforts that threatened pork barrel funds
provoked objection from the party rank and file, and moves toward
a tight money policy met with objections from overextended
business firms. As a result the economy continued to suffer from
difficulties that made it particularly vulnerable to the collapse of the
world market and the onset of world depression after 1929.

The Dual Structure

These same difficulties also contributed to the continuing concentration of economic power in the 1920s. As in the past the greatest
gains in profits, in wages and salaries, and in skills and technology
accrued to large-scale enterprises, who left agriculture and small
business wobbling in their wake. Particularly striking, however, was
the dramatic rise in importance of the zaibatsu, or financial combines, that had begun to take shape in the late Meiji period. Following the Russo-Japanese war both the Mitsui and Mitsubishi
concerns had undergone reorganization into highly centralized
business conglomerates, and in the wake of the World War I boom
they found themselves well supplied with large capital reserves. By
the 1920s these two zaibatsu, together with the Yasuda and Sumitomo interests, were generally regarded as the big four of the business world.

The zaibatsu grew in part through innovation, organizing new
firms and putting capital into new industries, such as chemicals
and electrical goods, that had promise of future growth. But they
also grew by the technique of corporate takeover, following the

principle that those who have, get. A zaibatsu bank or a zaibatsu-related firm would buy stock in an independent firm and then to protect its interests in the firm would advance it loans. By a gradual process of increased zaibatsu investment, financial control, and even manipulation of resource supplies, the once-independent firm would find itself hemmed in by the zaibatsu management, and eventually would end up woven into the total fabric of the zaibatsu complex.

The results were striking. In the late 1920s the Mitsui Holding Company, which had assets of around ¥50,000,000 on the eve of the world war, had increased its assets to ¥300,000,000. It controlled a network of direct affiliates and subsidiary firms with assets nearing 15 percent of the total of all business firms in Japan. This pyramidal corporate structure placed enormous wealth in the hands of zaibatsu families and enormous economic power in the hands of zaibatsu managers. The main concern of the top zaibatsu managers was the overall profitability of the combine. They often arranged for affiliates to sell their products to other zaibatsu affiliates or to buy supplies from them at prices that might be highly disadvantageous to the individual firm, but advantageous to the overall interests of the complex. They also interfered freely in the appointment and promotion of executives in the subordinate firms. On the whole, however, this concentration of decision-making and financial power paid off in stability and security over the long run. Since the zaibatsu could back individual firms with the resources of the whole system during hard times or a drop in demand the zaibatsu affiliates had greater survival power than ordinary firms during periods of economic slowdown. Their employees were also much better protected against economic fluctuations. At the same time the economic influence of the zaibatsu brought their top executives political influence as well. Since zaibatsu business decisions were bound to have a major effect on the economy as a whole party leaders and top officials were inclined to listen to their views.

In contrast to many other advanced industrial countries, however, the growth of industrial giants like the zaibatsu did not spell the end of small-scale enterprises. In the 1920s big business existed side by side with a vast number of small and medium-sized firms, creating what economists call a dual structure in the modern sector of the economy. The survival of small enterprises rested on their ability to adapt to the advance of technical change by substituting machinery for hand tools and electricity for human muscle power.

More important, small enterprises survived because they performed functions that complemented big business activities in many important ways. First of all, small- and medium-scale enterprise continued to dominate the production of basic consumer goods such as processed foodstuffs, housing, clothing, and items of daily use. Second, they were important in the production of many export commodities—silk yarn, cotton cloth, ceramic goods, and other "cheap Japanese gimcracks"—which were marketed abroad by zaibatsu affiliated trading companies. Finally, these small firms were also suppliers or subcontractors for large companies, performing certain production orperations less expensively in their small workshops than the larger firms could in their factories. Often, for example, they made machine parts assembled into sewing machines or heavy machinery in large plants. Since the small factory or workshop was as important to the development of the modern sector as the large plant, it is not surprising to find that in 1930 about 55 percent of the total urban working force were employed in small-scale workshops (under five employees).

Although their aggregate importance to the economy was great the individual small enterprises or workshops were often quite insecure and unstable. Typically, small entrepreneurs were capital-poor, operating with little extra cash or savings to spare, and often forced to borrow from small local banks. They were quite vulnerable to sudden changes in demand, especially if they were subcontractors for large firms. The canceling of an order could mean bankruptcy. At the same time, though small firms did not compete with large ones, they competed a great deal with one another in the scramble for business. In order to keep from going under they had to cut both profits and wages to an absolute minimum. Thus, despite the growth in the number of the small firms many of them were beset with more or less chronic uncertainty, frequent bankruptcy, and little economic influence. Since small-scale industry was a large employer these problems affected not only their owners but also their workers, who usually received lower wages, worked less regular hours, and enjoyed far less security than those in large factories and concerns.

Government policy, however, by and large neglected the problems of the small entrepreneur. Following the precedent established by the Meiji oligarchy the party cabinets of the 1920s continued to encourage bigness, cartelization, and the merger of large firms. While the government supported by votes in the Diet continued to lavish subsidies and tax relief on industries such as ship building, iron and steel, petroleum, air transport, and chemical dyestuffs, unorganized small business was left to fend for itself. In 1925 export guilds were authorized, primarily in an attempt to encourage small businesses to cooperate in the marketing of their products in the foreign market, but by 1930 only fourteen had been formed. Little or nothing was done to help those not engaged in foreign trade such as subcontractors for large firms, small retail shops competing with big city department stores, and producers of traditional consumption goods.

Urban Labor Unrest

The lagging economic growth of the 1920s took place also against a background of increased unrest among the urban labor force. Like so many of the other problems facing Japan during this period, the new labor problem grew out of the wartime boom, which created a sudden demand for factory workers, especially skilled male workers in the growing heavy industry sector. By 1919 the factory labor force was twice as large as it had been ten years before, and the majority of the new entrants to the labor market were men. Even inexperienced farm youths, fresh from primary school or a stint in the military service, had little difficulty in finding good jobs. From all over Japan, save the poverty-stricken Northeast, job-seekers poured into the cities from the countryside. Employers competed intensely for workers, and labor piracy was common. Under these circumstances, wages rose swiftly and workers could shift from job to job. A 1919 government report[1] lamented the inconstancy and prodigality of workers under boom conditions: "Habits of hard work and parsimonious saving are going out of fashion, and wasteful behavior rules the day. Workers simply go out for money without knowing where they are going or what they are going to do."

Labor affluence did not produce labor content, however. The sudden expansion of the working force and the sharp increase in demand for labor laid the foundations for a militant union movement. Prosperity bred new hopes and new concerns. Particularly important was the failure of wages to keep pace with rising prices and rising profits. As a result the number of strikes and labor disputes leaped from 50 in 1914 to 417 in 1918. Many were solved by peaceful bargaining or mediation, but employers and government officials alike became concerned about these stirrings of labor unrest. In 1919 a number of big businessmen organized the Kyōchōkai (Harmony Association) aimed at establishing "harmonious relations between capital and labor." Leaders of working class organizations responded with indifference or hostility.

The onset of the postwar recession only served to intensify labor militancy. When the boom collapsed the result was a rash of lay-offs and wage-cuts, and the number of labor disputes rose to 2,388 in 1919, more than five times more than the year before. Picketing, sabotage, and work stoppages became common, and tempers often flared on both sides. Many left-wing intellectuals and student activists began to join hands with leaders from the worker ranks to form labor unions. By 1921 there were about three hundred compared with a mere forty in 1917, and many of them were affiliated with the Japan Federation of Labor organized in 1919. Better organization meant longer and bitterer strikes. In 1920 disgruntled workers demanding better working conditions at the government's Yawata Steel Works, shut down its huge blast furnaces for the first time since they had been lit twenty years before. The following year 30,000 shipyard workers in the Kobe-Osaka area struck for nearly two months in the most prolonged and serious labor conflict of the pre–1945 period. Although the number of strikes declined somewhat, the union movement continued to grow in steady fashion throughout the 1920s.

The rise of unions, labor unrest, and industrial disputes disturbed political leaders. Some were shocked at the workers' "selfish individualism" while others worried that strikes meant lagging production or higher wages. Labor strife threatened both social stability and Japan's competitive position in world markets. The more conservative politicians were disposed to meet labor unrest with a policy of suppression. Hara Kei, for example, privately fulminated against "faint-hearted capitalists" who gave in to worker demands; and he frequently mobilized police and even army troops to combat striking workers. Government officials also gave covert support to strikebreaking organizations such as the Kokusuikai (National Essence Association), and encouraged employers to fire striking workers or refuse to reinstate them. Labor agitators and union organizers were frequently subject to arrest, particularly if they were known to have Marxist inclinations or Communist associations.

At the same time, however, there were also responsible political leaders and officials in favor of a more conciliatory policy toward labor. The Kenseikai-Minseitō leaders in particular argued that it was necessary to abandon a laissez-faire attitude toward the labor problem in order to restore social peace. In fact the Diet had already passed a factory law in 1911 that curtailed child labor, shortened the working day for women, obligated factory owners to support disabled workers and their families, and the like. Although hardly radical in its provisions, the Factory Law established a precedent for other legislation and created a body of reform-minded officials in the Home Ministry to administer it. By the mid-1920s the Diet began to produce a steady trickle of social welfare legislation designed to improve the lot of the working class—a labor exchange law, a national health insurance law, a minimum age law, and additions to the original factory law. Less successful were attempts to pass a comprehensive labor law to regulate the organization of labor unions and their activities. In 1926 the government of Katō Kōmei succeeded in repealing official ordinances that forbade strikes and set up official machinery for the voluntary arbitration of labor disputes. But an attempt to legalize labor unions in 1926 was unsuccessful—and so was another attempt three years later. The main obstacle to more extensive labor legislation was opposition from the big business community, especially the large manufacturers represented by the Japan Industrial Club and the Japan Economic Federation. Working with allies in the parties and in the Diet, as well as in the economic bureaucracy, these groups thwarted efforts to give unions official recognition or to legalize collective bargaining.

All this does not mean that employers, especially the large capital intensive firms, were oblivious to the need for some positive response to labor unrest. Throughout the 1920s skilled workers remained a valuable commodity and companies were anxious to keep them content and on the job. Companies worked hard to maintain worker loyalty by increasing wages, shortening working hours, improving working conditions, and providing workers with a host of amenities from low-cost company housing to company-paid excursions and lotteries. Equally important, more and more large employers provided workers with lifetime guarantee of employment and wage scales based on seniority. "Regular workers" were kept on the payroll even in slack times and were assured of higher wages the longer they stayed with the company. Some firms also instituted work councils, which afforded opportunities, albeit limited, for consultation between the representatives of labor and management. All these measures were useful in undercutting the labor movement. Company paternalism and welfare policies were a way of demonstrating to workers that labor unions and work stoppages were not the only way to improve their lot.

It seems likely that such conciliatory policies did more to inhibit the growth of class consciousness than policies of repression, which had the opposite effect. Nevertheless union activity, particularly in the mid-1920s, was responsible for many of labor's gains. Unions were most active in large-scale industries such as gas and electricity, transportation and communication, and heavy machinery manufacturing, where companies tended to adopt welfare policies. Working class organizations did not always force employers to make concessions, but their mere presence tended to make employers more responsive and more conciliatory.

The better paid, better treated, and more secure workers in large-scale industry still tended to remain in the minority, however. In 1928 over 42 percent of the factory labor force worked in establishments employing under one hundred workers, and nearly half were young women employed in the textile industry. Even in the large-scale firms many employees were classified as temporary workers, laid off in hard times. A sharp dichotomy was growing between the labor aristocracy and the mass of workers who were textile operatives, employees of small-scale firms, day laborers, and temporary workers in big companies. Left at the mercy of the labor market, relatively unprotected by either government legislation or company paternalism, and unable to organize themselves into unions, these workers often turned to the countryside in times of distress. They returned to their villages when urban prosperity faded, yet often found themselves unwelcome there too.

The Ailing Countryside

Of all the sectors of the economy, the countryside proved to be the least dynamic during the 1920s. To be sure, war brought prosperity to the countryside as it did to the rest of the country; and during the years between 1916 and 1920 most farm families were better off and more affluent than they had ever been before. The price of rice and silk worm cocoons skyrocketed, bringing in new cash income and stimulating production. Marginal land was brought into cultivation since now it could be farmed at a profit, and new advances were made in farming techniques (new threshing machines, mechanized irrigation pumps, and more widespread use of chemical fertilizers.) The wartime boom also created new opportunities for by-employment, and many farm family members took temporary jobs in industry during the agricultural off-season. The farm population, like the rest of the country, found much of its new affluence eaten away by rising commodity prices, but on the whole living standards rose markedly in the villages, enabling many peasants to buy clothing and other incidentals they had been unable to afford before the war.

The postwar economic reversal, however, affected the rural economy no less than the urban. After 1920 a long-term agricultural depression set in. The lagging industrial sector was less and less able to absorb surplus rural labor, and workers turned out of jobs in the cities drifted back to their native villages, adding new strains to farm family budgets. The peasants, however, suffered less from such hidden unemployment than from a long-term drop in the price of agricultural goods. The price of rice had shot up steeply during the war as demand exceeded domestic supplies. The resulting inflation of rice prices had led to the outbreak of rice riots in 1918. In response to this situation the government adopted a policy of increasing rice imports from the colonies of Korea and Taiwan to make up for the deficit in domestic food production. Colonial rice was cheaper because of lower labor costs, and the government took pains to assure that it would remain cheaper by regulating the flow of imports to keep the price down. This policy naturally benefited urban consumers, but it created hardship for the rural population within Japan.

Interestingly enough, the onset of agrarian depression marked an end to the growth of tenancy. Throughout the 1920s there was a slow but steady increase in the number of small- and medium-size owner-farmers. This group had made the most gains during the war years, since it was they, rather than the noncultivating landlords, who worked most assiduously at reclaiming new land, constructing new drainage and irrigation works, and improving farming techniques. By contrast, landlords found themselves faced with declining profits. With the decline in the rice price, rental receipts dropped and land prices leveled off. Since public sale of stock was commoner than before, other kinds of investment seemed more attractive to many landlords, especially those who had moved off to the city and no longer felt close ties with their native places.

In many areas the growth of tenancy disputes also made landlordism less attractive. The popular unrest that unsettled the cities in the postwar years spread to the countryside, and tenant farmers began to follow the example of their city cousins who struck for higher wages and better working conditions. The number of tenancy disputes rose from 84 in 1917 to 1,680 in 1921. In 1922 two Christian social reformers organized the Japan Farmers' Union, a nationwide organization of local tenant groups, which by 1924 claimed a membership of 53,000 in 500 branches throughout the country. The original goal of the organization was fundamental land reform. As one of its leaders proclaimed, "Like the peasants of Russia we must fight until we have land and freedom."[2] But this grandiose goal proved elusive early on, and by the mid-1920s the focus of the tenant movement was primarily rent reduction. Disputes were most common in the more urbanized and commercialized areas of western Japan where the rise of absentee landlordism had eroded the bonds of community and mutual responsibility that had continued to hold the village together in the Meiji period. When the relation between landlord and tenant became a purely economic one, unmitigated by landlord largesse or community leadership, a sense of rights quickened among the tenants. Between 1924 and 1926, the Diet passed a tenancy dispute arbitration law and instituted a program of low-interest government loans to facilitate tenant purchase of the land they farmed, in part to reduce tension in the countryside, in part to provide incentives for landlords to sell off their holdings.

Ironically, however, though the growth of tenancy was arrested, the general situation of the rural population continued to grow worse in the late 1920s as bumper crops further depressed the price of rice. Many farm families tried to make ends meet by cash cropping, especially through the raising of silkworms. By 1929 the production of raw silk was three times what it had been in 1914, and according to one estimate 40 percent of all farm families relied on silk cultivation as a source of extra cash. This made the countryside more dependent on world market conditions, since most silk went into the export trade. Unfortunately the development of rayon began to cut overseas demand, especially in the United States, the main importer of Japanese silk. By the end of the decade the price of silk was also in a state of decline.

The net effect of all these developments was to make life increasingly difficult for the 5.5 million farm families who lived in the countryside—about half the population. The government took some cognizance of the problem by increasing subsidies to agriculture in the late 1920s, but this policy had very little effect. The fundamental problem was the basic economic position of the peasant population. As small-scale and unorganized producers they were exposed to impersonal market forces over which they had no collective control. When the price of rice or silk dropped most peasants, instead of cutting production to force prices back up, worked even harder to produce more. The effect, of course, was to further aggravate the price decline. Lacking any collective leverage in the market and lacking any collective political influence, they remained socially powerless. As a result the problem of the villages remained unresolved, as did many other social and economic problems in the 1920s.

Urbanization and Middle-Class Life

Despite the existence of many basic social and economic problems the burgeoning middle class in the cities enjoyed continued prosperity. Although opportunities for dramatic personal success had declined by the end of the late Meiji period the expansion of the economy continued to create new white collar jobs. The ranks of the national civil service, local and municipal government officials, and company executives grew steadily. After the Russo-Japanese War salaries in business had become generally competitive with salaries in government service, and promising university students found themselves courted by private firms, who often helped students defray university expenses, and in extreme cases even offered the class valedictorian the hand of the boss's daughter to lure him into the firm. Since the paternalistic practices of guaranteed lifetime employment, seniority-graded salary scales, and generous fringe benefits had become quite common in large companies, life as a company employee—or "salary man"—was as attractive as a career in the bureaucracy. By the end of the World War, the salary man was a key new feature of the social landscape.

The emergence of the salary man was marked by new patterns of work and consumption in the cities. Most striking, of course, was the growth of new downtown business areas and commuter suburbs on the fringes of the city, especially in the great metropolitan areas. In Tokyo, for example, a large central railroad station was completed in 1913 and the nearby Marunouchi section soon became a major business hub, filled with the national headquarters of many major banks, insurance companies, and industrial concerns. During the 1920s the construction of new intercity lines by the national government and private municipal railway companies created new suburban residential areas, many of which were constructed in the wake of the 1923 earthquake, which had destroyed much housing in the central city. The older *shitamachi* section, where most commoners had lived in Tokugawa times, remained an area of small scale shops and working places, but the heart of the city shifted to the bustling business section crowded with salary men and office women during the day and the amusement areas frequented by company employees in their afterhours.

The lifestyle of the new middle class was marked by an avid taste for the modern and the up-to-date. The average member of the class regarded his lot in life as a great improvement over his father's, who was likely to be a peasant villager, and not necessarily a well-to-do one at that. He sought out symbols of his new respectability and success. For the upper echelons of the middle class, the starched collar (or *haikara*, "high collar"), shopping trips to the Mitsukoshi Department Store, and weekly visits to the Imperial Theater (modeled on the Paris Opera) became the marks of the cultured life. For the less pretentious, downtown shops and lesser department stores replaced small neighborhood shops for shopping, Western-style restaurants and cafeterias displaying gaudy models of their menus replaced noodle shops and sushi parlors for casual meals, and the trolley car and taxi replaced the ricksha as the main mode of local transportation. Middle-class children also were neater and cleaner than their country cousins, marching off to school in brass-buttoned Western-style school tunics or middy blouses in place of homemade kimonos.

If the new middle class was avidly up-to-date, it also displayed a continuing gluttony for self-improvement. Coming from the relatively settled and fixed ways of life in the provinces, many new city-dwellers were self-conscious about their new style of life. During the

First World War a flood of new magazines appeared to tell their middle-class readers how to lead a "cultured life" (*bunkateki sei-katsu*), dealing with everything from child-rearing and cooking to tips on how to master English or pass university examinations. Publishers also found that there was an almost limitless market for books among the culture-thirsty middle class. The number of retail bookstores jumped from 3,000 in 1914 to 10,000 in 1927. Some publishing houses like the Iwanami company bombarded the intellectuals with the latest translations of European philosophy and the most recent works on Japanese thought, but there was much more profit in publishing inexpensive works of fiction or multivolume "complete works" of famous authors, often prized as much for their appearance in the parlor as for their content.

All this was part of a more general emergence of a new popular urban culture, spurred by the spread of mass literacy and the growth of mass media. By 1920 there were 1,100 newspapers with a combined circulation of six to seven million. According to one estimate nearly half of the country's eleven million households subscribed to a daily paper. The large metropolitan dailies, which dominated the newspaper business, worked hard to attract readers by sponsoring airplane shows and baseball teams. New magazines appeared almost weekly. Intellectual journals like *Chūō Kōron* and *Kaizaō* were crammed with serious political analyses by men like Yoshino Sakuzō and serious fiction by writers like Tanizaki Junichirō, but a wider audience turned to monthlies like *Kingu* (*King*) magazine, which fed them a diet of lively features, patriotic essays, and action-packed light fiction. In downtown movie palaces and theaters the public could also thrill to the latest D. W. Griffith epic or Chaplin comedy as well as domestic products like *The Last Days of the Bakufu* or *Man-Slashing, Horse Piercing Sword*. Government-operated radio stations began regular broadcasts in the mid-1920s, and by 1928 about 500,000 households owned wireless receivers.

But if life in the cities represented an advance for its middle-class population there was a tackier side to it as well. The dance hall (with its hostesses), the chorus line (with its bare knees), and the cafe (with its willing waitresses) attracted pleasure-seekers at downtown amusement centers. In a mild way Japan even had a jazz age with its own version of flaming youth. The *mobo* and the *moga* (short for *modan boi* and *modan garu*, "modern boy" and "modern girl") flaunted convention by smoking cigarettes, drinking beer, and dancing cheek to cheek. Although, as one Japanese social critic noted, the *mobo* and the *moga* were "like cats without whiskers and tigers without teeth" when at home, their public behavior was a sign to many that popular morals were on the decline. Members of the older generation were unsettled by the dizzy pace of life of younger Japanese afflicted with the "modern disease," and many hard-pressed rural inhabitants were shocked, resentful, and frustrated at the contrast between city life and their own lot.

The surface affluence and frivolity of middle-class city life heightened its contrast with life in provincial towns and rural villages. The gulf was cultural as well as economic. Although city fever still drew rural youth to the cities and metropolitan areas, there was a widespread feeling that the values of city folk were corrupting the authentic core of Japanese society. Frugality, hard work, harmony, and decorum, so valued in the rural tradition, were threatened by the materialism, individualism, and decadence of urban society. This cultural gap was as important in fomenting and focusing discontent as the dual economy and imbalances in the distribution of national wealth and prosperity. The rhetoric of class struggle, so popular among urban intellectuals and reformers, fell on deaf ears among the farm population and even among less favored strata in the cities such as small shopkeepers, small businessmen, and their employees. Their inarticulate yet deeply felt discontent doubtless sprang in part from limited economic opportunities and advantages, yet it sought an outlet not so much in protest or overt struggle as in a renewed commitment to the Japanese spirit. When the economic crisis deepened after 1929, this discontent sought to purge itself not in strikes or street demonstrations but in mounting enthusiasm for renewed expansion abroad and return to a mood of national solidarity.

12

The Empire Between the Wars

The Japanese victory over Russia in 1905 had an enormous psychological impact on other Asians. It struck down the notion that Westerners were invincible and kindled hopes that the Western colonial yoke could be cast off. "Japan's example has given heart to the rest of Asia," wrote the Indian poet Rabindranath Tagore. "We have seen the life and strength are there in us, only the dead crust has to be removed."[1] From all over Asia, antiimperialist nationalists flocked to Tokyo to learn Japan's secret of success. The largest group came from China. The Ch'ing dynasty sent hundreds of young Chinese students to Japan in a belated attempt to initiate reform. Ironically, revolutionary ferment grew among these students, and anti-Ch'ing revolutionary leaders like Huang Hsing and Sun Yat-sen organized the T'ung-men hui, an anti-Manchu revolutionary group, in Tokyo in 1905. Other students came clandestinely to Japan, such as the young Annamese sent by Prince Cuong De as part of his resistance to French colonial rule. There were even students from Korea, dispatched by the Ilchin-hoe (Advancement Society), a group which favored annexation to Japan. All these young Asian nationalists saw Japan as a potential liberator of Asia, a notion shared by a great many Japanese as well. But events were soon to prove these hopes false. Although many Japanese continued to be Pan-Asianist in word, the Japanese government was emphatically imperialist in deed, working hand in glove with the very Western colonialist powers against whom the other Asian nationalist movements struggled. In the end it was simply not possible for Japan to be imperialist and anticolonialist at the same time.

The Continental Commitment

After the Russo-Japanese War the Katsura government took great pains to consolidate its battlefield victories by a cautious diplomatic offensive. It was careful to reassure the other imperialist powers, particularly Great Britain and the United States, which had done much to help finance the war. In 1906, when both countries complained that Japanese military occupation forces in Manchuria were restricting the activities of their businessmen, the cabinet and the genro agreed to a troop withdrawal, establishing instead a colonial administration in the newly acquired concession on the Kwantung Peninsula. At the same time, through a series of bilateral diplomatic agreements, the Japanese secured recognition of her rights there from the British, American, and French, and in 1907 concluded a secret agreement with the Russians to divide southern and northern Manchuria into separate spheres of influence for each. All these moves committed Japan more and more deeply to the diplomacy of imperialism, by which the Europeans and Americans attempted to reduce the possibility of conflict among themselves over East Asian problems. Business and economic competition continued apace but a moratorium was declared on the pursuit of new territorial gains in China.

The main focus of Japan's colonial interests after the war was Korea. In November 1905 Itō Hirobumi, backed by a Japanese occupying force, negotiated with the Korean court an agreement making the country a Japanese protectorate. Japan assumed responsibility for Korea's diplomatic relations and dispatched advisors to supervise its internal political, administrative, and military affairs. There were still strong pro-Japanese elements in Korea, but the new intrusion provoked sporadic but widespread anti-Japanese movements. In 1907 the Korean king dispatched a secret mission to the second Hague Peace Conference to protest against growing Japanese domination. In response Itō forced his abdication, disbanded the Korean army, placed Korean courts under Japanese judges, and

put a Japanese police force in charge of maintaining order. Few
were surprised in 1910 when the Katsura government announced
formal annexation of the country to Japan.

The colonization of Korea was harsh and brutal, very different
from the earlier development of Taiwan which flourished economically under development policies conceived by Gotō Shimpei, an
able colonial official. The main concern of General Terauchi Masatake,
the first Japanese governor-general in Korea, was suppression of a
popular anti-Japanese movement in the countryside, often led by
members of the old local elite class (*yang-ban*) who resented their
own loss of status and power. Between 1907 and 1911 the Japanese
authorities recorded 2,852 anti-Japanese disturbances, involving
141,185 Koreans. They responded by burning villages, executing
rebel leaders, and indiscriminate terror tactics. To contain and suppress Korean discontent Terauchi turned the country into a totally
authoritarian state, crushing not only dissent but all forms of
political activity. The native population was given no political rights,
newspapers and other organs of public opinion were placed under
strict control, and the ubiquitous military police kept a firm hand on
the local communities. Except for a handful of collaborators, the old
Korean ruling class ceased to have any political function and the top
posts of Korean government were occupied solely by Japanese.

The Japanese colonial government probably treated the Koreans no
more harshly than the early Meiji government had treated its own
people, and possibly no more harshly than an indigenous Korean
modernizing regime would have. But being foreigners and outsiders,
the Japanese showed little concern for Korean interests, and the
Japanese presence generated enormous hostility. So did the Japanese
settlers and carpetbaggers who began arriving in the country in large
numbers. In 1910 there were already 171,000 Japanese living in
Korea, and by 1918 there were 336,000. Most enjoyed political
influence unimaginable for the Koreans themselves, and most lived
at a much higher standard of living. By contrast many Korean peasants through ignorance, misinformation, or deception lost their
land during nationwide land surveys carried out by the Japanese
between 1911 and 1918 in order to modernize the financial system.
Much of this land not only found its way into the hands of Korean
landlords but was also bought up by Japanese owned land companies. The Oriental Development Company, a semiofficial firm
established in 1908 to aid Japanese business expansion in Korea,
was the most important of these. It soon became a major economic

force in Korea, channeling capital into the development of Japanese-owned companies there, branching out into investments in Manchuria and North China by 1918.

The Japanese penetration of Manchuria was subtler and more complicated than the takeover in Korea, since Japan's rights there ultimately rested on treaties with the Chinese government. The original aim in acquiring the Manchurian foothold had been strategic, but gradually Japan began to acquire an economic stake there as well. The main instrument for economic expansion was the South Manchurian Railway Company, a semigovernmental corporation established with government capital in 1906. Half the stock belonged to the government and the rest was put on public sale. Most of it was bought up by small and medium size investors rather than the zaibatsu or large banks, but zaibatsu trading companies and other affiliates moved into the Manchurian market once the Japanese presence there stabilized. Government banks also used their capital to underwrite private Japanese investment in Manchuria, hoping to meet the competition of Western business interests there as well as in north China.

Economic ties between Japan and the continent grew steadily in the decades after 1905. At the turn of the century, Japanese investment had been negligible, perhaps around $1 million, but by 1913 it had already reached $220 million and was growing by leaps and bounds. Most of it was concentrated in Manchuria, but from 1914 it also grew in the treaty ports, especially Shanghai, where Japanese private interests began to set up cotton textile mills to sell in the Chinese market. Naturally trade increased as well. The Japanese began to import raw materials and the volume of trade quadrupled between 1899 and 1913. By the early 1920s China (especially the north provinces and Manchuria) became the chief supplier of Japan's coal, iron ore, and cotton fiber imports. To be sure, Japanese trade and investment in China still lagged behind the other powers, especially Great Britain, but they still added up to a substantial set of economic interests. Protection of these interests was as important to many private business concerns as protection of the strategic line of interest was for the military and naval high commands.

By the last years of Meiji, Japanese foreign policy increasingly hinged on defense of her colonial possessions, Taiwan and Korea, and protection of her special rights and interests in China. These basic goals were agreed on by a wide consensus within Japan and in this regard nearly all Japanese were imperialist in outlook. Few questioned the desirability of the continental commitment or suggested abandoning the newly acquired territories. But by the same token there was far less agreement on how best to achieve these goals and deep-seated disagreements over basic imperialist strategy. A polarity emerged between those who stressed the need to cooperate with the other imperialist powers and those who said Japan should go it alone.

The multilateralist viewpoint was mainly associated with the diplomat corps, dominated by professional officials, nearly all recruited from the Imperial University. By training and experience they thought of Japan as basically a Western power, whose diplomatic interests were closer to those of the Europeans and Americans than to those of the Chinese or other Asians. They accepted the rules of the imperialist game already laid down by the Westerners. They agreed to the principle, embodied in the "Open Door" policy, that no single power should upset the status quo in China by establishing exclusive spheres of influence or making territorial acquisitions there, and they felt that the imperialist countries should act as a bloc in dealing with the Chinese government. Confident of Japan's ability to hold her own in the world of international politics by diplomacy, they tended to stress the tactics of negotiation rather than the use of military force in achieving Japan's purposes. In this they carried on the traditions of diplomatic caution backed by national strength, that was the *leitmotiv* of oligarchic foreign policy.

By contrast, the unilateralist school of thought tended to emphasize the special character of Japan's position in Asia. While the multilateralists thought of Japan as a naval and mercantile power, basically similar to the United States and Great Britain, their opponents saw it primarily as a continental power with interests and needs substantially different from the Westerners'. Borrowing a leaf from the pan-Asianist gospel, they stressed the common heritage of language, race, and culture that Japan shared with other Asians, and with the Chinese in particular. At the same time they emphasized the greater importance of mainland Asia to Japan's defense and security. While vast distances separated the Europeans and Americans from East Asia, the Japanese were cheek by jowl with the continent and affected far more immediately by internal political and economic developments there. Tanaka Giichi noted that Japan had closer diplomatic and geographical ties to China than other nations; and he felt that therefore Japanese rights and interests, more than other countries', should be expanded in China. He described this task as a right and a duty. Such views, which were especially strong in the army, implied Japan should have a predominant position in Asia and the Westerners a secondary one. Consequently the unilateralists felt little need to follow the Westerners' diplomatic lead, and urged that Japan pursue an independent policy suited to her own interests.

The cleavage between these two orientations toward foreign policy—and all the intermediate shades between them—became particularly acute as oligarchic influence declined. The genro had clearly been in command on foreign affairs down to the post-Russo-Japanese War years, presiding over the conduct of war and the making of peace, but by the Taishō period foreign policy decision-making became a complicated struggle among a welter of forces—the cabinet, the foreign office, the military services, and the Diet as well as the surviving genro themselves. The decline of genro influence was signaled in 1914 by the refusal of Foreign Minister Katō Kōmei to circulate key dispatches to them or to ask for their counsel when Japan entered the war against Germany. Although the genro retaliated by forcing Katō out of office they never really regained the initiative, and in 1917 a special new body, the Extraordinary Council on Foreign Affairs, was set up to coordinate conflicting viewpoints in a way the genro no longer could. It floundered on for a few years but was finally disbanded in 1922.

In any case the unity of purpose that characterized Meiji foreign policy had vanished by the decade between 1910 and 1920. Japanese foreign policy came to be marked by enormous fluctuation and uncertainty shaped by the conflict of competing countercurrents within Japan. The government steered first toward one pole, then the other, wobbling between cooperation and autonomous action and sometimes seeming to pursue both simultaneously. The army, enjoying constitutional autonomy from the civilian government, often acted quite independently. The result was a kind of dual diplomacy. As Yoshino Sakuzō noted in 1920, ". . . Japan has two representatives in China, the consuls representing the Foreign Office and the men who are over there in large numbers representing the General Staff. When the consuls point to the right, the men representing the General Staff point to the left. And so the Chinese are saying, 'What is Japan doing, anyway?'"[2] The question admitted of no easy answer because the Japanese were not always sure themselves.

The China Problem

If the central problem of Meiji foreign policy has been the fate of Korea, the central problem of Taishō diplomacy was the fate of China. In October 1911 a republican revolutionary movement, partly under the leadership of Sun Yat-sen, overthrew the Ch'ing dynasty. The upheaval excited Japanese anxiety. As long as the Ch'ing had been in power Japanese interests on the mainland seemed relatively secure. The Manchus had guaranteed the Japanese foothold in Manchuria and they remained militarily weak, unable to challenge the foreign presence. On both counts they were easy for the Japanese to deal with. The revolution, however, introduced new uncertainties. The republican revolutionaries were ardent nationalists determined to build a strong and modern "new China" capable of ending the shameful Chinese subjugation to the imperialist powers, but proved inept as nation builders. Far from rescuing China from her plight, the revolution plunged the country into even graver political chaos. A republic was proclaimed in 1912, but real power lay in the hands of Yüan Shih-kai, the strong man who commanded the only modern fighting force in China. When conflict broke out between Yüan and the revolutionaries, China entered a period of civil strife in which it lacked both political stability and a strong national leadership.

The political uncertainties in China were echoed by an indecisive and confused Japanese response. When the revolution actually broke out in 1911, army leaders hoped to detach Manchuria from the rest of China, genro like Yamagata favored intervention on the side of the Ch'ing, and supporters of Sun Yat-sen favored aid to the revolutionaries. All hoped the revolution would produce a China friendly to Japan but they entertained radically different notions of who Japan's Chinese friends were. As it turned out, the Japanese government decided not to intervene in the revolution at all. Rather it chose the path of caution, waiting to see how the other imperialist powers would react. It soon became clear that the powers, Great Britain in particular, did not care who ruled China as long as it was ruled by a stable regime willing to recognize the imperialist privileges granted by the Ch'ing government. Since the most likely leader for such a regime was Yüan, president of the "republic," an international consortium in 1913 offered financial assistance in the form of a "Reorganization Loan" of £25,000,000. Continuing the pre-revolutionary policy of cooperating with the other powers, Japan joined the consortium with a contribution of funds.

With the outbreak of World War I, Japan suddenly made an about-face shift in China policy, choosing to pursue its own interests without consulting the powers. The decision to enter the war on the side of the Allied powers in 1914 enabled Japan to seize the German concessions on the Shantung peninsula. Since the Europeans were wrapped up in problems of their own, the war also provided the opportunity for Japan to steal a march in consolidating its position in China. In January 1915 the Japanese government presented the Yüan government with the so-called Twenty-One Demands, a draft treaty providing for an overall settlement of many issues pending between the two countries. The first fourteen demands called on China to confirm Japan's position in Shantung, extend the leaseholds in Manchuria and grant Japanese new rights there, place the rich Hanyehping iron mines under monopoly control of a Sino-Japanese joint venture, and to guarantee no leaseholds be given to any other power in Fukien province opposite Taiwan. All these measures were aimed at consolidating the existing Japanese foothold in China. But the last set of demands, separately called requests, provided for placing Japanese advisors in key government agencies, compulsory purchase of arms from Japan, and the granting of new residence rights and other privileges to Japanese nationals. In effect these demands, included largely as the result of army pressure on Foreign Minister Katō Kōmei, would have made China a Japanese protectorate. Although Yüan eventually agreed to the first set of demands he skillfully used Western indignation at Japan's unilateral actions to avoid agreement on the last set.

Despite the hostile reaction to the Twenty-One Demands by the other imperialists, especially the United States, the Japanese continued to fish in the troubled waters of Chinese politics. After Yüan's death in 1916, China was plunged into a prolonged struggle among regional warlord cliques, all fighting for control over the vestigial central government at Peking. Some elements in the army general staff hoped to detach Manchuria and Mongolia from China by backing independence movements launched by local warlords there, but these attempts ended in failure. In 1917 the Terauchi government returned to the policy of backing a strong man. Through a private emissary, the government advanced a loan of ¥45,000,000 to Tuan Ch'i-jui, Yüan's successor at Peking, ostensibly for the development of railroads and repair of flood damage, but in fact to subsidize Tuan's military campaigns against rival warlords. Tuan proved no more successful in uniting the country than Yüan, and the so-called Nishihara loans served to link Japan with political forces deemed the most reactionary and destructive forces by many Chinese. Suspicions about Japan's real intentions toward China, especially among the new generation of educated Chinese, fed a rising tide of anti-Japanese sentiment. It finally exploded on May 4, 1919, when thousands of Chinese students, merchants, and workers staged demonstrations all over China in protest against the decision of the Versailles Peace Conference to leave Japan in control of the Shantung territories.

Equally disastrous was the ill-fated Siberian expedition following the outbreak of the Bolshevik Revolution in 1917. Seizing on the opportunity provided by the political disorder in Russia, the army general staff proposed dispatching a military expedition to occupy the trans-Siberian railway line as far west as Lake Baikal. The project was supported by Foreign Minister Motono and Home Minister Gotō Shimpei, who entertained hopes of setting up a pro-Japanese puppet government in eastern Siberia and a Japanese sphere of influence in Mongolia and Northern Manchuria. This grandiose scheme was opposed by political party leaders such as Hara Kei and Katō Komei, and even by Yamagata Aritomo, who feared the scheme might provoke the United States. Cooler heads prevailed, and Japanese troops were sent to Siberia in August 1918 only as part of an Allied expedition to rescue Czech forces stranded there by the revolution. Using its discretion in operational decisions, the army mobilized an enormous force, far larger than those of the other Allies, and maintained them in Siberia even after the Americans and the other Allies withdrew their troops in 1920. The expedition accomplished little, but it cost Japan dearly in lives (3,500 dead) and money (¥700 million).

The Washington System

The end of World War I brought a return of Japanese diplomacy to a moderate policy of cooperation with the powers. In large measure the shift was a reaction against the unilateralist policy of playing the lone wolf on the continent, a policy which invited Western suspicion and Chinese hostility without significantly enhancing Japanese interests there. By contrast, the tremendous expansion of trade with China and the rest of Asia during World War I had convinced many that economic diplomacy could be as advantageous to Japan as military posturing and territorial expansion. Men like Hara Kei began to advocate the idea of economic expansionism through peaceful penetration of overseas markets both in China and the West. Naturally this notion enjoyed the support of the business community as well. As a result domestic pressures began to build for a less belligerent and self-serving China policy.

At the same time the Allied victory in the war gave currency to Wilsonian ideals in diplomacy. At the Versailles Peace Conference the Western powers seemed ready to base the postwar world order on the principles of national self-determination, international peace, and collective security arrangements. To be sure, they showed no readiness to give up their colonial possessions, but at least they seemed willing to preserve a peaceful international status quo through multilateral international agreements rather than through balance of power politics. Professional diplomats in Japan, like Makino Shinken, were convinced that Japan's best interests lay in accommodating her foreign policy to the new diplomacy.

The new assessment of the world situation was embodied in Japan's participation in the Washington Conference of 1921–1922, convened in order to establish a new international order in East Asia. The conference reached several important agreements which established a new framework for Japanese foreign policy in the 1920s. First of all, the conference reaffirmed the principles of the Open Door policy: the territorial integrity of China and the recognition of commercial equality among all nations trading there. As an indication of her good intentions Japan unilaterally agreed to give up the Shantung territories acquired from Germany, to relinquish certain rights wrested from China during the Twenty-One Demands, and to withdraw from Siberia. Second, the powers indicated their resolve to end their competition for influence in China and to work for the establishment of a stable government there. Implied was a willingness to work toward the eventual abolition of extraterritoriality and the restoration of tariff autonomy to China, both keystones of the unequal treaty system. Finally, the conference also reached an agreement on naval arms limitations, the Five Power Treaty, which established a 5:5:3:1.75:1.75 ratio of capital ship tonnage for Great

Britain, the United States, Japan, France, and Italy. The intent
was to head off an incipient naval arms clash that seemed to be
developing between Japan and the United States at the end of the
war. The naval ratio resulted from a compromise by the Americans
and the British who agreed to build no new fortifications west of
Pearl Harbor in the Pacific, or east of Singapore. Since the Japanese
fleet would be equal in size to the combined Pacific fleets of the
Anglo-American powers, and hence strong enough to defend her
home islands and colonial possessions, Japan accepted the inferior
ratio. In fact, it established a Pacific naval balance of power compatible with Japan's own security.

The Japanese acceptance of the Washington system reflected a
realization that the alternative would be a costly and purposeless
arms race. Further territorial expansion on the continent was no
longer a realistic option, and it made more sense to defend Japan's
national security there through a peaceful collective security arrangement. Within the context of this new arrangement Japan began to
strengthen its political and economic ties with China. The main
advocate of the new foreign policy was Shidehara Kijūrō, Foreign
Minister during the Kenseikai-Minseitō cabinets of the 1920s (1924–
1927, 1929–1931). Shidehara was no less committed to maintenance
of empire than anyone else, but his main priority was to protect
and expand Japan's overseas trade, especially with China. To this
end he emphatically rejected needless saber-rattling and bellicose
gestures in China, maintaining a policy of strict non-intervention in
China's domestic troubles. He even refused to go along with a British
suggestion for a show of force by the powers when antiimperialist
riots, such as the May 30 movement in 1925, threatened Japanese
life and property in China. He did not regard Chinese nationalism
as a significant political threat to Japanese interests in the mainland,
and wished to maintain a sympathetic attitude toward the rising
power of the Kuomintang.

The goal of peaceful coexistence and coprosperity with China
had its limitations, however, and so did Shidehara's willingness to
cooperate with the other powers on China policy. Both foundered
on Shidehara's reluctance to make any concessions to Chinese
nationalism that worked to Japan's economic disadvantage. When
an international tariff conference was held at Peking in 1925 Japan
stubbornly resisted the return of tariff autonomy to the Chinese
for fear that a rise in tariffs might make Japanese goods, especially

textiles, less competitive. Shidehara also opposed Chinese efforts in the late 1920s to build railway lines in competition with the South Manchurian Railway.

Whatever its merits, Shidehara diplomacy did not reflect a national consensus. To many it appeared a weak policy, sacrificing national security and national honor to pursuit of international harmony, a goal many regarded as highly unrealistic will-o'-the wisp. While Shidehara assiduously cultivated close ties with the Americans and the English, he made little or no protest against their racialist immigration policies, especially the American Exclusion Act of 1924, which all but halted Japanese immigration to the U.S. These policies were a serious affront not simply to rabidly nationalistic Japanese, but to those with a commitment to a liberal sense of justice. Furthermore, many were concerned about Shidehara's nonchalant attitude toward the growing antiimperialist militance of Chinese nationalism. In 1924, the Kuomintang, re-organized with help from the Soviet Union, had proclaimed a policy of revolutionary diplomacy, aimed at ending the old imperialist privileges. In the summer of 1926 Kuomintang armies under the leadership of Chiang Kai-shek launched a northern expedition against local warlord regimes in an attempt to end civil disorder within China and bring the country under centralized leadership. As China seemed to move more and more rapidly toward unification, many influential Japanese, both civilian and military, feared that confrontation between Chinese nationalist sentiments and Japanese imperialist privilege was in the offing.

Against the background of these sentiments, in 1927 Seiyūkai Premier Tanaka Giichi proclaimed a new "positive policy" toward China. Tanaka's policy did not represent a 180-degree shift in direction away from Shidehara diplomacy, since the new premier recognized the need for economic expansion and felt that cooperation with the Anglo-American powers was essential for an effective China policy. But Tanaka's "positive policy" was different in two important respects: first of all, Tanaka felt that Japan had more than simply a material stake in China, and when the northern expedition seemed to threaten Japanese residents there he twice dispatched Japanese troops to protect them; second and perhaps more important, Tanaka felt that Japan's interests in Manchuria were fundamentally separate and distinct from those in the rest of China. Even if the Kuomintang established itself as the legitimate government of China, he felt it was necessary that Manchuria be kept outside its jurisdiction. While maintaining relatively friendly relations with the new Kuomintang government of Nanking Tanaka intrigued to keep Manchuria under the control of a local warlord, Chang Tso-lin. Whether this would have proven successful in the long run is moot since already in the late 1920s elements in the Japanese army were plotting a revolution in Japanese foreign policy that would overturn the Shidehara-Tanaka line of moderation.

Army Discontent

The triumph of diplomatic moderation in the 1920s was accompanied by the relative decline in the political fortunes of the army. There was a general revulsion against militarism at the end of World War I. The Japanese army had brought a fair measure of unpopularity by its stubborn, costly, and ultimately futile adventure in Siberia. Moreover, in face of the recurring financial instability of the early 1920s strong pressure built in the Finance Ministry and the business world for a reduction in military spending. The army was an easy target for advocates of government economy since Russia, the prime hypothetical land enemy, was weakened by revolution and civil war. The navy had agreed to arms limitations at the Washington conference, and it was only fair that the army be required to make sacrifices as well. In 1922 the cabinet of Admiral Katō Tomosaburō, the head of the Japanese delegation to the Washington conference, began a series of cuts in military spending, down from 39 percent of the national budget in 1919 to about 16 percent from 1923 to 1931. In 1924–1925, the Katō Kōmei cabinet accomplished a major cutback reducing the army by four divisions, or about 35,000 men, including several thousand officers.

The retrenchment policy was not entirely to the disadvantage of the army. It kept army spending from increasing but it did not reduce the absolute size of the army budget. War Minister Ugaki Kazunari (1924–1927) used retrenchment as an excuse to effect major reforms in the army structure and to reduce the influence of older conservative generals. Savings brought about by manpower cuts were used to modernize the army, shifting away from an infantry base to a mechanized one relying on motor transportation and the use of new tactical weapons such as tanks, machine guns, long-range artillery and airplanes. As a result the army was better

prepared to fight for the new kind of warfare that developed during
the European conflict. At the same time, in an attempt to create
a stronger civilian constituency for the army and to provide employment for cashiered officers, Ugaki managed to introduce military
training into the middle schools and to reorganize the local army
reserve associations among the factory workers as well as among
village and rural populations. Despite the apparent disadvantages of
the retrenchment program, the army became more efficient and
more closely linked with the mass of the population during the
mid-1920s.

The retrenchment policy nonetheless did create much resentment
in the officer corps, which directed its discontents against civilian
domination of domestic policy and the diplomatic moderation of
Shidehara. Many officers, including those in the highest echelons,
felt Shidehara diplomacy was excessively naive and potentially dangerous. They did not believe that the world had ushered in a new
era of international peace and harmony. Both the "Anglo-American
imperialists" and the "Bolsheviks" in Russia and China seemed to
be pursuing their own particular interests with slight regard for
international cooperation. Moreover, just as leaders in the Meiji
period had absorbed Western imperialist doctrines of national
security, so the more informed and up-to-date officers in the 1920s
came under the influence of the theory of total war. This view held
that in modern times wars were not won on the battlefield alone,
but on the homefront as well. Without a total mobilization of the
civilian population, and more crucially, a strong and autonomous
industrial base, victory was not possible. Many army leaders, including Ugaki's gifted lieutenant, Nagata Tetsuzan, felt that the
temporary peace of the 1920s should be used to prepare the country, internally and externally, for a global conflict that was sure to
come in the long run.

By the late 1920s the primary focus of army anxiety was Manchuria. If Japan were to create a self-supplying, self-sufficient economic sphere in preparation for total war in the future it would have
to include Manchuria, an area with vast resource reserves of iron
and coal, and Mongolia, a natural buffer against the Soviet Union.
Some officers also thought Manchuria could become important as a
source of food supply and as an outlet for excess population unable
to find employment in Japan itself. As Kuomintang armies swept
ever closer to Manchuria, certain young staff officers, particularly

in the Kwantung army, felt the need for urgent action. Like Tanaka Giichi they wished to keep Manchuria out of Chinese hands but unlike Tanaka they were willing to use military force to do so. In June 1928 a group of Kwantung army officers secretly engineered the assassination of the Manchurian warlord, Chang Tso-lin, in hope of precipitating a Japanese military occupation of the area. The plot failed when the Tanaka cabinet, profoundly upset despite all its talk of a positive policy, refused to take advantage of the situation. If anything, the incident severely damaged Japan's position in Manchuria since Chang's son, Chang Hsueh-liang, established closer ties with the Kuomintang to protect himself from the Japanese.

The growing sense of alarm among the army leadership was deepened by other developments. On the one hand the persistent economic troubles of the 1920s finally reached crisis proportions. After a decade of civilian temporizing the Hamaguchi government in 1929 finally decided on a thorough-going deflationary policy marked by severe budget cutbacks, rationalization of heavy industry to increase productivity, and a return to the gold standard to establish stability in foreign trade. The government anticipated that these policies would bring a drop in prices and employment but they did not foresee the October 1929 crash of the New York stock market or the onset of a general world depression. The result of this unfortunate convergence was a sudden plunge into hard times. Manufacturers cut production, workers were laid off in large numbers, wage cuts were common, and the number of striking workers doubled. More serious were the effects of the world and domestic depression on small-scale enterprise and on the rural population. The sharp drop in the employment in the textile industry flooded the villages with returning workers; the rice price index (1926 = 100) dropped to 67.7 by late 1930, and 49.2 in late 1931; silk prices fell equally drastically; and a serious crop failure in northeastern Japan cut the harvest to 50 to 70 percent below normal. The condition of much of the population was summed up by the comment of one small-scale wholesale dealer in Kyoto: "We have grown accustomed to falling prices. We sell an item of ¥100 at ¥80 so that we can eat . . . We are nothing but a group of hungry demons."[3] Neither the Hamaguchi government nor its civilian predecessors were totally responsible for this economic disaster, but they did little to alleviate its consequences. Though the party cabinets of the 1920s—like the oligarchs and clique governments—were willing to bail out failing business firms with easy credit or to encourage the concentration of large-scale enterprise they took no very consistent or effective actions to relieve the lot of the peasant, the working man, or the small entrepreneur. It was not difficult for army officers, and many others as well, to blame social distress and economic chaos on civilian and party rule.

At the same time the party governments of the late 1920s seemed increasingly oblivious to the problem of national security. In 1929 the Tanaka cabinet agreed to the Kellogg-Briand pact outlawing war as part of its continuing effort to maintain the international framework of peaceful cooperation and collective security. To make matters worse, at the London Naval Conference of 1930, the Hamaguchi government agreed to new naval arms limitations. Going against the advice of the navy general staff, the Japanese delegation agreed to a 10:6:6 ratio with Great Britain and the United States in heavy cruisers, a 10:6:6 ratio in light cruisers and other vessels, and parity in submarines. The consequence was a major constitutional crisis. The navy objected that the civilian cabinet had violated its right of direct access to the throne, and the Seiyūkai, for purely partisan reasons, took up the cry in the Diet. Premier Hamaguchi pushed through ratification on the grounds that the cabinet had the right to conclude treaties after consulting the military authorities in proper fashion, and after a bitter struggle, he secured Privy Council approval. The victory of the government only deepened the anxieties of the military for not only did the episode commit Japan to self-restraint in military preparation it also called into question the fundamental principle of military independence from civilian influence.

The stage was set for army action. Concerned over the deteriorating position in Manchuria, staff officers in the Kwantung army, acting in concert with ranking members of the general staff, had already laid plans for the seizure of Manchuria. But the demand for expansion abroad had become linked with plans for a military coup d'état at home. In March 1931, hoping to bring about a major national reconstruction, a group of field-grade staff officers in Tokyo laid the groundwork for an army revolt to oust the civilian politicians who seemed incapable of dealing with either the economic crisis or unconcerned over threats to national security. Arrogant, contemptuous of civilian rule, and deeply involved in plans for the seizure of Manchuria, they aimed at the establishment of a military dictatorship under the leadership of War Minister Ugaki. Ultimately the plan was thwarted by the opposition from the top army leadership, including Ugaki, who refused to become involved, but the incident was hushed up, as the assassination of Chang Tso-lin had been, and the conspirators went unpunished.

Nevertheless plans for the Manchurian takeover moved ahead. On the evening of September 18, 1931, officers from the Kwantung army garrison at Mukden dynamited a few feet of the South Manchurian Railway near the city. Claiming that the explosion was the work of Chinese saboteurs, the Kwantung army declared a state of emergency. Japanese troops seized control of Mukden, and within a few weeks the Kwantung army, backed by the tacit consent of the general staff and aided by the dispatch of a division from Korea, had occupied most of south Manchuria as a "defensive measure." The civilian government at Tokyo, headed by Premier Wakatsuki and including Foreign Minister Shidehara, worked hard to contain the hostilities, but they were powerless to reverse the *fait accompli.* The war minister, as well as members of the general staff, kept assuring them that military action in Manchuria would be limited in scope. By the time it became clear that such was not the case it was too late for the government to act without loss of face. There were also many civilian politicians, including Home Minister Adachi Kenzō, in sympathy with a militant and aggressive policy in Manchuria. But even if the cabinet had not been divided against itself, it was apparent that the Kwantung Army was determined to push ahead whatever the wishes of the Tokyo government. As one officer remarked to the Japanese consul at Mukden, if the civilian government objected to its policies, the Kwantung army was prepared to secede from Japan. Perhaps decisive international action might have blocked Japanese military expansion in Manchuria, but since no foreign power including the Chinese themselves did more than make verbal objection, the deed ultimately went unchallenged. Willy-nilly the Kwantung army had brought about a diplomatic revolution that colored every aspect of Japanese politics for the next decade and a half, and eventually brought the total war so long anticipated by army leaders.

13

Militarism and War

The Manchurian crisis not only overturned the cooperative diplomacy of the 1920s, it also brought an end to domination of politics by civilian politicians. The decade following 1931 was marked by a retreat from the relative freedom of the 1920s, a deepening commitment to aggression abroad, and a search for new forms of national leadership. Many observers discerned in these trends the "rise of fascism," parallel to developments in Europe, but it would probably be better to describe the 1930s as a period of militarism in the broadest sense of the word. Under the pressure of international crisis the country was gradually transformed into a garrison state dominated by militaristic politics and militaristic goals. This militarism was confined not simply to the professional officer corps, but infiltrated every corner of society, often finding its most enthusiastic supporters among civilian elements. The whole country gradually geared itself for what many felt was the greatest national crisis since the Meiji Restoration, carried away by feelings that Japan's survival was at stake.

The Nationalist Reaction

The groundwork for the mood of the 1930s had been long in the making. It was basically shaped by the official morality propagated through the elementary education system since the 1890s. The traditionalist ideas of social harmony, of duty and self-sacrifice, of loyalty to the emperor and obedience to parents, and of the special character of the Japanese kokutai were thoroughly embedded in the minds of most Japanese. Originally propagated by the government to shore up popular resolve in a time when Japan was protecting its fragile new national independence, these ideas were easily diverted to mobilizing popular support behind a policy of expansion abroad and political reorganization at home.

During the 1920s these ideas were also diffused by nostalgic and conservative right-wing movements, alarmed by the spread of "degenerate habits" and "dangerous ideas" among the populace. In the eyes of the right the country was going to rack and ruin. Intoxicated by the hedonistic doctrine of individualism, the younger generation was being lured by radicalism. "Bolsheviks" and "Reds" spread their sinister ideas of class struggle, and unrest was everywhere evident among the normally docile masses. To combat these ominous trends, which augured a decline in national unity and the spread of social divisiveness, right-wing elements rallied into new political groupings. Some were organizations of long standing, like the Local Reservist Associations (Zaigogunjinkai) or the local Youth Associations (Seinendan), organized under Home Ministry auspices in late Meiji to buttress the official morality propagated by the schools and to organize the population against an incipient socialist movement. Others were antilabor groups, like the Kokusuikai (National Essence Society) directed at curbing the new left wing through strike-breaking and strong-arm intimidation of individuals suspected of harboring "dangerous thoughts." Finally there were more respectable "educational" groups, such as the Kokuhonsha (National Foundation Society) which recruited backing among leading bureaucrats, businessmen, politicians, and military men and aimed at combatting the "decline of traditional morality" and the spread of subversion. All these groups were basically conservative, interested in preserving the social and institutional status quo.

But there also emerged in the 1920s a radical right wing, equally alarmed by the problem of national disunity but inclined to place much of the blame for it on those in positions of power. The right-wing radicals were convinced that the pursuit of profit, materialism, and self-interest had deflected the nation's leaders from pursuing the public good and protecting social harmony. The zaibatsu expanded ruthlessly, heedless of the social consequences; the political parties, shot through with corruption, pandered to special interests; and the older generation of nonparty officials and politicians clung doggedly to their positions with scant regard for the plight of the common people. While the plutocrats, peers, and party leaders went their self-serving ways, the rest of the country was sinking into poverty and discontent. Government officials summarized the views of one group of right-wing terrorists as follows:

> The political parties, the zaibatsu and a small privileged group attached to the ruling classes . . . pursue their own egotistic interests and desires, to the neglect of national defence and to the confusion of government. As a result national dignity is lost abroad, while at home the morale of the people collapses; the villages are exhausted, and medium and small industry and commerce have been driven to the wall.[1]

In sum, hard times, unemployment, and rural starvation signaled the decadence of the ruling class and the triumph of private interest over public good at the highest level of leadership. To the radical right the failure of the privileged classes to deal with the nation's multifaceted crises meant they had forfeited their right to rule in the emperor's name.

Although members of the radical right wing shared a revulsion for those in power they were divided in their visions of Japan's future. Some were agrarian romantics, like Gondō Seikyō, violently hostile to "Prussian" statism. They hoped for a revival of the local village community through greater decentralization of political power, local economic self-sufficiency, and a general redress of the imbalance between city and country. Such views appealed not only to rural elements but also to those urban dwellers denied the benefits of middle class status, who were carried away by a nostalgic enthusiasm for the simple, natural, and healthy values of rural life.

Their model of the good society was the village. For other right-wing theorists it was the barracks. Kita Ikki, an influential national socialist thinker, preached a highly centralized form of state social-ism aimed at mobilizing the energies and strength of the nation by tight authoritarian controls over all aspects of society, politics, and economy. His goal was a holistic society, free from class conflict and united under direct imperial rule, capable of liberating Japan's "700 million brothers in Asia" from the bonds of colonial rule. These state socialist ideas gained currency among disgruntled army officers already convinced of the need for building a state easily mobilized for total war, and also among reform-minded civilians who rejected left-wing ideas. But in many right-wing tracts both agrarian romanticism and nationalist socialism were mingled together in glassy-eyed rhetoric with more regard for emotional logic than rational consistency.

In their critique of capitalism, their attack on party rule, and their advocacy of social reform, radical right-wing thought converged with that of the left. Indeed this intellectual convergence made it possible for many left-wing activists of the 1920s to convert to the right wing in the 1930s. But more significant was a radical difference with respect to goals and tactics. For one thing, the right wing was not so much indignant over the misery of the common people in itself but rather was alarmed at the effects this misery had in weakening Japan vis-à-vis the outside world. Concern for social suffering was shaped mainly by anxiety about Japan's national strength and the right wing goal of domestic reform was social harmony and national unity, not social justice. The right-wing radicals also made no attempt to organize the masses or build up a popular movement. Instead they favored the elitist tactics of personal terrorism and military coup d'état. To some extent this indifference to the tactics of mass organization was fostered by a mystique of personal heroism and a lust for self-glorification, paradoxically fed by the idea of selfless personal devotion to nation and emperor. But it was also fostered by the realization that terrorist tactics were more realistic than the tedious process of building mass support. As the experience of the proletarian parties had demonstrated, the entrenched political parties held a firm grip on the electorate, and the mass of population living in the country responded to the direction of local political bosses and "men of influence." The privileged classes were also in firm control of the police, the courts, and the other instruments of state power. It seemed futile to fight the entrenched elite on its own ground and far more effective to resort to illegal, extraconstitutional, and elitist tactics. Consequently most members of the civilian radical right felt the greatest hope for bringing about national reconstruction lay in a military coup to overthrow the "selfish cabal" leading the country.

The Manchurian crisis, coupled with deepening rural depression, spawned an atmosphere of crisis, anxiety, and uncertainty in which right wing ideas flourished. By early 1932 patriotic associations, national socialist political parties, chauvinist religious sects, and crank right-wing study groups began to proliferate in droves. Between 1932 and 1936 membership in such groups rose from 300,000 to over 600,000. Often led by professional right-wing ideologues and sometimes by former leftist elements, they drew support from social strata most resentful of the corrupt parties, the zaibatsu, and the "evil advisors" of the throne—namely, the lower-middle classes in both city and country, petty officials, small shopkeepers, retired military officers, elementary school teachers, small landowners, the bosses of small-scale workshops, army reservists, and the like. These social elements were well enough educated to have absorbed the official cult of loyalty to the throne but not well enough educated to doubt its mythical bases. Beset on all sides by economic difficulties and resentful of their plight, they contrasted their own attachment to traditional virtues with the evidence of moral failure and political corruption in high places. They also poured invective on the "foreign" or "Western" values of selfish individualism, materialism, and liberalism associated with the ruling classes. Divided and fragmented and lacking access to power, these small patriotic groups represented a kind of "little man's fascism." Occasionally they had some small political impact. In 1935, for example, a grass roots movement centering on the Local Reservist Associations succeeded in prompting the expulsion of Minobe Tatsukichi, a prominent liberal constitutional scholar, from the House of Peers. But in general, the main role of these groups was anesthetizing public opinion to the dangers of a reckless foreign policy by constantly lauding the superiority of Japanese spirit, proclaiming the infallibility of the Imperial Way, and clamoring for a clarification of the national polity.

The Shōwa Restoration

The Manchurian incident brought an end to the era of party rule and ushered in a period when political violence was so constant that one foreign journalist referred to Japanese politics as "government by assassination." Terrorism had made its first appearance in November 1930, when a young right-wing fanatic gunned down Premier Hamaguchi in protest over the London Naval Treaty. It escalated with the officers' plot against the cabinet attempted in March 1931 and a similar one the following October. These two abortive colonel's revolts stimulated bolder and more violent activities by junior officers who thought of themselves as latter-day samurai, heir to the radical loyalist tradition of the 1850s and 1860s. Convinced that Japan was once again threatened by danger from without and troubles at home, they sought to bring about a "Shōwa Restoration" to save the nation from its plight. The Shōwa emperor was to be rescued from the entrenched civilian elite as earlier the Meiji emperor had been rescued from the tyranny of the bakufu.

The radical young officer movement, recruited from lieutenants and captains in line companies rather than from the more responsible field grade staff officers in army headquarters, often acted in concert with civilian radical rightists like Gondō Seikyō and Inoue Nisshō. They began a campaign of assassination and personal terror aimed at wiping out the civilian domination of government. Beyond that their goals were rather vague. "We thought about destruction first," one of them later confessed. "We never considered taking on the duty of construction. We foresaw, however, that once the destruction was accomplished someone would take charge of the construction for us."[2] In 1932 young naval officers joined with members of a civilian right-wing group, the Blood Pledge Corps (Ketsumeidan), to carry out the systematic elimination of the country's top financial and political leaders. Their efforts culminated with the assassination of Premier Inukai Tsuyoshi, the Seiyūkai president, on May 15, 1932. The radical young officers and their civilian allies were not without sympathizers in high places, the most conspicuous being War Minister Araki Sadao, who publicly praised the actions of "these pure and naive young men." "They are not actions for fame or personal gain, nor are they traitorous," he commented. "They were performed in the sincere belief that they were for the benefit of Imperial Japan."[3] These sentiments were doubtless shared by the burgeoning right-wing movement as well.

But General Araki's views by no means prevailed among those in positions of responsibility. The assassination of Inukai ended the constitutional practice of appointing party cabinets, but it did not lead to a loss of civilian control. Prince Saionji, still surviving as genro, felt that the parties had lost the initiative in foreign policy and credibility in domestic policy but he was appalled at the insubordination of the Kwantung army, the military's bellicose attitude toward the outside world, and the spread of political terrorism. Acting on the advice of the *jūshin* ("senior officials"), an informal group of court officials and former cabinet ministers, Saionji decided the best course of action would be to establish a neutral, nonpartisan "national unity" cabinet resting on a coalition made up of the political parties, ranking civilian bureaucrats, and the military services. From 1932 until 1936 Japan was governed by two such cabinets, led by retired admirals, the first under Saitō Makoto, and the second under Okada Keisuke. The army had a significantly larger voice in both cabinets but it was still forced to compromise with the other elite elements.

The failure of the 1932 assassination plots to achieve a major reorientation of Japanese politics simply fed the fires of radicalism among the young officers. Not only did the privileged classes retain control of the country, but the senior ranks of the army (including even those who had joined the abortive 1931 plots) remonstrated against the lack of discipline in the lower echelons. Young officer frustration was further deepened by a struggle for power at the highest levels of army leadership. The retirement of General Ugaki as War Minister in 1931 led to factional in-fighting among the generals and leading staff officers. On one side were ranged the generals of the Imperial Way Faction (*Kōdōha*), who controlled key posts in the army high command. Their leader was War Minister Araki Sadao, a man given to sombre pronouncements about the efficacy of the Japanese spirit in solving the country's ills and consequently popular with the radical young officer movement. Araki was opposed by a powerful coalition of elements in the General Staff, who opposed his lenient attitude toward the radicals, felt him to be a weak advocate of army interests in the cabinet, and disliked his spouting of right-wing rhetoric. They also disliked his belligerent anti-Soviet attitudes and feared that he and the other Imperial Way generals lacked a sufficient understanding of modern military theory. Instead of creating machinery for long-term economic planning and national mobilization, the Imperial Way generals were content to rely on "spiritual mobilization" as preparation for war. The anti-Imperial Way generals gradually whittled away the power of Araki and his followers but supporters of the Araki clique struck back in August 1935 by assassinating Nagata Tetsuzan, who was regarded as the evil genius of Araki's opposition.

The radical young officer movement made a last desperate effort to bring about national reconstruction in early 1936. On February 26 elements in the First Division at Tokyo led by radical young officers attempted a major military insurrection. Nearly fifteen hundred troops seized the government nerve center in Tokyo while carefully organized assassination bands attempted to murder a group

of top national officials, including the premier, key cabinet ministers, members of the imperial court bureaucracy, a number of ranking army leaders, and even the genrō Saionji. The rebels announced
their intentions to save the nation by removing the "traitors and evil-
doers surrounding the Throne," thus paving the way for national
renovation. Faced with this unprecedented military rebellion from
below, many army leaders, perhaps sensing an opportunity for a
take-over of the government, took no action to put it down. But the
emperor was personally aghast at such a major breach of army discipline and the navy, incensed by assassination attempts on senior
admirals like Premier Okada, former Premier Saito, and Grand
Chamberlain Suzuki, moved warships into Tokyo Bay with guns
trained on the rebel strongholds. The rebellion quickly collapsed, the
troops returned to their barracks, and the leaders of the rebellion (as
well as Kita Ikki) were summarily executed by army firing squads.

The radical movement to carry out a Shōwa Restoration failed to
achieve its goal, but the terrorism of the early 1930s had not been
without effect. Civilian politicians, both in the parties and the
bureaucracy, were severely shaken by the officer plots. The influence of political parties, tainted by the failures of the 1920s, slowly
declined. Fewer and fewer party men were invited to become cabinet
ministers after 1932, and fewer and fewer ambitious officials showed
an interest in joining the parties. In the face of right-wing terrorism
the political parties also found it difficult to recruit business or
bureaucratic support. In the wake of the incident of May 15, the
large zaibatsu—first Mitsui, then Mitsubishi—gradually but deliberately withdrew financial support from the parties and in late 1932
the Saitō government also moved to end the patronage power of the
parties by trimming the discretionary power of the cabinet to
appoint prefectural governors and local police officials. Although
the parties still continued to lobby for local interest groups and
obtained funds from "new zaibatsu" involved in war industries, it
was clear to most that party influence was on the wane, and there
was very little the parties could do to reverse the trend. Having risen
to power through compromise the parties now found themselves
squeezed by those who sought to compromise with the army instead.

As the influence of the parties declined the influence of the army
increased. Using the February 26 meeting as an excuse, the army
leadership began to restore discipline within its ranks, to put an end
to factionalism, and to press for the economic reorganization neces-

sary for full-scale military mobilization. In the winter of 1936 a clean-up campaign weeded out radical elements in the junior ranks and forced into inactive status generals who had sympathized with the radicals. To exclude the purged generals from important political posts, the army managed to restore the requirement that the War Minister be on active status, a regulation that gave the army the same veto power over the formation of cabinets that it had enjoyed down until 1913. Quite apart from its new legal powers, the army also began to speak out with an authority born of its increasing indispensability in making national policy. With the future direction of Japan's continental policies still unresolved, the opinion of the military now carried great weight, since it would have most of the responsibility in carrying this policy out. Indeed, as one Diet member noted, it had become "the driving force in politics."

The China Quagmire

 The central reason for increased army influence in national politics was the deeper and deeper commitment of Japanese military power and national prestige on the Asian mainland. After the establishment of the puppet state of Manchukuo under Kwantung army auspices in 1932 its defence and maintenance as an "independent" state became a basic axiom of Japanese foreign policy, accepted by the Saitō cabinet and all those that were to follow it. Criticism from abroad, whether it took the form of diplomatic nonrecognition of Manchukuo or overt condemnation of Japanese aggression by the League of Nations, only served to bolster this commitment. Against a background of rising anti-Westernism and antiforeignism in the press and public opinion, the Japanese government resorted to truculent self-justification that became increasingly shrill as the decade wore on. Leading officials and government publicists, resuscitating Pan-Asian doctrines that had enjoyed a vogue since the turn of the century, spoke of Japan as a champion of "Asia for the Asiatics" and described her policies on the mainland as a "Japanese Monroe Doctrine." What Japan was doing on the mainland, they argued, was no different from what the United States had done in Latin America for over a century.

This confident rhetoric masked enormous confusion, uncertainty, and cross purposes at the high echelons of government in Tokyo. Aside from the maintenance of Manchukuo in the face of increasing diplomatic isolation and Anglo-American hostility there was no clear consensus on national goals. In January 1932, when fighting broke out between Chinese and Japanese forces in Shanghai, one faction of the army, led by Nagata Tetsuzan, urged an expansion of military operations in China proper. But there was considerable opposition to such a move among other responsible officials. The finance ministry objected that it would place an unbearable strain on the economy; the navy high command, as well as the foreign ministry, feared that it would provoke hostilities with the British and the Americans; and the Imperial Way generals in the army thought it would deflect energies from preparation for conflict with the Soviet Union. All these considerations, coupled with the factional struggle in the army and the overturn of cabinets, kept the government in Tokyo from making any precipitous foreign policy moves.

In contrast to the hesitation of civilian officials in Tokyo, the Kwantung Army, with the backing of elements in the central army high command, continued to nibble away at Chinese territory. Claiming the military necessity of defending Manchukuo's borders, Kwantung Army forces moved into Jehol in the winter of 1933. In April the Japanese signed the Tangku truce agreement with the Chinese government, under which the Japanese area of occupation was extended to the Great Wall and a demilitarized zone was established in north China around Peking. On the move again in 1935, the Kwantung Army managed through military pressure and negotiation to expel Kuomintang party organization and troops from Hopei province as well. Encouraged by their successes, local Japanese commanders in the fall of 1935 began to promote a "north China autonomy movement," encouraging dissident Kuomintang generals to launch "independence movements," in the hopes of creating a buffer zone for Manchukuo. Their aim was to keep the Chinese divided and weak and to link the resources of north China to the Manchurian economy, perhaps in preparation for further moves into Mongolia. In short, while the authorities in Tokyo debated local armies on the mainland made national policy by default.

These tactics of creeping aggression were successful largely because there was no effective resistance to the Japanese by forces within China. Chiang Kai-shek was well aware of Japan's military superiority and he was further plagued by the Kuomintang's inability to create a stable central regime commanding widespread popular loyalty. The Kuomintang's main preoccupation in the early 1930s was eradication of Communist bases in south China. Chiang's armies were tied down by extermination campaigns that left no leeway for confrontation with the Japanese. In 1935 Chiang even made overtures to Tokyo for a Sino-Japanese Treaty of Friendship. But the "long march" of the Communists to Yenan in 1934–1935, coupled with mounting anti-Japanese sentiments among certain Kuomintang generals and among the students, put Chiang under heavy internal pressure to reverse his priorities. In December 1936 Chang Hsueh-liang forcibly detained Chiang during a visit to Sian until he finally agreed to cooperate with the Communists in a united front against Japanese aggression. This shift in the position of the Nanking government seriously increased the likelihood of a major Sino-Japanese conflict.

When the clash finally came it caught the newly formed Konoe Fumimaro government almost by surprise. On July 7, 1937, a minor skirmish occurred between Chinese and Japanese troops at Marco Polo Bridge near Peking. The local commanders succeeded in arranging a truce but the Nanking government decided to demonstrate its willingness to stand up to the Japanese by sending new troops into the area. The Konoe government, no less concerned to make a show of strength, replied in kind, and soon a full-scale undeclared war was underway in north China. When Chinese bombers attacked the Japanese settlement in Shanghai in August 1938 both sides had reached the point of no return. The war spread quickly as the better-armed and better-trained Japanese forces advanced southward into Chinese territory. Although the army had neither long-range plans for operations in China nor extensive stockpiles of equipment and materiel Japanese forces drove steadily toward the capture of Nanking, the Kuomintang government's capital. Exultant field commanders, meeting little effective resistance, sent back reports of victory after victory and confidently predicted that Chiang could be defeated in six months.

The Konoe government, caught up in its own enthusiasm and reassured by army authorities that each next campaign would surely smash Chinese resistance, continued to authorize new operations. Significantly, however, many officers in the general staff, including men like Ishihara Kanji, one of the planners of the Mukden incident, were opposed to this reckless expansion into south China. Skeptical of the view that China would collapse under a series of punishing blows, they were well aware of the difficulties of fighting in the vast geographical expanse of China and they knew that Japan was not prepared economically and industrially for a full-scale war there. Moreover, they feared that if the China war were not quickly brought to an end preparations for a possible clash with the Soviet Union would be put in jeopardy. Consequently they urged that no further military advances be made, that the status quo be maintained in north China, and that peace negotiations be opened with Chiang Kai-shek.

The early military successes in China, especially the fall of Nanking in December 1937, only made the Konoe government more inflexible. In January 1938, after an unsuccessful attempt to secure Chiang's recognition of Manchukuo and the demilitarization of north China, the Konoe government finally burned its bridges by announcing its unwillingness to negotiate further with Chiang and its hopes for the emergence of new regimes in China friendly to Japan. In effect Konoe committed Japan to military subjugation of Chiang instead of a negotiated end to the hostilities. The decision proved disastrous for the Japanese simply lacked the ability to succeed in such a policy. Adopting a scorched earth policy and the tactics of attrition, Chiang retreated to the interior city of Chungking. Japanese armies continued to win battles, capturing the great industrial-commercial complex at Wuhan in October 1938, but they were unable to win the war.

A "reform government," staffed by a number of pro-Japanese officials who had served earlier in warlord regimes, was established to administer Japanese-occupied areas. Eventually it was reorganized under the leadership of Wang Ching-wei, a former protégé of Sun Yat-sen and a rival of Chiang Kai-shek, who defected from the Kuomintang government in hopes of arriving at some accommodation with the Japanese. But the Japanese were unable to generate much popular support for their puppet regime or to convince many of its independence.

By the summer of 1939 the worst predictions of the general staff had come true. After two years of hard fighting the momentum of the Japanese offensive operations had nearly come to a halt. The Japanese controlled the main coastal cities, the area around Peking, the Wuhan industrial complex, and most major railway lines. Japanese bombers harassed the Kuomintang base at Chunking, but Chiang's government, ensconced beyond the Yangtze River gorges, was safe from land attack. In Japanese-occupied territories local guerrilla movements, sometimes led by Kuomintang elements, and sometimes by Communist, carried on underground warfare against Japanese forces. And to make matters worse, in mid-1938 and again in the spring of 1939 clashes with Soviet troops on Manchurian borders renewed anxieties over the possibility of war with Russia. Despite the heady confidence of the first months of the war Japan had reached a military stalemate from which there was no simple promise of escape.

These dismaying realities did not blunt enthusiasm for war within Japan. In part it was stirred up by the propaganda efforts of the government, beginning with a "national spiritual mobilization movement" organized in the fall of 1937. Official pronouncements portrayed the war as a struggle to liberate China. In November 1938 Premier Konoe announced Japan's hope for the establishment of a "new order in East Asia," based on "cooperation" of Japan, China, and Manchukuo. He pointed to the common interests of China and Japan as have-not nations, excluded from their rightful place in the world by the white imperialists. In his rhetoric the unexpected war was transformed into a struggle by the Japanese to end Western influence and domination in China and the Japanese were depicted as allies of the Chinese people in their struggle against Chiang Kai-shek, the foreigners' "running dog." The notion of a new order was belied by the army's exploitative economic policies in China, the ruthless pacification campaigns against Chinese guerillas, and the economic dependence of Japan herself on the Westerners, especially the United States for war materiel. But these facts were ignored by the mass of the population, who were convinced of the high moral purposes of Japan's "Holy War," moved by the bravery and sacrifice of her troops, and confident in the superiority of the Japanese Way. As in 1894 and 1905, a surge of renewed national confidence and a sense of national purpose gripped all but an insignificant handful of people.

At the same time it should be remembered that the outbreak of the China war coincided with the final recovery of the economy from the hard times of the early 1930s. From 1932 onward the finance ministry under Takehashi Korekiyo pursued a reflationary policy based on an expansion of the national budget (especially in support of the Manchurian enterprise), deficit spending, aid to farmers, and a de facto devaluation of the yen. By 1936 unemployment dropped, domestic consumption rose, and real incomes went up. Although prices rose sharply and shortages occurred in certain consumer goods after the outbreak of war in 1937 the country was enjoying a mild prosperity. An expanding military budget, which swelled from ¥450 million in 1931 to ¥1.4 billion in 1937, created new jobs, promised new profits for both large scale industry and small-scale entrepreneurs, and guaranteed a market for food produced by the farm population. It was not difficult for most people to associate foreign adventure with good times. In any case bombs were falling on Chinese cities, not on the Japanese, and life continued more or less unchanged. To be sure there were troops dying in China, but triumphant news dispatches from the front made even their sacrifices worth while. Yet to suffer personal hardship, the majority of the Japanese sat idly by as the nation sank deeper and deeper into the bog.

Wartime Politics

In spite of the near unanimity behind the war effort national leadership remained highly fragmented. In contrast to the fascist regimes in Europe, no dominant personal leader or dictator emerged, nor did any popularly based totalitarian movement. Rather, the highest levels of government were beset by constant but rarely successful attempts to establish within the framework of the constitutional structure the same kind of collective leadership that had guided Japan through its two earlier wars. The weight of army influence increased under the pressure of war, but it was not able to dominate the domestic politic scene as the oligarchs had a generation before. On the contrary, many elements, particularly the older party leaders, resented army influence and did their best to thwart the army's efforts to gain control over the state apparatus. The military leadership found itself stumbling over the same constitutional obstacle that had earlier troubled both clique government and party cabinets.

The main bone of contention between the army and the other elites was the army's efforts to build a national defense state capable of carrying on a total war effort. Its goals were increased military expenditure and an orderly expansion of industrial sector to give Japan a self-sufficient materiel base for an extended war. For the army this meant an end to economic liberalism (that is, a competitive, laissez-faire economy), the introduction of central planning, state controls over industrial production, and perhaps the nationalization of certain key industries. Although the Diet readily approved increased funds for military expenditure from 1933 onward the army's plans for massive administrative and economic reforms designed to create a national defense state met with opposition in many quarters. The parties resented the army's plans for placing enormous economic and administrative controls in the hands of cabinet-controlled economic agencies; entrenched bureaucrats feared their powers would be undercut by the elimination of old ministries and the creation of new economic machinery; and big business was opposed to any sort of controls on its profits and business decisions and feared that overly large budgets would lead to inflation. During the 1937 Diet session criticism of the army was so bitter that the Seiyūkai and Minseitō issued a joint declaration demanding the resignation of the army-backed premier, General Hayashi Senjūrō.

The jūshin had attempted to patch over this mutual distrust by recommending the appointment of Prince Konoe Fumimaro as Premier. Konoe, a protégé of Saionji, was regarded as the man of the hour. Personally aloof, but well connected with elements in the army, the bureaucracy, and the Diet, he seemed to be the only individual leader capable of bringing some unity to national politics. He was known to be a strong opponent of "Anglo-American Imperialism" and to have a strong interest in domestic reform. Taking advantage of the sense of urgency created by the outbreak of war with China, the Konoe government, prompted by the army and supported by a group of reform-minded young bureaucrats, moved to centralize economic controls in the hands of the cabinet. In October 1937 the Cabinet Planning Agency (Kikaku-in) was created with responsibility for devising plans for economic mobilization. As the result of its work a whole series of new laws regulating everything from foreign trade to currency control were put into effect. But the main goal of the agency, staffed by a new breed of economic bureaucrats oriented toward centralized economic planning and enjoying the full backing of the army, was to eliminate the waste and duplication of a competitive free economy by giving the cabinet wide discretionary powers in allocating resources, capital, and manpower in the wartime situation. In the name of the war effort they tried to by-pass the Diet, dominated by vested business and economic interests.

All this smacked of "state socialism," abhorrent to both the parties and big business, who resisted the proposals for a National Mobilization Law finally sent to the Diet in February 1938. The main support for the law came from the left-wing proletarian parties, who welcomed the law as a step toward social reconstruction and the restriction of capitalism. It was finally approved by the Diet, but only after the entrenched parties had extracted certain concessions from Konoe. The government promised not to apply the law for the duration of the China incident, provided for government consultation with the Diet and the business community, and left out any provision for the regulation of private profits. The army's demand for the creation of a highly centralized national defense state was thus diluted by compromise with the parties, big business, and conservative elements in the bureaucracy. By contrast, none of these elements made any strong objection when the government put into effect those provisions of the law affecting wages, hours, and contracts of workers, despite its promise not to apply the law during the China incident.

Political conflict still continued at the top. During the three years following the Marco Polo Bridge incident the country went through four Premiers and five cabinets, a token of habitual in-fighting within the elites. The cabinet fought the military high commands over foreign policy, the army struggled with the navy over funds and strategic plans, and the obstreperous Diet slowed down the passage of legislation. The diplomatic corps was divided against itself, and the business community counseled caution and restraint. By the end of 1939 a desire to end this unseemly squabbling led many to call for the establishment of a new political order aimed at transcending bureaucratic or partisan interests and restoring cooperation and harmony to national politics.

There were several approaches to building a new political order. Elements in the army, disgusted with the disruptive, selfish, and "foreign" tactics of the parties, wanted a Nazi-style one-party state to mobilize the population behind the war effort. Certain civilian politicians, drawn from both the proletarian parties and the radical right, wished to build the new political order from the bottom up, as a mass party resting on local popular organizations. Finally, many members of the established parties wanted to create one big party able to resist pressures from the military, by merging progressive elements in the Seiyūkai and Minseitō. In the summer of 1940, as a prelude to the establishment of a new political order under the leadership of Prince Konoe, all the major political parties dissolved themselves, bringing to its logical conclusion the decline that had begun in 1932.

The new political order that finally emerged, however, was not a new political party capable of mobilizing the masses or exercising control over the formulation of national policy. Rather it was the Imperial Rule Assistance Association, a sprawling and unwieldy national organization set up in the fall of 1940. From the beginning the organization was beset by a struggle among the diverse groups that had urged the destruction of the political status quo and the creation of a new political order—the army, the politicians, and the civil bureaucracy. Eventually the bureaucrats in the Home Ministry won out, converting the IRAA into a nationwide organization that meshed with the existing bureaucratic structure. The *ex officio* president of the Association was the Premier, and its local branches were headed by the prefectural governors. Its basic function was to increase popular identification with the state and to expedite the downward flow of official orders and regulations.

The whole population belonged to the organization either as members of some centralized functional association (for example, the Imperial Rule Assistance Youth League, the Agriculturalists' Patriotic Association, or the Writers' Patriotic Association) or as members of local neighborhood groups called *tonarigumi*. The neighborhood association, designed to by-pass local political party machines or other nonstate groups, was made up of about ten households, which were required to hold monthly meetings and to report to village or town associations at the next administrative level. Because it challenged a variety of established political interests, from the political parties to extremist right-wing groups, the IRAA was subjected to considerable public criticism, especially in the Diet. Some said that like the bakufu it stood between people and emperor, others attacked it as a "lair for communists," and still others complained that it was both expensive and unconstitutional.

The new political order represented by the IRAA was therefore a far cry from the fascist one-party dictatorships of Europe. It is not difficult to understand why this was so since social and political conditions were very different from either Hitler's Germany or Mussolini's Italy. First of all the cult of imperial loyalty had the effect of thwarting the appearance of a charismatic popular dictator. Since the focus of popular loyalty was the emperor, it was difficult, if not impossible, for a strong fascist mass leader to emerge in Japanese politics. Even if such a potential dictator had managed to succeed, inevitably he would be second-best to the emperor, and ultimately

responsible to him. Second, a fascist regime based on a mass movement was doomed by the lack of an adequate social base for such a
movement. If the politics of the 1920s had shown anything, it was to
demonstrate how difficult marshalling a popular movement could
be. The only mass movement that had shown any degree of success
at all in pre-1940 Japan was the labor movement, and even at its
peak it had been able to recruit only 7 percent of the industrial labor
force. In the depths of the depression when so many were drawn to
the Nazi party and other fascist groups in Europe, individual Japanese were not so completely rootless and helpless. In contrast to
people in the highly urbanized and industrialized societies of the
West they could turn to family, neighborhood, or village for support
in time of economic want and psychological uncertainty. Finally,
the ideological atmosphere was not conducive to fascist ideas. Both
the Fascist Party in Italy and the Nazis in Germany had proclaimed
themselves, at least in their early stages, to be revolutionary, socialist,
and anticapitalist. Such ideas were not likely to make much headway
in a population long indoctrinated with the values of loyalty, obedience, and harmony. In a sense Japanese society was in many ways
too "underdeveloped" to support a fascist movement.

Consequently although fascist political groups did exist, they
never achieved the critical size necessary to gain power either at the
polls or in the streets. The regime that presided over Japan during its
slow descent into militarism represented no radical break in style
from those that had led the country since the turn of the century. It
rested on an uneasy coalition of the brightest and the best in the civil
bureaucracy, the military hierarchy, the political parties, and the
business world—they had worked their way upward through regular
channels of elite recruitment by dint of ability and hard work. They
were respectable, not agitators and demagogues, and they modestly
regarded themselves as servants of the nation. Unfortunately, as
events were to prove, all their ability and all their sense of public
service provided no guarantee against national disaster.

14

The Pacific War

Just as the defense of Manchuria had become axiomatic after the Kwantung Army's *fait accompli* in 1931, victory over China became a national goal no longer questioned in public after 1938. In a curious reversal of rational policy making, battlefield victories shaped strategic planning, strategic planning shaped foreign policy, and foreign policy dictated domestic reform, all because the China War generated policy commitments that could not be gracefully repudiated. To be sure the cabinets of the late 1930s could have extracted Japan from its uncomfortable position on the mainland by a unilateral withdrawal or by softening its terms to the Chiang government. But to suggest either course of action bordered on treason. In February 1940 when a Minseitō member, Saitō Takeo, suggested on the floor of the Diet that Japan simply did not have the capacity to defeat the Chinese he was expelled from his seat by an overwhelming majority vote. Far from contemplating a negotiated peace in China, planners in both the army and the navy by 1940 had begun to think of expanding the war into Southeast Asia in order to crush Chinese resistance once and for all.

The Road to Pearl Harbor

The idea of a move southward gained currency after the outbreak of war in Europe in late 1939. The early victories of Germany culminating in the fall of France in June 1940 opened new and intoxicat-

ing perspectives for the military. With France and Holland under
Nazi control and England beseiged by the German air force, an Axis
victory in Europe seemed imminent. The European colonies in South
and Southeast Asia lay weak and unprotected, a power vacuum
tempting to the Japanese. In late July 1940 the Konoe government,
after consultations with the army, agreed that the time had come to
strengthen ties with the Axis as preparation for establishing military
bases in French Indochina and for securing access to the rich natural
resources of the European colonies. A foothold in Southeast Asia
would enable the Japanese to cut off Chiang's supply routes from
the south, to obtain a staging area for new campaigns in south China,
and to secure control of rubber, tin, and oil resources essential for
achieving military victory against the Kuomintang. The government
hoped to secure these ends by diplomatic means. Accordingly, in
September 1940, after receiving the assent of the pro-Nazi Vichy
government in France, Japanese troops moved into northern Indochina. A few days later the government signed a tripartite mutual
defense pact with Germany and Italy, aimed at deterring intervention
by the United States, the only major nonbelligerent world power,
from interfering in either the European War or in the Sino-Japanese
conflict.

This new turn of events set Japan on a collision course with the
United States, which began to show political support for the Chiang
regime and sympathy for the "brave Chinese." Committed to the
increasingly bankrupt principle of peace through international agreement, the Roosevelt administration had already made clear its disapproval of Japanese aggression against China in the famous "quarantine speech" of October 1937. While Japanese leaders had begun to
tout Japan's role as liberator of Asia, the American president spoke
of the need to stop an "epidemic of world lawlessness." To bring a
change in Japan's China policy the United States adopted a slowly
escalating program of economic sanctions similar to the one suggested by the American Secretary of State in 1931. In the summer of
1938 Washington placed an embargo on shipments of aircraft, arms,
and other war materiel to Japan; in July 1939 it abrogated its commercial treaty with Japan so that it could legally expand its economic
warfare; and in the fall of 1940 the president terminated the export
of scrap iron and steel to Japan. These moves perplexed and irritated
the Japanese leaders, who felt the United States had no substantial
economic or security interests in East Asia to compare with Japan's.
Failing to appreciate the emotional logic behind the American

actions they could only conclude that the United States was moved by arrogance, a sense of racial superiority, and a selfish and intransigent hypocrisy. In short, the Americans loomed as the main stumbling block to a successful military solution of the China problem.

Despite this basic inability to understand the American position the Konoe government still nurtured hopes that Japan might be able to extract itself from China with American help. In March 1941 the Japanese began diplomatic talks with the Roosevelt government in the hopes of securing its good offices in pressuring Chiang to accept Japan's terms and in guaranteeing the shipment of war goods. In April Ambassador Nomura set forth proposals that clearly reflected a Japanese willingness to disengage from the war by nonmilitary means: a negotiated withdrawal of Japanese troops from China, Chinese recognition of Manchukuo's independence, a merger between the Chiang government and the pro-Japanese puppet regime at Nanking under Wang Ch'ing-wei, and a joint Sino-Japanese anti-Soviet pact.

From the outset, however, the Americans made clear that they were as uncomprehending of Japan's emotional logic as the Japanese were of theirs. For Roosevelt and Hull, the China war was neither a holy war nor a war for the liberation of Asia, but rather a simple case of "totalitarian aggression." In response to the Japanese proposals Hull set forth the American position—respect for the territorial integrity of other nations, respect for the principle of nonintervention in the affairs of other countries, respect for the principle of equality among nations, and the nondisturbance of the status quo in the Pacific except by peaceful means. In effect these high-flown principles meant a complete American refusal to recognize any of Japan's de facto gains since 1931, a position that hardly augured well for the future of the U.S.-Japan talks.

While pursuing talks with the Americans the Konoe government also tried to mend fences with the Soviet Union, still regarded by the army as a major military menace. The signing of the nonaggression pact between Hitler and Stalin in 1939 had modulated the fear of Russia but the Japanese still wished to protect their northern flanks in the event of a new move into Southeast Asia. In April 1941 the two countries finally concluded a neutrality pact. More effective in neutralizing the Soviet Union, however, was the German invasion of the country two months later. With Soviet troops diverted from the border of Manchukuo and Mongolia to the European front, the

Japanese no longer had to fear the possibility of a confrontation there.

Relieved of this anxiety, in July 1941 the Konoe government, at the prompting of the army, finally decided to move troops into southern Indochina as preparation for possible operations against the Dutch East Indies. The United States responded by freezing Japanese assets in the United States and imposing an embargo on the export of oil to Japan. At American prompting Great Britain, the British Commonwealth nations, and the government of the Dutch East Indies followed suit, cutting 90 percent of Japan's oil imports. This sudden escalation of economic warfare was intended to deter Japan from further rashness but it had precisely the opposite effect. Without oil imports Japan's whole war machine would have to come to a halt everywhere, including China, within a matter of months. The Konoe government was now forced to choose between abandoning the military gains of the past decade or seizing the Dutch East Indies at the risk of war with the Americans. The likelihood of a victory in a conflict with the United States seemed problematical to many leaders, especially the navy high command, but the alternative of submitting to the demands of the "white imperialists" was equally hard to stomach.

The oil embargo pushed the Japanese government inexorably toward a decision for war. The navy high command, which had tended to urge caution and restraint in dealing with the Americans, concluded that if war were to come it had better begin before Japan's precious oil reserves were exhausted. The army leadership, which had a much less acute sense of Japan's military limitations, agreed, and in early September 1941, the government made a tentative decision to go to war by the end of October. The decision, however, was made contingent on one last attempt to cut through "ABCD (American-British-Chinese-Dutch) encirclement" by further negotiation. Premier Konoe proposed to meet directly with President Roosevelt, but when the American government rebuffed him he decided to resign.

His successor was War Minister Tōjō Hideki, an ardent spokesman of the army's hardline position. As a last gamble the Tōjō government sent to Washington a proposal to withdraw from Indochina if the United States agreed to end the oil embargo, help Japan get oil supplies from the Indies, and help Japan in achieving a diplomatic end to hostilities in China. In November 1941 the Roosevelt administration indicated once again that it would accept nothing less than a return to the pre-1931 status quo, the withdrawal of Japanese troops from China, Manchuria, and Indochina, and Japanese recognition of the Chiang Kai-shek government. The irresistible force had met an unmovable object. Faced with diplomatic stalemate the Tōjō government decided to break off formal diplomatic talks with the Americans and to make a preemptive strike against American forces in the Pacific. On Sunday, December 7, while secretaries in the Japanese embassy rushed to finish typing the final note to Secretary of State Hull, a striking force of carrier-based Japanese planes swept out of the sky in a surprise attack on the great American naval base at Pearl Harbor. The "wanted, unwanted war" had begun.

The decision for war with the United States was not chosen, but was rather, as Roberta Wohlstetter has put it, "forced by the more terrible alternative of losing status or abandoning the national objectives."[1] These national objectives were likewise not entirely the product of conscious or deliberate decisions but rather had grown like a cancer following the Manchurian incident. The Japanese leaders rarely considered whether their national objectives were compatible with those of other nations or whether their goals were in and of themselves feasible. But even if they had the implications of abandoning them would have been clear. It would have meant the Japanese would have to accept national humiliation or the role of a second-rate power, and neither of these was acceptable to most Japanese.

War in the Pacific

The Japanese did not enter war with the United States as blindly as they had stumbled into the China war. Long-range plans envisaged a strategy similar to the one that had led to victory in the Russo-Japanese war. Counting on Japan's advantages of surprise and superior preparation, the Japanese plans aimed at forcing the larger and stronger United States to the negotiating table before it could mobilize its full strength. A series of lightning-fast amphibious operations were to establish a defense perimeter stretching south and westward from the Marshall Islands in the Central Pacific down through the Indonesian archipelago to Malaya and Indochina. Once secured, this perimeter was to be held against American counterattack while German armies completed the conquest of Europe. Japanese planners

expected that the United States, when finally faced with the overwhelming strength of the Axis powers in both Europe and Asia,
would finally be forced to negotiate a peace settlement that would
leave Japan in control of a Greater East Asia Co-Prosperity Sphere,
an economic and military geopolitical bloc under Japanese hegemony.
In short, Japanese war plans optimistically envisaged a limited war.

The Japanese strategy was bold and dangerous but in the early
months of the war it seemed to be succeeding. In the first days of
war Japanese planes swiftly neutralized Anglo-American forces in
the Pacific by the devastating attack on Pearl Harbor, air strikes
against the American air base at Clark Field in the Philippines, and
the sinking of the British warships, the *Prince of Wales* and the
Repulse. With the Japanese in control of both superior air and naval
power in the West and Southwest Pacific the way was open for a
series of amphibious landings in the Philippines, the Dutch East
Indies, and Malaya. A Japanese overland offensive also set out from
Indochina across Thailand to Burma. The succession of early victories
went off like clockwork—the British naval base at Singapore fell in
February 1942, the Dutch East Indies were under Japanese control
by the end of March, the last American redoubt at Bataan in the
Philippines was taken in early April, and the Burma Road supplying
China from the south had been cut by the end of May. By the spring
of 1942 amphibious operations also had established a string of island
bases in the Southwest and Central Pacific—Guam, Wake Island, the
Solomons, the Gilberts, the Marianas, and northern New Guinea.
Japanese troops even had a tiny foothold in American territory on
the westernmost tip of the Aleutian chain in Alaska. The great
defensive perimeter was now complete.

Long-term plans called for welding the vast new area of Japanese
conquest into a Greater East Asia Co-Prosperity Sphere, a large-scale
version of the autarkic economic bloc that originally inspired Army
staff officers in the late 1920s. In November 1942 a Greater East
Asia Ministry was established to deal with national governments
within the area, but real control was in the hands of local Japanese
occupying forces. The goals of the Japanese in the Co-Prosperity
Sphere tended to be self-contradictory. On the one hand, in order to
obtain local support and cooperation the Japanese stressed to indigenous leaders their "anti-imperialist" goals of driving Western colonialism out of Asia. Wherever possible they tried to encourage local
anticolonial nationalist movements, to set up independent native

regimes, and to arrange ceremonial visits of native leaders to Japan. On the other hand the Japanese were equally interested in exploiting the rich economic resources of the newly occupied areas in order to supply the war effort with oil, tin, rubber, and other crucial materials. In short, the necessities of war forced the Japanese to practice what they had preached against, and they soon found themselves taking over the roles of the European colonial officials, policemen, and plantation managers they had ousted. This contradiction became increasingly evident as the war turned against the Japanese, who were forced more and more to substitute coercion for cooperation with local regimes.

Quite apart from these difficulties, however, the Japanese simply did not have the capability to hold on to Co-Prosperity Sphere over the long run. The Japanese planners had envisaged fighting on interior lines to defend the great perimeter, moving mobile defensive forces to points under American counterattack. But the Japanese merchant marine fleet was barely adequate to maintain supply lines to the Pacific outposts. Moreover, Japanese industry lacked the productive capacities to support their farflung forces in a war of attrition. American industrial potential outstripped Japan's in every essential war materiel and on the eve of the war in 1940 most Japanese imports of oil, steel, and heavy machinery had come from the country she chose to fight. As one astute observer has noted, "It was a tragic paradox that Japan should have gone to war with the one nation upon which she was most heavily dependent for materials essential to successful prosecution of the war. Of all the folly that may be charged against the military leaders of Japan, their failure to realize fully this inherent weakness in their economic plans is the greatest."[2] As events were to prove, Japan was economically outstripped to begin with, and steadily lost ground thereafter. Japanese war production expanded at a much slower rate than that of the United States, and her military technology began to lag behind as the Americans developed and refined new tools of war such as radar and long-range bombers.

The assumptions behind the Japanese war plans began to crumble in the summer of 1942. The critical turning point came with the battle of Midway in June. The Japanese naval high command had planned to lure the Americans into a decisive naval battle that would smash the remainder of the American Pacific fleet, including the aircraft carriers that had escaped destruction at Pearl Harbor. As luck would have it the Americans had broken Japanese naval cipher codes and were well aware of the Japanese plans. The Japanese not only lost the advantage of surprise but American carrier-based planes used this intelligence to make a devastating attack on the Japanese fleet instead, sinking four irreplaceable aircraft carriers. The Japanese command over both the air and the sea in the Pacific was thoroughly shaken.

The military initiative now shifted to the Americans, who began a counteroffensive, hacking away at the weak outer points of the Japanese perimeter. During 1942–1943 one American island-hopping thrust arched across the central Pacific while another struck out from New Guinea toward the Philippines. By June 1944 Allied forces had reached Saipan, putting the Japanese home islands within range of American bombers, and the following October forces under General Douglas MacArthur had landed on Leyte to begin a reconquest of the Philippines. American amphibious operations were orchestrated with American submarine warfare against the supply lines of the Co-Prosperity Sphere. Japanese planners had thought that the Americans, who condemned the use of submarines as inhumane at prewar disarmament conferences, would not rely on underwater warfare. But American submarines preyed on unescorted Japanese merchant vessels with aplomb, sailing to the very mouth of Tokyo in order to disrupt Japanese shipping. The Japanese were unable to produce ships as fast as they were sunk, with the result that Japanese industrial production reached a plateau in 1943 and declined steadily thereafter. The limited war had become a war of attrition.

By mid 1944 it was clear that a Japanese victory, even negotiated at the bargaining table, was beyond Japan's grasp. In June 1944 Allied landing in France presaged the eventual collapse of Japan's European allies and foreclosed the possibility of an American stalemate there. At the same time war reached the home front with the mounting of an American air offensive against the Japanese home islands. In the summer of 1944 American planes made their first major strike against the Yawata steel works in Kyushu and by late fall American incendiary raids escalated. At first American bombers attacked military targets and installations around Tokyo and other urban centers, but slowly American planes began to step up nighttime raids against the civilian population. In early March 1945 a fire

raid in Tokyo created a ghastly holocaust that in a single night left
78,000 dead, 43,380 injured, and 1,500,000 homeless. The beginning
of the end was in sight.

The Home Front

The outbreak of war with the United States in 1941 had been met
with wild public exhilaration. The government had already saturated
the population with anti-Western propaganda as part of its spiritual
mobilization campaigns in the late 1930s, and the confrontation
with the United States let loose a flood of bottled-up emotion. The
Asian David had finally struck a blow against the Western Goliath.
A heady mixture of pent-up frustration, hurt pride, anti-Westernism,
and political mysticism convinced many that Japan stood on the
verge of a great and sacred enterprise, and reports of early victories
blaring over radio loudspeakers confirmed the rightness of the war.

In a deeper sense the intensified war effort helped to reintegrate
Japanese society, still scarred by the social divisions of the 1920s and
the economic hardships of the early1930s. Despite a tightening of
government censorship and an increase of government regulations
controlling every phase of daily life public morale remained high.
The activities of the neighborhood associations involved the mass of
the home front population in communal efforts in all aspects of
life—the distribution of rations, the sale of war bonds, the collection
of scrap, farewell parties for new recruits, air raid drills, and the like.
Many enjoyed an experience of self-rule they had not known before.
There is even evidence that in some areas the associations challenged
the prerogatives of established village elders and landlords by ele-
vating to positions of responsibility more modest members of the
community. Voluntary activities, prompted by patriotic concern,
became common, and even women were called in to do many jobs
left vacant by the departure of men to the front. The war effort
became a part of daily life as a Japanese, and at first the common
people willingly endured the temporary burdens it engendered.

By contrast bureaucratic squabbling and political in-fighting continued at the top levels of society. To some extent Premier Tōjō had
attempted to put an end to the intramural elite conflicts that had so
confused politics in the late 1930s by making himself into a strong
man. Publicly he was self-effacing, insisting he was merely an ordinary citizen doing his job at the emperor's request. (As he told a

group of Diet members in early 1943, "I am of an entirely different character from the gentlemen in Europe who are known as dictators.")[3] But in fact Tōjō was an adept bureaucratic politician who gathered larger and larger powers to himself. Initially he assumed control over the War Ministry as well as the premiership, and *ex officio* served as head of the Imperial Rule Assistance Association. When a new Munitions Ministry was established in November 1943— to supervise a total mobilization of the war economy through allocation of raw materials, establishment of production schedules, regulating wages, and the like—Tōjō became its head and in early 1944 he also assumed the post of army chief of staff. He was ruthless in disciplining his critics within the military establishment (by sending them to the front) and careful to build his own personal clique (by placing subordinates in key positions).

But it was still beyond the capacities of any single individual to hold together the welter of competing political power centers that constituted the national leadership. The Diet did not actively challenge the Tōjō cabinet, especially after the elections of 1942, when excessively liberal or critical Diet members were weeded out by a system of government recommendation. Even so, nearly one-fifth of the nonrecommended candidates succeeded in winning, and the old political parties, though officially dissolved in 1940, retained shadow organizations and links with their old constituencies. The zaibatsu likewise supported the war effort but nevertheless continued to pursue their own advantage and interest, resisting bureaucratic and military efforts to take over direct management of their firms. When government economic planners tried to spur production in 1942–1943 by encouraging economic rationalization through company mergers, zaibatsu concerns used the opportunity to absorb smaller companies and amalgamate their own enterprises. At the same time the Tōjō government, realizing the importance of the business community to the war effort, continued to rely on business and financial leaders for advice on economic policy. The civil bureaucracy jealously guarded its prerogatives when new wartime ministries, such as the Greater East Asia Ministry or the Munitions Ministry were established, and interministry jurisdictional conflicts continued. Finally, and perhaps most surprising of all, army-navy rivalry, a constant factor in prewar Japan, continued to vex the planning of military operations and the allocation of strategic materials. The two services even refused to standardize equipment, with the result that an otherwise identical item might require left-hand threaded screws if supplied to the navy and right-hand threaded screws if supplied to the army.

By 1944 these internal political strains coupled with the worsening military situation in the Pacific and the continuing American sea blockade led to rapidly deteriorating conditions on the home front, especially in the cities. Public entertainment places were closed down and even prostitutes were pressed into service as factory workers; food supplies began to dwindle, and by the end of 1944 rations of meat, fish, and fresh milk had all but ceased; growing malnutrition led to a rise in the incidence of tuberculosis, rickets, and adolescent eye disease; taxes soared, prices increased, and black markets flourished; and even university students, the promise of the future once exempted from military conscription, were recruited for service at the front. As the intensity of American air attacks increased in 1944 and 1945, life grew ever more desperate in the cities, and those with a roof over their heads counted themselves fortunate. Nearly 10,000,000 Japanese, out of fear or out of necessity, evacuated to the countryside to stay with friends or relatives. Large bombed-over sections of Tokyo became desolate. Stray dogs did not even roam the streets, for those who had not been eaten had starved to death. Everywhere a democracy of suffering prevailed.

Yet still the social fabric continued to hold. Political tension never broke into open conflict, riot, or antiwar movements, nor did there emerge a domestic underground antigovernment conspiracy such as the one that nearly cost Hitler his life in July 1944. Part of the explanation lies in the pervasive attitudes that continued to undergird Japanese society even as it was sinking into destruction. As one journalist later recalled,

> Despite the fact that there wasn't even one article which seemed believable throughout the entire wartime Japanese newspapers, we tried to force ourselves to believe and to be ready to die. If a parent were on the verge of bankruptcy and told a transparent and painful lie, would it be possible for a child to expose the secret? All the child could do would be to die silently with this parent, submitting to his fate.[4]

As a result, even though defeat loomed more and more probable by 1945 young men willingly hurled themselves in *kamikaze* planes at American naval vessels, and women, old people, and children began to train with sharpened bamboo spears to meet the final American onslaught.

The Surrender of Japan

The Japanese leadership found it no easier to bring an end to the Pacific War than to the China War. Although victory was out of the question the alternative was not acceptable. In 1944 some responsible officials, including the court bureaucracy and many of the jūshin, began to contemplate the possibility of a compromise peace. The fall of Saipan, coupled with internal cabinet conflicts, enabled the jūshin to ease Tōjō out of power in July 1944. This might have been an occasion for responsible officials to make approaches to the Allies, but the army was determined to continue prosecution of the war even in the obviously unfavorable circumstances the country now found itself. The new premier, General Koiso Kuniaki, announced the unanimity of the "Yamato people" in their determination to fight the Anglo-American enemy to the end, and the pro-peace elements found themselves thwarted.

The main external obstacle to a negotiated peace was the declaration of the Allied leadership that it would accept only an unconditional surrender from the Japanese. The psychological effect on the Japanese leaders was to rein in even the pro-peace elements, since all responsible officials, whatever their views on the desirability of continuing the war, insisted on the preservation of the imperial institution as a minimal condition for surrender. The doctrine of unconditional surrender made it difficult for the Japanese to approach the Americans, the British, or the Chinese, but there was still a possibility that the Russians might be persuaded to act as a go-between with the Allies. In April 1945, when the island of Okinawa finally fell to U.S. forces, the jūshin nominated as premier Suzuki Kantarō, a private advocate of an honorable peace. This intensified debate between the peace advocates and the army diehards. In early June the Supreme Council for the Direction of the War decided to prepare for a final battle of the homeland, hoping to inflict enough losses on American invading forces so that they would abandon the unconditional surrender policy. In late June, as a sop to the peace party, it also authorized quiet approaches to the Russians to ask for help in mediating peace. Much to the disappointment of the Japanese emissaries, the Russians were not very responsive. Unknown to the Japanese, at the Yalta Conference in February 1945 Stalin had already agreed to enter the war against Japan within three months of German surrender.

When Stalin, Truman, and Churchill met in July 1945, they issued the Potsdam Declaration, reaffirming the demand for unconditional surrender. The Suzuki government rejected it, for all practical purposes dashing the hopes of a negotiated peace once and for all. Given the inability of the army to admit its defeat and the unwillingness of the pro-peace party to take decisive action, a final end to the war awaited American initiative, which would clearly have to be military. Since a direct landing on the Japanese homeland was likely to result in heavy American losses, President Truman authorized the use of the newly developed atomic bomb in an effort to compel Japan's surrender. On August 6 the city of Hiroshima was left a flattened pile of rubble by the first atomic explosion in history. Two days later, the Soviet Union, anxious to be in on the final division of spoils, issued its promised declaration of war, and sent its troops across the Manchuria border. On August 9 a second atomic bomb fell on Nagasaki. The utter destruction flamboyantly threatened in the Potsdam Declaration now seemed a matter of time.

Even these catastrophic events failed to sway military opposition to surrender. The war minister and the chiefs of staff insisted that conditions be attached to American demands for surrender. The deadlock was broken only when the emperor himself, at an Imperial conference, urged the acceptance of surrender subject only to the condition that his prerogatives might not be affected. The Americans replied that the emperor would be placed under Allied control and that his eventual fate would be determined by the Japanese people, an ambiguous response that prompted renewed debate among the Japanese leadership. On August 14 the emperor intervened once again, soberly urging his ministers to accept unconditional surrender and taking the final responsibility for a decision no one else dared to make.

The larger significance of the Pacific War has been a matter of debate over the last generation, and will doubtless be debated for generations to come. During the war years it was common for most Americans to regard the war as part of a global conflict between the forces of "fascist totalitarianism" and the forces of "democracy." But clearly this view obscures the differences between the ambitious aggressiveness of Hitler and the less grandiose goals of the Japanese leaders, who sought to avoid the war until the last. It also obscures the differences between the demonic personal rule of the Nazi dictator and the constitutional fragmentation that prevailed in Japanese politics even after war broke out. On the other hand the wartime Japanese view that Japan was fighting to liberate the oppressed peoples of Asia from "Anglo-American imperialism" or to protect them against the "threat of Bolshevism" is equally unsatisfactory. As things turned out the war did help topple Western colonial empires in Southeast Asia and stimulated nationalist independence movement there. But it should be obvious that the Japanese thrust into the area was prompted less by a sense of Japan's antiimperialist mission than by strategic and economic considerations. Perhaps the real significance of the war was that it represented a way of resolving certain basic problems rapid modernization had engendered—the imbalance between Japan and her weaker neighbors, the equally large imbalance between Japan and the West she admired yet distrusted, and the imbalance between Japan's aspirations and her capabilities. War was a costly way to resolve these problems, but in the end defeat may have proven worth the price for the generation to come.

15

Occupation, Reform,
and Recovery

On August 15, 1945, the emperor's thin, reedy voice crackled over radio loudspeakers announcing Japan's decision to surrender to the Allied powers. Children stood half-comprehending, and adults with bowed heads and tears, as the emperor spoke of his determination to "endure the unendurable." For the first time in its history Japan stood as a defeated nation. All the wartime suffering, sacrifice, and hardship had ended in disastrous failure. The cost in human life had been enormous. Over 2,300,000 men (about one in every five households) had been killed or wounded in battle since the outbreak of the China incident. Manpower losses were so fearful that by 1945 fifteen-year-olds were being recruited. At home 800,000 civilians were injured or killed in air raids and nearly a third of the population had lost their homes. Tokyo, once a metropolis that rivaled London or New York, was a wasteland of rubble and ash, and Hiroshima and Nagasaki lay flattened by atomic blast. The country was prostrate economically, its factories at a standstill and its food supplies barely sufficient to keep its people alive. The mass of the population were exhausted, disillusioned, and apprehensive, glad that the suffering was at an end but fearful of what was to come next.

The American Role

In spite of the total material and psychological collapse of Japan, defeat ushered in an era of sweeping change more radical than any the country had experienced since the early years of Meiji. The main agent of change, however, was not native but foreign. Japan's wartime elite had been tainted by defeat, and popular opinion ran against those who had been responsible for the national disaster. "I worked like a slave until the very last day, when the emperor made his broadcast terminating the war," wrote one indignant citizen. "Wasn't it government officials who played the major role in weakening Japan's fighting strength . . .?"[1] In place of the discredited national leadership came the American occupation forces led by General Douglas MacArthur, Supreme Commander for the Allied Powers (SCAP). They represented the only effective authority in the country. American troops everywhere were visible symbols of the occupation's military power; and their leader was vested with legal powers that virtually made him sovereign. Even the emperor was obliged to call on MacArthur to pay his respects, leaving little doubt in anyone's mind about who was in charge of the country. The American occupation therefore commanded far more authority in 1945 than the new imperial government had in 1868 and it was able to impose change from above far more rapidly.

The Americans were not pragmatic revolutionaries like the oligarchs, but idealistic reformers. Their goal was to create a "democratic and peace-loving" Japan. This was a reversal of the wartime plans of President Roosevelt and his intimates, who had favored a harsh and retributive settlement with Japan. By mid-1945, however, the uncooperative attitude of the Soviet Union in the occupation of Germany had persuaded American officials that a vengeful peace would serve no useful purpose and that constructive reform would be the best guarantee against a recurrence of Japanese aggression against Japan's neighbors in Asia. In many ways the occupation resembled the "benevolent colonialism" the United States had pursued in the Philippines, where over the decades it had prepared its "little brown brothers" for independence and self-government. Its policies were shaped by the same mixture of political idealism and cultural condescension that characterized American Asian policy since the days of the Open Door. MacArthur himself epitomized the basic American attitude. A conservative at home, he was liberal by Japanese standards for he ardently believed in the superiority of the "American way of life"—democratic self-government, personal freedom, and supremacy of law. He was confidently patronizing toward the political "immaturity" of the Japanese, and convinced that their "Oriental psychology" made them susceptible to leadership by the resolute and dynamic Americans. The lower echelons of the SCAP hierarchy, entrusted with detailed formulation of policy, were no less imbued with the same reforming vigor. Civilian-soldiers drawn from every conceivable walk of life—lawyers, labor union officials, school teachers, bank managers, businessmen—they shared MacArthur's confidence in the ability of the United States to reshape Japanese society.

Most occupation officials, from MacArthur on down, had similar views on what had led Japan into war and totalitarianism. First of all, they believed that an old guard that included not only the army, civilian fascists, and right-wing extremists, but also the zaibatsu, the bureaucracy, and the peerage had consciously and deliberately planned aggression against China and the United States. "Liberal" and "peace-loving" elements were to be found only in the political parties, the moderate left wing, and the diplomatic corps. Second, the power of this old guard was buttressed by the emperor system created by the oligarchics—an autocratic constitution, an independent military, an undemocratic educational system and a "Shinto" myth of imperial divinity. Third, this emperor system was in turn sustained by an archaic and feudal social order, which exploited both peasant and industrial worker to maintain the strength of the army and its allies in bureaucracy and big business. Many felt that the economic backwardness of the peasantry in particular was the main bulwark of prewar authoritarianism. Finally, since political oppression and social exploitation at home had made possible aggression and expansion abroad, the re-emergence of a militaristic Japan could be prevented only if the nation were made into a democracy. In retrospect many of these assumptions seem quaint but they represented the consensus on which SCAP policy decisions were based.

Since SCAP headquarters took most of the initiative, reform tended to be a one-sided process, but it would be wrong to regard the Japanese as either passive or resistant toward change imposed by the Americans. From the beginning many prewar liberals and social democrats were agreed on the need for major social and institutional change. They did not always see eye to eye with the Americans on the degree of reform or its direction, however. Many reforms, from constitution revision to land reform, were first undertaken by the Japanese without SCAP prompting, only to be overwhelmed by more far-reaching policies designed by the Americans. At the same time many SCAP programs were formulated with the participation of interested Japanese. Those who collaborated with SCAP were a varied group. At the highest level, prewar diplomats of a pro-British or pro-American stripe, such as Shidehara Kijūrō, Ashida Hitoshi, and Yoshida Shigeru, assumed positions of leadership, and English-speaking members of the Foreign Ministry ran the Central Liaison Office, the main go-between for SCAP in its dealings with the Japanese bureaucracy. Prewar party politicians of the moderate left and other liberal academics, intellectuals, and officials also helped SCAP drafting reform legislation and programs.

Doubtless the most important figure to work with the Americans was Yoshida Shigeru, who served as premier during much of the occupation. If MacArthur represented American idealism, Yoshida embodied Japanese pragmatism. Like many prewar moderate liberals, he saw no need for sweeping political reorganization and felt that patchwork repair of existing institutions was sufficient. His main goal was not so much social and political change as the rebuilding of an independent and economically strong Japan. He once confided to an intimate that his policy was to win by diplomacy what had been lost by war. He found many SCAP programs excessive, naive, and unsuited to Japanese conditions. Nevertheless, he was also aware that the Americans were conquerors and that he would have to bend their intentions to his own purposes if he were to succeed. Like many Japanese collaborators he cooperated publicly with SCAP but tried to moderate its efforts behind the scenes by raising doubts about the feasibility of certain reforms and by continually diverting SCAP's attention to the problems of economic recovery. He also played on growing American fears of rising Communism in Asia, in Japan and on the continent. Since many reforms subtly changed form through the channels of the Japanese government, many SCAP officials became convinced that sinister and reactionary forces were at work to sabotage American efforts. But on the balance, except perhaps in the area of economic policy, the Americans had their way throughout the occupation.

Political Democratization

The occupation began its effort to democratize Japan by dismantling the repressive and militaristic institutions of the prewar system. In the fall of 1945 SCAP released all wartime political prisoners (many of them Communists), disbanded the Imperial Rule Political Association, abolished laws used to repress and control public opinion, eliminated the apparatus for police surveillance of "dangerous thoughts," prohibited official patronage of the Shinto religion (judged to be a prime source of ultranationalist thought), abolished the general staff as well as war and navy ministries, and ordered the enactment of female suffrage.

To safeguard against back-sliding into militarism SCAP also conducted a draconian purge of wartime political and economic leadership. First to go were top leaders like Tōjō Hideki, arrested for trial on charges of war crimes and crimes against humanity. Most Japanese expected the arrest of these top leaders but in October 1946 the occupation began a more controversial bloodless purge of those suspected of militaristic tendencies. Nearly 210,000 business executives, journalists, right-wing leaders, schoolteachers, officials and former military personnel were barred from public office or from positions of public responsibility because of their alleged involvement in the war effort. According to one estimate about one out of every four top business executives was forced into retirement, and so were many members of the wartime Diet. Curiously, however, only 145 civilian bureaucrats were purged, and nearly half of these suffered because they belonged to the Martial Arts Association, an athletic club whose name was more sinister than its activities.

In the midst of this massive assault on the supporters of the emperor system, the position of the emperor himself came into question: was he to be included among the war guilty or not? During the war a vocal group in Washington, particularly pro-Chinese officials in the state department, had advocated trying the emperor as a war criminal. Joseph Grew, prewar ambassador to Tokyo, however, succeeded in convincing the American government that abolition of the imperial institution and public prosecution of the emperor would thwart reform and reconstruction by stirring up social and political unrest. The emperor himself was apparently willing to abdicate the throne as expiation for his responsibility, but SCAP felt it more useful to keep him in office, partly out of deference to the popular need for a central national symbol, but partly because he personally seemed well suited to the role of a constitutional monarch. The price exacted for retaining the imperial institution was its complete demythologization. On New Year's Day 1946 the emperor formally renounced all claims to divinity, and during the months that followed he appeared in fields and factories all over the country, clad in battered fedora and rumpled business suit, establishing himself as a somewhat awkward and thoroughly human public figure.

The main thrust of political democratization centered on revising the constitution. At MacArthur's prompting the Shidehara cabinet proposed a draft constitutional revision to SCAP in February 1946. The SCAP government section, however, judged the Japanese draft altogether too cautious since it made few changes in the emperor's legal powers, subjected basic civil rights to restriction by statute law, and failed to abolish the armed forces. Laboring six days and resting on the seventh, the SCAP government section produced a draft of its own, written just in English. The SCAP draft was submitted to the Diet for approval as an amendment to the Meiji constitution; and it was eventually approved in November 1946 despite heated debates over how it might affect the *kokutai*. Although ostensibly adopted in accordance with the "will of the Japanese people," the new constitution was clearly of American origin. Indeed, one man in the street, when queried by a roving reporter on his reaction to the document, is said to have replied, "Oh, has it been translated into Japanese?"

Nevertheless, the new constitution did effect a massive restructuring of the Japanese political system. First, it reduced the emperor to a mere "symbol of the state and the unity of the people" and restricted his functions to purely ceremonial duties. Second, it abandoned Japan's right to maintain land, sea, and air forces as well as other war potential and it renounced "forever" resort to war as a means of solving international disputes. Third, it eliminated non-parliamentary organs of state such as the privy council and the military high command, which had shared power with the cabinet and the Diet. Fourth, it declared as "eternal and inviolate" the "fundamental human rights" of the Japanese people, including some, such as the right of collective bargaining, not guaranteed by the American constitution. Fifth, it established a British-style cabinet system, resting on the principles of parliamentary supremacy and cabinet responsibility to the Diet. The premier was to be elected by a majority in the House of Representatives, and that he or she was obliged to resign from office or dissolve the Diet if he or she received a vote of no confidence. Finally, the position of the lower house of the Diet was strengthened. The House of Peers was replaced by a popularly elected house of councillors, and the House of Representatives empowered to override the decisions of the upper house by a two-thirds vote.

The occupation followed the British constitutional model in altering the institutions of the central government but it turned to American precedents when changing other aspects of the political structure. The constitution established an independent judiciary under a supreme court, which was given the power of judicial review on the constitutionality of Diet legislation. In hopes of breaking the hold of the central government over the provinces and encouraging local self-government the constitution also provided for popularly elected local prefectural governors. Other laws passed in conjunction with the constitution gave increased tax powers to prefectural governments, and following the model of American federalism put both police forces and schools under the control of local governmental bodies. The result was a curious hybrid between British-style parliamentarianism and American-style federalism.

But if SCAP-sponsored political reforms destroyed most of the state structure built by the Meiji oligarchy there was one element left largely untouched—the civil service bureaucracy. To be sure, bureaucrats were declared to be public servants rather than Imperial officials, but for the most part the bureaucracy remained unaffected by the reform whirlwind. It preserved both its autonomy from political appointments and its elitist recruitment procedures. This was hardly surprising since SCAP governed Japan through the existing administrative structure rather than American military government teams like those operating in occupied Germany. Some ministries were abolished, including the Home Ministry, but officials who had staffed them simply moved into newly created agencies. Bureaucratic morale remained undiminished, resting on confidence that civil service expertise and connections were essential to running the country. All attempts at major civil service reform therefore met with firm resistance. Many bureaucrats also took advantage of the purge of professional politicians from public office to move into party politics. Indeed, professional bureaucrats who entered the Diet eventually became a key factor in postwar politics.

Social and Economic Reform

The policy of democratization was not limited to formal political institutions. The occupation authorities assumed that political democracy needed the nurture of a "democratic" social environment as well. However, since it was not clear how best to create such an environment, social reform emerged in a piecemeal and uncoordinated fashion, the product of programs initiated independently by various sections of SCAP headquarters, very much like the American New Deal that was shaped by a welter of competing agencies in the 1930s. Some of these programs aimed at a fairer distribution of national wealth in order to elminate social inequities held responsible for the rise of "fascism" in prewar Japan. Others sought to promote the growth of popular social forces able to defend the new democratic political structure against conservative reaction or conservative backsliding. Finally, some programs aimed at encouraging the spread of "democratic" values and ideals among the people, especially the younger generation. In combination these various programs added up to a massive assault on the prewar social order.

The attack on economic inequality was embodied in a vigorous program of economic deconcentration intended to break the economic and financial power of the zaibatsu and other large business concerns. This policy reflected the belief that the zaibatsu had been active supporters of aggression in the 1930s but it was also inspired by the ideology of free competition and distrust of monopoly that underlay antitrust legislation in the United States. The earliest phase of the policy, and the most lasting in its effects, was the dissolution of the zaibatsu. Zaibatsu holding companies were outlawed, zaibatsu family stocks were virtually confiscated for public sale, and zaibatsu family members were prohibited from working for firms they had once controlled. These measures struck the prewar plutocracy an economic blow from which it never really recovered. At the same time the complex networks of affiliate companies formerly dominated by zaibatsu holding companies were split apart. Some large firms such as the Mitsubishi Trading Company were divided into a number of smaller companies. To prevent reconcentration of economic power SCAP sponsored the passage of antimonopoly legislation prohibiting unreasonable restraint of competition and established a Fair Trade Commission to enforce its provisions.

While the industry and financial section of SCAP waged its war on economic concentration the agricultural section promoted a thorough-going land reform program aimed at eliminating tenancy, creating a larger owner-cultivator class, and encouraging the growth of a more prosperous countryside. There were no specific American precedents for such reform, but many SCAP officials felt poverty in the countryside had bred right-wing radicalism. The Japanese, mainly out of sentiments of social justice and a desire to increase rural productivity, had begun planning land redistribution in 1946, but SCAP found the Japanese proposals wanting. The Diet, still heavily influenced by landlord interests, had weakened a bill sent it by the Yoshida cabinet, so SCAP pressured for the passage of a stronger legislation in October 1947. The land reform law compelled landlords to sell land to cultivating tenants so as to eliminate absentee landlordism and curb the economic power of village landlords large enough to dominate their neighbors. Under its provision, about 4.3 million farmers, or roughly 70 percent of the total, purchased new land at extremely low prices, often with low interest government loans. Tenancy was virtually eliminated as a result (46 percent of the cultivated land was tenant farmed in 1946, but only 10 percent in 1950), and the prewar landlord class went the way of the prewar plutocracy. Statutory limitations on the size of land holdings guaranteed that landlordism would not re-emerge in the future.

The SCAP labor section, staffed mainly by former union officials and labor experts, undertook to create an independent trade-union movement, protected from legal harassment by government or business. MacArthur, never a conspicuous friend of the union movement in the United States, made it quite clear that SCAP considered strong unions essential to the creation of antimilitarist, progressive, and democratic public attitudes. In late 1946, under pressure from SCAP, the Diet passed a slew of laws legalizing labor union activity, guaranteeing the right to strike and collective bargaining, setting standards for working hours and conditions, and providing for the mediation of labor disputes. Fired by a missionary zeal to breathe life into the infant labor movement, SCAP labor officials made the rounds of factories with Japanese labor organizers in tow to set up new worker organizations. Having no one else to rely on, they often used the services of Communist organizers, recently released from political prison. (Shiga Yoshio, one of the main postwar leaders of the Communist party, toured major ports and harbors in an American LST in order to revive the Seaman's Union.) As the result of such efforts, by the end of 1946, the labor union movement, which had ceased to function during the war, recruited 4.8 million workers into 17,000 unions, many of them under control of Communist leaders.

The occupation also created another constituency for "democracy" by overhauling the educational system at all levels. The prewar system had carefully routed the elite toward higher technical schools and national universities, while the rest of the populace received basic elementary education along with a heavy dose of official values. In contrast to this meritocratic system SCAP educational reforms aimed at the American goal of education for all. The old multiple track school system was replaced by an American-style single track system, education was made compulsory through ninth grade, and a large number of new "lunch box" universities were newly established at the prefectural level. Apart from this attempt at social leveling, the Occupation also sought to alter the content of education, particularly at the elementary levels. The old ethics courses were eliminated from the curriculum, textbooks stressing nationalistic myths and militaristic virtues were banned, and new courses in social studies were introduced. Just as the Meiji leaders had hoped the schools would create patriotic subjects, ready and willing to sacrifice themselves without hesitation for country and emperor, the Americans hoped they would create "responsible citizens" with a strong sense of personal rights and capable of self-government. The older values were easily eliminated, especially since they had been discredited by the defeat, but the new civic virtues often failed to take hold, leaving many young Japanese without any set of publicly sanctioned ideals.

On the whole the Americans were successful in convincing young Japanese that "democracy" was good and "feudalism" was bad. Most were aware that life had been less than perfect in the prewar period and were willing to accept American guidance. Intellectuals, free from the restraints of thought control and the pressures of popular nationalism, also welcomed "democracy" with the same uncritical enthusiasm that once inspired men like Fukuzawa Yukichi to spread the ideas of "civilization and enlightenment." The collapse of the old official orthodoxy led to much soul-searching and criticism of the traditional value system. On the negative side, men like Maruyama Masao exposed the pathology of prewar ultranationalist thought, deplored the lack of a "modern spirit" in Japan, and generally attacked the "feudalistic" character of Japanese society. On the more positive side, "democracy" and "democratization" became facile and often half-understood catch words, used to justify everything from the establishment of PTAs in local schools to easy divorces. Eventually there would be a reaction to superficial democratization but in the early days of the occupation the mood of self-criticism and openness to the outside facilitated SCAP's efforts.

Economics, Recovery, and Reaction

The massive flood of reform from 1945 through 1947 took place against a sombre background of economic hardship in which most of the population was faced with the problem of economic survival. The nation's productive capacities had sunk far below prewar levels. Agricultural production in 1946 was about 60 percent of what it had been in 1941, and industry was nearly at a halt on account of war damage or SCAP prohibitions on strategic production. Nearly six million Japanese were repatriated from overseas war zones and former colonies, and millions of newborn Japanese came into the world after the war's end. Food shortages were severe, and malnutrition widespread. Many Japanese scavenged leftover rations from American billets. The shut-down of industrial production likewise created unemployment and the shortage of all basic consumer goods created a runaway inflation.

The American government sent food and medical supplies to Japan to prevent disease and unrest, but otherwise did little to alleviate these bleak and harsh economic conditions. A frankly punitive economic policy toward Japan was spawned by American indignation at the harsh treatment meted out by the Japanese to the Chinese and other occupied peoples. In December 1946, for example, the Pauley reparations mission recommended that the greater part of Japan's industrial plant be dismantled for reparations to other countries, on the grounds that there was no reason why the Japanese should enjoy higher living standards than the Asian people who had suffered from Japanese aggression. Pervasive economic hardship, however, was an ideal breeding ground for social discontent, particularly in the cities. Although the rural population was relatively well-off, able to live on its own produce and profit from sky-rocketing food prices, the urban working class was beset by unemployment, inflation, and black-market profiteering. Leaders of the burgeoning labor movement, moved both by genuine concern over worker hardship and by a desire to promote more radical change than that sponsored by the occupation, began to organize protest movements, foment strikes, and organize demonstrations demanding increased food supplies. At May Day in 1946 one banner proclaimed, "Food not constitutions."

The Japanese government, under the leadership of Yoshida Shigeru, feared that strikes and popular disturbances would put an undue strain on the already prostrate economy. Bitterly hostile to "troublemakers" in the union leadership and their supporters in SCAP, in January 1947 Yoshida announced that striking workers would not be paid. Picking up the gauntlet, a coalition of labor union leaders announced their intention to call a general strike. The more moderate among them hoped to force Yoshida to retract his action and perhaps resign from office, but extremist elements, especially the Communist union leaders, hoped to precipitate a revolutionary crisis.

The pending general strike forced SCAP to choose between the "democratic" unions and the conservative government. Not surprisingly, since Yoshida had won MacArthur's confidence as a trustworthy and cooperative leader, SCAP decided to back him up by ordering the announced general strike to be called off. This decision marked a turning point in SCAP policy. In the face of disruptive union tactics some of MacArthur's intimates questioned the wisdom of encouraging a strong and militant labor movement as a counterbalance to "reactionary" and "feudal" forces. When Communist leaders in the government worker unions (which accounted for about 40 percent of the labor movement) continued to hold out for a general strike, SCAP deliberately reversed its early labor policy by directing the Yoshida cabinet to curtail the right of government workers to strike or bargain collectively.

Support for Yoshida's tough antilabor stand coincided with a more general shift of emphasis in SCAP policy from rapid institutional change to a policy of promoting social and economic stability. This shift was largely the result of the cold war. By the end of 1947 the coalition that defeated the Axis had splintered into two opposing camps, the "Communist bloc" led by the Soviet Union and the "free world" led by the United States. Against the background of this global confrontation the American government began to view Japan less as a potential threat to world peace than as a potential and very useful ally. The dramatic deterioration of the Kuomintang government in its civil war with the Chinese Communists strengthened the idea that Japan might become a base for American power in its confrontation with Communist expansionism in Asia. In early 1947 Secretary of State Dean Acheson spoke of making Japan into "the chief factory in Asia," and in early 1948 Secretary of War Kenneth Royal declared that Japan should be made a bulwark against "totalitarianism" in Asia. The American image of Japan had turned full cycle. Although the policy of democratization was not abandoned the American government began to think more seriously about restoring Japanese economic strength, and perhaps military strength as well. By early 1948 the economic policies of SCAP reflected this change in outlook. The program of economic deconcentration was slowed down since it was clear that large firms, with their greater efficiency and technical expertise, would have to play a major role in rebuilding the economy. Vigorous trust-busting was incompatible with the recovery of private enterprise. The list of over a thousand firms originally scheduled for deconcentration was whittled down to a mere eighteen. At the same time SCAP abandoned its earlier laissez-faire policy toward inflation, black-marketeering, and the wage-price spiral afflicting the economy. The Dodge Mission, dispatched by the American government in 1949, urged the Japanese government to take stringent measures toward inflation and to adopt more conservative fiscal policies in order to rebuild the country's economic potential.

The new American policy meshed neatly with Premier Yoshida's desire to regain Japan's independence and international position through economic strength. The government, whose deficit finance policy had exacerbated inflation, balanced its budget, rigidly curtailed expenditures, and bent every effort to stabilize the yen. Yoshida also used the Dodge mission recommendations as a weapon in his war with the labor movement. Government economizing efforts included the dismissal of 250,000 government workers, many of them union activists. Private industry followed suit. Faced with this new challenge, from mid-1949 extreme left-wing leaders staged violent and desperate demonstrations all over the country. Far from weakening the government, this round of left-wing violence gave SCAP an excuse to carry out a second purge. This time, however, those ousted from positions of responsibility were not "feudal," "militaristic," or "reactionary" elements, but rather "reds" and "radicals."

The change in SCAP policy also coincided with the emergence of renewed divisiveness within the left-wing. Moderate social democratic elements held the militant tactic of head-on confrontation with management and government to be reckless and irresponsible. By the same token militant left-wing leaders, especially the Communists, argued that the gradualist tactics of the social democrats would lead to compromise with reactionary forces. By late 1947, just when the government and SCAP began to move against the radical left, moderate labor leaders called for a democratization of the union movement to wrest power from the "elitist" Communists. In 1950, with the encouragement of SCAP, which even aided in recruiting, the moderates succeeded in organizing the General Federation of Labor (Sōhyō), which split away from Communist-affiliated union confederation. The Socialist Party, organized in 1946 out of the remnants of the prewar proletarian party movement, likewise split into two contending factions, which were unable to reunite until 1955.

Independence and the "American Umbrella"

By 1950 the reins of power rested firmly in the hands of Premier Yoshida, who had skillfully identified himself with the SCAP reform programs, yet kept himself discreetly independent by arguing against the excesses of many SCAP measures. Gathering around himself Diet members newly elected in the postwar elections and recruiting as his lieutenants a group of promising young ex-bureaucrats, Yoshida created the Liberal Party as his organizational basis. His parliamentary opposition was weak, divided between the Socialists and the Progressives (later the Democrats), who had been barely able to maintain a coalition government in 1947–1948, and he had little difficulty in handling the Diet. A vigorous and domineering man who suffered neither fools nor rivals gladly, Yoshida established himself as a one-man leader. Even though he was at times cavalier in his parliamentary tactics and arrogant toward the public, he was probably the most effective political party leader since Hara Kei.

Yoshida's main goal was to achieve a peace settlement with the United States. In this his views coincided with those of General MacArthur, who had always favored a quick termination of the occupation and the restoration of normal diplomatic relations between Japan and the outside world. The problem, however, was to assure that Japan would remain solidly in the ranks of the free world nations once she recovered full sovereignty. The Americans, after consulting with the British, finally decided to conclude a peace treaty with Japan even if the Soviet Union refused to go along. Some

Japanese political leaders feared that a separate peace with the United States and the other "free nations" might provoke the Russians, but Yoshida, with his strong anti-Communist outlook, felt no such apprehensions. On the balance the advantages of friendly relations with the Americans outweighed the disadvantages of Soviet hostility. Alignment with Great Britain and the United States, he wrote, "is not essentially a question of either dogmas or philosophy, nor need it lead to a subservient relationship; it is merely the quickest and most effective—indeed the only way—to promote the prosperity of the Japanese people."[2] The Yoshida foreign policy was a latter-day variant of Shidehara diplomacy.

Although Yoshida and the Americans were agreed on the desirability of a separate peace treaty they differed in their views of Japan's future. For the United States the treaty was a means of securing American supremacy in the Pacific; for Yoshida it was a way of laying the groundwork for future economic advance. This difference became apparent in discussions of Japan's military security after conclusion of a peace treaty. Yoshida was willing to accept the continuation of American military bases in Japan, to protect Japan and to contain Asian Communism, but he balked at American suggestions that Japan rearm itself. Conventional rearmament, he felt, would jeopardize economic recovery and in any case was quite futile in a nuclear world. He may also have seen that a new Japanese army might be more useful to the Americans than to the Japanese, who could count on the Americans to come to Japan's defense in case of international crisis. Far from being an American puppet, Yoshida was a nationalist of a very subtle sort.

The upshot of Yoshida's negotiations with the Americans was a delicate compromise embodied in the San Francisco Treaty and the Mutual Security Treaty signed in September 1951. No punitive economic restrictions were placed on Japan and no promise of massive rearmament was extracted from her. On the other hand, Yoshida had to make a certain number of concessions: the Japanese were to expand the paramilitary police reserve force to guarantee domestic order within Japan; the Americans were allowed to retain control of Okinawa for use as a major military base to contain China; a sizeable American military force was permitted to remain on Japanese territory; and Japan was forced to recognize the Kuomintang regime on Taiwan as the legitimate government of China. In short, by solidly wedding Japan to the American bloc, Yoshida had bought Japan

restored sovereignty, freedom from the economic burden of rearmament, and a political atmosphere favorable to economy recovery
and growth.

Soon after the conclusion of the peace treaty Yoshida's political
fortunes began to decline. His long and comfortable grip on power
provoked criticism. One-man rule had been highly suitable in the
days of the occupation, when Yoshida stood as a buffer between
SCAP's good intentions and Japanese realities; it was not so popular
once the Americans were gone. Yoshida's personal testiness, his
reliance on an inner circle of cronies, his contemptuous treatment of
the Diet, and his flagrant use of administrative discretion to prevent
the arrest of his follower, Satō Eisaku, for bribery, led to mounting
popular dissatisfaction and cost the Liberal party votes. Yoshida's
dominant position among the conservatives was also weakened by
the return of many de-purged prewar politicians to the Diet after
1951. Indeed about one-third of the conservative party men elected
in the first post-Occupation election of 1952 came from this group.
Older leaders, such as Hatoyama Ichirō, a Seiyūkai veteran, challenged Yoshida's position and Yoshida could no longer protect himself, as he often did during the occupation, by the implicit backing
of MacArthur.

The opposition to Yoshida took the form of a nationalistic reaction
against his pro-American foreign policy. After seven years under
American rule, many Japanese demanded greater independence for
Japan politically as well as legally. The left protested that the peace
settlement had made Japan subservient to the United States and
called instead for a policy of cold war neutrality or friendship with
the "progressive bloc" led by the Soviet Union. On "bloody May
Day" in 1952, thousands of demonstrators clashed with police on
the plaza of the Imperial Palace in protest against the peace settlement. In the years that followed left-wing demonstrations against the
presence of American forces, against the enlargement of American
bases, and against American testing of nuclear weapons in the Pacific
became endemic. On the right, Yoshida's conservative opponents
raised another kind of nationalist protest against overdependence on
the "American umbrella." Their goal was not neutralism but the attain-
ment of military autonomy through revision of the antiwar constitution and the signing of a peace settlement with the Soviet Union to
attain diplomatic autonomy. In the end nationalism of the right and
of the left cancelled each other out, since the Socialists helped to

prevent constitutional revision and the conservative nationalists checked the development of close ties with the Soviet bloc. For better or worse, even after Yoshida fell from power in late 1954 Japan remained the "workshop in the American lake," relieved of international responsibility by the American alliance and free to pursue Yoshida's goal of economic growth.

16

The Reluctant Giant

In 1956 a flurry of newspaper and magazine articles expatiated on the theme that the war was finally over. This mildly ironic comment was prompted by the issuance of the government's economic white paper, which pointed out that both GNP and national income had reached prewar levels the previous year and argued that the postwar decade of recovery was over. It also proclaimed that the country was moving into a new stage of high economic growth, a prediction many felt overly optimistic. The developments of the next decade confirmed the estimate, however. By 1968 a remarkable economic upsurge had made Japan the third largest industrial nation in the world, at once the object of envy and astonishment abroad. To many outside observers Japan's rise from a nation humbled in defeat to a powerful force in the world market seemed nothing short of miraculous. Perhaps more surprising, though, was the fact that the Japanese seemed unwilling to use their formidable economic power as a means of achieving international influence or of building up political-military power. Signs of national pride and self-confidence were everywhere evident, from the massive effort to host the Olympic Games in 1964 to the staging of Expo '70, but foreign policy was tempered by restraint and caution. Memories of 1945 lingered on, and so did Japanese dependence on the United States. For all her economic strength, Japan remained a reluctant giant, hesitant to cut a swath in the stage of world politics as she had in the world market.

The "Economic Miracle"

From 1954 to 1967 the GNP of Japan grew at an average annual rate of about 10 percent faster than any other national economy in the world and about three times as fast as the United States. To be sure, this remarkable performance was without historical parallel, but it has to be placed in a larger perspective. Unlike its Asian neighbors Japan did not have to build a modern economy from scratch. The country inherited abundant human resources from the prewar period—a highly educated population, wide diffusion of technical skills, a pervasive achievement ethic, a large and experience manager-ial class, and a tradition of government patronage of industrial development. The economy's foundations were solidly established and the Japanese merely needed to repair and add to the structure. It should also be pointed out that Japan was not alone in breaking records. During the years of Japan's "economic miracle" nearly all the economies of Western Europe grew much more rapidly than they had before World War II. As one economist has put it, Japan's "miraculous growth" was merely "an extreme case of a general phenomenon."

In many ways postwar economic growth was facilitated by a new set of advantages Japan had lacked before the war. First, wartime devastation proved a blessing in disguise. The destruction of obsoles-cent plants and machinery made it possible for the Japanese to catch up on a backlog of technology during the postwar period. Since Japanese businessmen acquired this technology by licensing arrange-ments with foreign firms, they got it at bargain prices, without the need for heavy investment in research and development. Japanese technicians were also often able to refine and improve upon even the most advanced Western techniques just as they had in the Meiji per-iod. Second, the abolition of a military establishment meant that capital, skills, and energy once channeled into war and empire build-ing could now be devoted to the expansion of the civilian economy. In 1938 about 16 percent of Japan's GNP was absorbed in military expenditure but by 1968 only about 0.8 percent was. This gave Japan an advantage over either the United States or the Soviet Union, both of whom acquired enormous economic burdens along with their new position as the world leaders. Third, after the sudden baby boom of 1946–1948, Japan experienced a dramatic slowdown in popula-tion growth. The war, of course, had killed off many potential fathers, but rather more important was the Eugenics Protection Law of 1948, which facilitated legal abortions. Passage of the law brought a sudden and dramatic drop in the birth rate, relieving the pressure of population growth on the economy. From 1955 to 1960 population grew only at the rate of 0.8 percent per year or less than half the rate in the 1920s. Finally, the postwar world economy was relatively free of protectionism that characterized the 1930s. A generally rising volume of international trade was a great advantage to Japan, whose prosperity had always been heavily dependent on foreign trade since World War I.

As in the past, the government played a key role in promoting economic growth. Japan did not have a command economy as did China or the Soviet Union, where the full power of the state backed economic directives, but the Japanese government did attempt to guide private enterprise by a complex mixture of planning, persuasion, and control. The basic goal of government policy was to promote exports in order to pay for the import of raw materials and manufacturer's products. Japan simply lacked domestic sources of oil, iron ore, cotton, soybeans, and other basic resources essential to economic expansion. The result was an "export or die" psychology that led the Japanese to expand their exports at double the world rate.

The techniques used by the government to achieve its end were varied. The Economic Planning Agency, an outgrowth of wartime attempts at centralized control over production, periodically issued national economic plans, indicating the most desirable direction for economic growth to take. Although the government plans were not enforceable, private business firms tended to rely on government forecasts in making plans for investment, hiring, and output. Since the planning process involved extensive formal and informal consultation between the economic technocrats and the business community it is not surprising that the government plans coincided with those of private business. Aside from planning the government used other more direct methods to shape the direction of economic development. Rigorous import controls protected certain domestic industries from outside competition, limitations were placed on the importation of foreign capital, and growth in selected industries was promoted by generous credit from government banks, special tax relief, depreciation allowances, and government purchase of stock.

The economic bureaucracy favored certain kinds of business over others. Sometimes aid was given to declining industries like coal mining on the grounds that they were essential "basic industries" or that their employees faced hardship. But more usually government aid was extended most generously to infant industries using imported technology or industries with high growth potential in both world and domestic markets. On the whole, men, resources, and capital were channeled into heavy industry rather than into consumer goods industries—cotton textiles, ceramics, bicycles, and the like—that had produced the staples of the prewar export trade. In the 1950s and early 1960s the government encouraged the growth of iron and steel, shipbuilding, trucks and buses, television and radios, optical equipment, and the like, all of which had begun in prewar days. Once these industries were well established by the late 1960s, however, emphasis shifted to complete new kinds of production such as computer equipment, private automobiles, and petroleum, none of which had been important before the Pacific war. By contrast few government advantages were given to industries that were inefficient, whose prices were not competitive in the world market, or which were no longer considered prestigious.

The success of the economy did not depend on government leadership alone. Just as a new economic technocracy had emerged in government the business world saw the rise of a new generation of business leaders who moved into the vacuum created by the occupation purges and dismantling of the zaibatsu. Some were new entrepreneurs like Matsushita Kōnosuke, who moved boldly into new industries such as electronics. Others came from the middle levels of the old managerial elite, freed from the constraints of the seniority system or the domination of the zaibatsu family interests. The new business leaders shared with the economic bureaucracy an expansionist outlook which stressed high profit rates less than growth itself. Private firms, controlled by professional managers rather than stock holders, often cut their profits to narrow margins in order to lead their industry production or market share. In pursuit of rank rather than profit, companies did not pay big dividends but constantly plowed profits back into further expansion of plant and productive capacity. Indeed, from 1953 to 1965 gross investment accounted for about 28.3 percent of the GNP, a rate much higher than any other industrial nation. Company executives operated in a general atmosphere of business optimism, confident that the economy would continue to grow. They were more inclined to take risks than most

Western European or American businessmen and their optimistic
expectations usually came true, further stimulating expansion, even
if it meant operating with huge debts. On the whole the business
community in the 1950s and 1960s was dominated by confident
plungers, certain they were riding the crest of an economic boom,
and the more conservative government planners constantly had to
worry about overexpansion and the overheating of the economy
resulting from business zeal.

Not too surprisingly, the economic upsurge of the 1950s and
1960s was accompanied by the re-emergence of industrial gigantism.
In the postwar period, *keiretsu* or "business groups" enhanced
Japan's competitive position through economies of scale as the
zaibatsu had in the prewar period, but they were very different in
character, strategy, and structure from the zaibatsu. In the first place
they were knit together less by the preponderant strength of a holding company than by ties of mutual convenience and interest. The
large bank or industrial concern that stood at the center of most
keiretsu had no absolute control over the policies and personnel of
affiliated firms, and member firms could withdraw from the keiretsu
to find capital, credit, and cooperation elsewhere if it seemed more
advantageous. While the old zaibatsu tended to dominate a particular
industry such as paper manufacturing the keiretsu usually tried to
draw into its ranks as many different industries as possible, following
a "one-set-of-everything" principle. Consequently there tended to be
much more competition between the postwar keiretsu than there had
been between the prewar zaibatsu. A chemical firm belonging to the
Sumitomo group would try to beat out a chemical firm belonging to
the Mitsubishi group by keeping its prices lower, the quality of its
products better, and the share of the market larger. The result was a
pattern of oligopolistic competition. A small number of large firms
competed intensely to reduce cost and improve quality. Since such
competition centered on building market shares or pursuit of industry rank rather than a high rate of profit it may have stimulated the
economy by producing strong incentives for investment in technical
or organizational innovation.

Labor also made its contribution to economic growth, probably no
less significant in many ways than that of business or government.
The high level of education, dedication, and efficiency of the Japanese factory workers was the envy of Western business executives
forced to deal with fractious labor unions and worker resistance to

productivity-boosting technical innovation. With the exception of West Germany probably no other Western economy was as free of crippling labor struggle during the 1950s and 1960s as Japan. Despite the militant slogans and theoretical anticapitalism of the large labor federations the Japanese union movement was usually cooperative with management. Unions served as spokesmen for individual workers' grievances and lobbied for better working conditions but they were not overly aggressive about wage demands. Large labor federations like Sōhyō engaged in regular spring offensives for wage contracts with leading industries (such as steel) to set a general model for wage negotiations, but most wage bargaining was done on the level of the individual firm. Since Japanese unions were typically enterprise unions, made up of all the employees of a single firm, whether white or blue collar, workers tended to identify more strongly with their companies than did workers in the United States or Great Britain. The lifetime employment system heightened worker loyalty to their firm, making them reluctant to bite the hand that would feed them until retirement, and union leaders were usually lower ranking white collar workers with a good idea of their company's financial limitations. For both these reasons, when enterprise unions negotiated with company executives on wage demands, they tended to think foremost of the firm's overall profitability and stability rather than the interests of the workers alone. Although union members tended to follow the political lead of the large federations they remained closer to their companies on economic questions. As a result, the businessman's wage bill was kept lower than it might have been had the unions adopted a stronger "antiboss" attitude or attempted to resist technical innovation by insistence on feather-bedding.

The Politics of Confrontation

The gradual return of prosperity was slow in making its mark on politics. The mid and late 1950s were a period of marked ill feeling in the Diet. In the autumn of 1955 conservative forces, divided into a variety of parties since the war, joined forces to form the Liberal Democratic Party. It was organized in response to pressure from the business community, which wanted a strong conservative party in control of the Diet to check the growing electoral strength of the Socialists (reunited once again) and to correct excesses of occupation policy such as the antimonopoly law. Leadership of the party at first lay in the hands of older prewar politicians like Hatoyama Ichirō, Ishibashi Tanzan, and Ogata Taketora, who had been eclipsed first by the purge and then by Yoshida Shigeru's one-man rule. Gradually, however, as these men died off or faded into semiretirement power shifted into the hands of ex-bureaucrats who had entered postwar politics under the patronage of Yoshida. Kishi Nobusuke, a former member of the wartime Tōjō cabinet, served as party leader from 1957 until 1960, and he was succeeded by two former Finance Ministry officials, Ikeda Hayato in 1960, and Satō Eisaku in 1964. The predominance of ex-officials reflected a reversion to the 1920s pattern of party leadership. Familiar with the ins and outs of the bureaucracy, experienced in administration, and well connected with both business and bureaucratic circles, the ex-officials possessed skills and opportunities lacked by those who had risen through local or Diet politics.

The new conservative coalition was soon engaged in a series of acrimonious clashes with the Socialists. The main domestic issue at stake was whether the democratic reforms of the occupation would be preserved or whether the country would follow a "backward course" toward the re-establishment of a highly centralized autocratic regime on the prewar model. The LDP took the position that many occupation reforms had been hastily conceived, were inappropriate to Japan's special circumstances, and ought to be modified in accordance with administrative rationality. Certain of the party's leaders, nostalgic for a more orderly and disciplined past, also hoped to restore sovereignty to the emperor and to restore the nation's right to maintain armed forces through a revision of the constitution. The Socialists were alarmed at these signs of conservative back-sliding. They felt that the occupation reforms had laid the foundations for a freer and more democratic society. By allying with the Communists they managed to block the two-thirds majority needed to carry out constitutional revision, but they were overwhelmed by the LPD on other questions.

Beginning with an attempt to recentralize the national police force in 1954, the conservatives introduced a whole series of antioccupation measures—the substitution of bureaucratic appointed school boards for locally elected ones, the establishment of a centrally administered teacher rating system, measures to strengthen the power of the police and the organization of a new central agency to supervise local government. These were modest changes, but to the left wing they seemed to herald a return to the bad old days of the 1930s. The intensity of confrontation between the LDP and the Socialists on these issues was out of all proportion to their probable impact on society, and bore little relationship to public sentiment. Opinion polls usually showed that most citizens were evenly balanced on either side of these questions, with a substantial minority largely indifferent. Nevertheless these disputes led to deepening Diet disorder and hostility between the two major parties. On the one hand the Socialists made no pretense of being a "loyal opposition." They openly and deliberately disrupted Diet proceedings by boycotting committee hearings or storming the speaker's platform in the House of Representatives. Police sometimes had to be summoned to the Diet floor to extricate an embattled conservative politician. On the other hand the LDP, with its Diet majority, rode roughshod over even nonpartisan objections to their measures. With the Socialists resorting to physical disorder and the LDP exercising a "tyranny of the majority," there was little consensus on the rules of the parliamentary game, let alone on substantive issues.

The politics of confrontation were even more pronounced on questions of foreign policy. While the Socialists continued to advocate some sort of neutralist policy, the LDP stood firmly behind a policy of gradual rearmament and military alliance with the United States. After the establishment of the Self-Defense Agency in 1954 the LDP gradually began to increase the size and firepower of the National Self-Defense Forces, relying on the advice of American military personnel and using American-made military equipment. Liberal Democratic foreign policy also faithfully followed Washington's lead. The LDP cabinets maintained correct but distant relations with the Soviet Union even after signing a peace treaty in 1955; they continued to recognize the Kuomintang regime of Chiang Kai-shek as the only legitimate government of China; and they voted consistently with the Americans in the United Nations. The only exception to this pattern was the attempt by LDP politicians to open trade with the People's Republic of China. The United States repaid the LDP government's loyalty by acting as Japan's sponsor into various international organizations such as the International Monetary Fund and World Bank, the GATT, and the OECD, all of which facilitated recovery of Japan's international respectability and the enhancement of Japanese foreign trade. Less directly, the political-military alliance with the United States guaranteed Japanese entry into American consumer and capital markets.

By contrast the Socialists carried on an active and persistent campaign in the Diet to block the expansion of the Self-Defense Forces. Outside the Diet they mounted popular demonstrations to protest against American nuclear arms tests, American bases, and against American servicemen involved in crimes against Japanese citizens. Some left-wing leaders of the party, to demonstrate their solidarity with the "progressive bloc," made pilgrimages to Moscow and Peking. During a visit to Peking in 1959 Asanuma Inejirō, a Socialist leader, made a joint declaration with Chinese officials that "American imperialism" was the joint enemy of the Chinese and Japanese people. The Socialist campaign against LDP foreign policy probably had more appeal than its battle against the "reverse course" in domestic policy. Even though most Japanese were friendlier toward the United States than toward her cold war rivals there was much popular resentment at the continuing presence of American military forces in Japan and at Japan's obvious dependence on the United States for military security.

The LDP-Socialist confrontation finally reached the boiling point in 1960 over renewal of the Security Treaty with the United States. Popular doubts about the value of the treaty were considerable. Many people questioned the wisdom of tying Japan to American strategic policy in Asia. Such a commitment might involve Japan in an international conflict where American interests were more at stake than Japan's. Confidence in American military superiority was shaken by the Soviet launching of Sputnik in 1957, and faith in American integrity was eroded by the U-2 incident in 1960. The United States was neither as comfortably omnipotent nor assuredly reliable as it had seemed a decade before. Despite these general misgivings the Kishi government committed itself to ratification of the renegotiated treaty. With little regard for the necessity of public debate, Kishi, an adroit tactician but arrogant public figure, rushed the revised treaty through the Diet, brooking no opposition and skillfully by-passing Socialist obstructionist tactics. The public response was the largest and most widespread popular political demonstration in Japanese history. Almost every day during May and June of 1960 hundreds of thousands of union members, students, white collar workers, intellectuals, and housewives staged massive demonstrations outside the Diet building. On June 4 over 5.5 million workers staged a general strike. The treaty was ratified by the LDP majority anyway, but the antitreaty struggle, prompted to a large extent by a feeling that the LDP had behaved undemocratically, indicated the extent of popular disillusionment with the conservative hegemony.

The Kishi government fell as a result of the Security Treaty riots, but the LDP continued in power. Nevertheless the party leaders decided to mend their ways. Ikeda Hayato, the new premier, abandoned the imperious ways of Kishi for a new low posture in the Diet. He was conciliatory toward the left and showed greater public concern for the lot of the common man. In a conscious effort to shift attention from the issues that had so troubled the 1950s Ikeda announced an "Income Doubling Plan" that promised to double the incomes of the Japanese people during the next decade. The main emphasis of the policy was to expand production, to develop both overseas and domestic markets, and to maintain a high rate of economic growth. The broad gauge appeal of such a program was obvious. Its promise of material prosperity was aimed at the aspirations of the average wage-earner; its stress on increased production and a high level of investment appealed to the business community and the financial community; and its emphasis on a high growth rate appealed to the economic nationalism of both the public and the economic technocrats. The shift to interest in economic issues, *leitmotiv* of LDP policy during the next decade, signalled the onset of a calmer and more moderate political atmosphere.

The Affluent Society

During the 1960s the mass of the Japanese people finally began to experience the benefits of economic growth. The postwar economic boom resulted in unprecedented popular prosperity. The fear of joblessness so acute in the early 1930s and again in the immediate postwar years had all but vanished. The high rate of industrial expansion coupled with the sudden drop in the birth rate began to produce labor shortages in the early 1960s that all but wiped out unemployment. The late 1950s and early 1960s also saw a precipitous rise in wages and personal income. In 1955 the average worker in firms with over 30 employees earned ¥ 18,300 per month, but ten years later in 1965 this had more than doubled to ¥ 39,400. In contrast to pre-war days when most personal wealth was in the hands of landowners, businessmen, and stockholders, it was distributed much more widely among ordinary wage-earner and "salary men." In 1934–1936 41.2 percent of all personal income took the form of wages, while 23.4 percent was earned as rent, dividends, or interest; in 1964 the wage share had increased to 61 percent while the share of return on personal investment dropped to less than 10 percent.

Affluence in the cities, among factory workers and the white collar classes, was paralleled by an improvement in the lot of the rural population. Tenancy had all but vanished by the mid 1960s (down to a mere 2 percent of the farm population), and rural prosperity grew steadily. In the immediate postwar period serious food shortages in the cities gave farmers new opportunities for profit, but more important in the long run was the growing productivity of the individual farmer. Growth in agricultural productivity was largely a byproduct of the occupation's land reform program. Former tenant farmers, now in full possession of the land they cultivated, had greater incentives to increase production. They no longer had to share the fruits of their labor with a landlord. Many farmers began buying new small-scale farm machines—power operated cultivators, tractors, and tillers not much larger or more powerful than those used by the American suburban gardener. These little machines enabled many farm families to spare one or two of its members for outside jobs that increased family income. Along with mechanization there also came the use of new insecticides that cut crop losses and new fertilizers that improved yields.

The LDP governments did their best to promote rural prosperity. Largely as a means of building rural electoral support postwar governments protected farmers against the vagaries of the market by paying a guaranteed rice price. Over the years it rose steadily until in the 1960s it was three times the world market rice price and government storehouses were filled with supplies sufficient to satisfy several years of domestic demand. The rice price support policy was economically inefficient since it discouraged farmers from diversifying into other needed food crops, but its social benefits to the countryside were unquestioned.

The general economic expansion helped to reduce the prewar contrast between country and city. Economic growth created new opportunities for industrial employment, and the lure of the city with its bright lights, good wages, fixed hours, and freedom pulled many young people away from the relatively long hours and heavy work on the farm. The farm population, which accounted for nearly

half the population in the 1930s, shrank to 34 percent in 1955 and
19 percent in 1970. Even those who remained in the country tended
more and more to be part-time farmers. Many heads of farm households commuted to work in near-by towns and factories, while the
women and older members of the family worked the family plot.
This work style, called "mama-grandma-grandpa agriculture" (*san
chan nōgyō*), became especially widespread after many firms deliberately moved plants to rural and provincial areas to capitalize on the
labor supply there. In any event, by the late 1960s only a minority
of farm families relied on farming exclusively for their income, while
the majority earned as much if not more from nonagricultural jobs.
The rural population therefore came to enjoy living standards very
similar to that of the urban population, and the diffusion of rural
television likewise closed the cultural gap that once separated country cousin from city cousin.

The new popular affluence was accompanied by a decline in the
old morality of personal frugality long exploited by the government
to encourage patriotic dedication. "Luxury is the enemy" had been
a wartime slogan, but many Japanese now seemed eager to get their
hands on every creature comfort they could. A sudden expansion in
demand for consumer durable goods, often called a consumer revolution, manifested itself first in the mid 1950s. In 1966, as the result of
the pursuit of the "three electric treasures," 94 percent of all Japanese households had television sets, 76 percent had washing machines,
and 61 percent had refrigerators. By the late 1960s the market for
private family automobiles began to grow as well. Yet material comfort was still largely confined to items of personal use. Housing
remained scarce in the cities, where it was most in demand, and
many Japanese wage-earners had to crowd their families and their
"electric treasures" in small "2DK apartments" (two rooms plus
dining-kitchen area). Similarly, except for public transportation the
improvement of public services lagged behind many other industrial
nations.

This imbalance between the boom in personal consumption and
continuing inadequacy in many public services perhaps reflected the
relatively low level of public spirit or public concern among Japanese
wage earners. During the late 1950s and 1960s most Japanese were
absorbed in pursuing private goals and their horizons did not much
extend beyond home and workshop. Few were interested in service
to society. In place of the wartime ideal of "self-sacrifice for the good

of the whole" (*messhi hōkō*), the period saw the birth of "my-home-ism" (*mai-homu-shugi*), a retreat to private concerns, the pursuit of material comfort, and the enjoyment of the amenities of middle-class life. As Ronald Dore has neatly summarized it, most Japanese sought "a cosy little home in the suburbs, a pretty wife, a couple of kids, and an occasional game of golf."[1] Many, moreover, seemed to feel they had achieved their modest aspirations. A public opinion survey of 16,000 respondents in 1967 revealed that 88 percent considered themselves middle class, 60 percent were content with their present living standards, and 44 percent felt their living standards were likely to improve in the future. In a sense, my-home-ism was the little person's counterpart of the economic nationalism pervasive in the government technocracy and the business managerial class.

Beneath the spread of popular affluence, however, the traditional work ethic remained as strong as ever. Indeed it helped to account for the affluence. Japan was still, as one observer put it, "a nation of compulsive over-achievers." Office lights in downtown Tokyo usually burned well into early evening, and the six-day work week was the rule in nearly all companies and government offices. The most striking manifestation of the work and achievement ethic was the continuing mania for education, now perhaps more intense than ever as middle-class aspirations broadened to include most of the population. Parents of all economic strata pressured their children from kindergarten onward to get into the "proper schools" in preparation for entry into a "good university," the key to a successful middle-class career. The aggressive "education-mad mother" (*kyōiku mama*), herding her children from school to English tutor to piano lessons to evening homework, was a stock figure in popular journalism. Ambitious youths, especially in the last years of high school, crammed their heads with facts in preparation for "entrance-examination hell." It was a testimony to the persistent drive for success, achievement, and status that most families put up with this despite its costs in money, frustration, and family tension.

The Politics of Affluence

The prosperity of the late 1950s and 1960s doubtless contributed to the continuing dominance of the LDP, if only by guaranteeing the society against violent economic changes that might have upset its hegemony. But, like the prewar entrenched parties, the LDP did not seem to capture the hearts and minds of many voters. In 1970 when a weekly magazine asked a number of Tokyo inhabitants what came to their minds when they heard the word *politician*, the replies—"tax thieves," "two-faced," "rotten," "greedy," and so forth—indicated a fair degree of malaise. Active dissatisfaction with the political system was perhaps as rare as enthusiastic support for the conservatives, however. A minority of student radicals took to the streets with helmets and wooden staves, disrupted traffic and clashed with riot police in protest against everything from crowded classrooms to the Vietnam War. Many Japanese showed sympathy for student goals and admiration for their sincerity, but few approved student tactics of violence and disruption.

The most significant index of voter apathy, indifference, or distrust of the ruling conservatives was to be found in the steady decline of popular electoral support for the LDP during the late 1950s and early 1960s. Conservative forces won 63.2 percent of the popular vote in the general election of 1955, but the LDP share of the vote dropped to 57.8 percent in 1958, 57.5 percent in 1960, 57.6 percent in 1963, 48.8 percent in 1967, and 47.6 percent in 1969. To a large extent this decline in electoral support reflected changing demographic patterns. Although the party continued to monopolize votes in rural areas it lost strength in rapidly growing metropolitan areas where voters tended to be younger, cut off from village roots, and generally more susceptible to the appeal of the progressive parties. The LDP was able to maintain its majority in spite of this demographic shift because the districting system was heavily weighted in favor of the rural voter. It also used electoral tactics more skillfully than its opposition.

Increasing fragmentation of the opposition into a number of small parties also helped maintain LDP dominance. When the party was organized in 1955 it really faced only one opponent, the newly unified Socialist Party. By the 1960s this situation changed considerably. The socialists, whose unity had been an off-again-on-again affair since 1945, split once again in 1960. Moderate elements within the party, discontent with the doctrinaire left-wing dominant in the party leadership, organized a separate Democratic Socialist Party in January 1960, considerably weakening the Socialist bloc at the polls. So did the ossification of the Socialist leadership into a kind of left-wing establishment, unable to pry itself loose from an *immobilisme* nurtured by attachment to outdated political slogans and rhetoric. The

Socialists' heavy pessimism about the future of capitalism seemed out of place in the prosperous 1960s, and their attacks on LDP policy smacked of a dreary ritualism. One faction of Socialist leadership under Eda Saburō attempted to refurbish the party's organization and image by making broader and less ideological appeals to the electorate, but on the whole it was unable to achieve much.

While the Socialists floundered, the Communist Party began to recover its strength. It did so largely by trading its earlier stance as militant crusader for a more moderate position. It cultivated a public image as a basically benign, fair-minded, and pragmatic party, interested less in ideological orthodoxy than in improving the lot of the masses. Communist Party posters in the early 1950s showed angry factory workers flexing their biceps beneath unfurled red banners, but by the mid 1960s they were peopled by smiling youths looking confidently toward the future or cheery grandfathers cuddling bright-eyed youngsters. By formally cutting ties with both Moscow and Peking, the Communists also established their independence from outside influence, a factor that made many less reluctant to support the party.

The fragmentation of the left was further complicated by the rise of the Komeitō (Clean Government Party), a new party that sprang into being in 1964 as the political arm of the Sōka Gakkai, the largest of Japan's postwar new religions. The Sōka Gakkai flourished in the rapidly growing urban areas where the LDP vote was diminishing. It drew into its ranks urban migrants cut off from their rural roots but unable to achieve the comforts of middle-class life. These lonely or disoriented social underdogs were largely ignored by the unions or the organized left. They found a sense of belonging in the Sōka Gakkai, which built solidarity by rigid discipline, intensive indoctrination, and all-embracing claims on its members' lives. When the Komeitō was formed the Sōka Gakkai membership automatically became its constituency. The new party also attracted the protest vote against the other parties. In the 1967 election, the Komeitō won twenty-five seats in the Diet (5 percent of the popular vote), and two years later it won forty-seven seats and more than doubled its popular vote, making it the third largest party after the LDP and the Socialists. In policy, it tended to adopt majority opinions as reflected in opinion surveys, and in tactics it usually cooperated with the LDP, perhaps with an eye to eventual coalition.

Despite its declining popularity, the LDP remained in power under the leadership of Satō Eisaku, who served as premier from 1964 to 1972, longer than any other man had held the post since the establishment of constitutional government. Though he did not enjoy great personal popularity Satō was an astute ex-bureaucrat turned politician who enjoyed the backing of the business community and knit together a solid coalition of factions in his party. His main accomplishment was a modest reassertion of Japan's voice in world affairs, a policy supported by an increasingly nationalistic public. It was also a policy encouraged by the United States. In the wake of the 1960 treaty riots, responsible officials in Washington, including President John F. Kennedy, realized that Japanese friendship ought not be taken for granted as it had been in the 1950s. New efforts were made under the Kennedy administration to renew the "broken dialogue" with Japan at all levels.

By the mid 1960s, as the United States became more bogged down in the Vietnam War and as Japan became ever more prosperous, the American government tried to encourage the Japanese to take a more active role in promoting the economic development and military security of free world forces in the Western Pacific. In response to American prompting the LDP government under Satō normalized relations with South Korea, increased foreign aid and investment in Taiwan, and moved in to support the newly established Suharto regime in Indonesia. The American goal was to have Japan share more of the burden and responsibility as America's partner in the containment of Asian Communism, but the Japanese goal was to establish a greater freedom of action within the framework of the American alliance. This subtle shift in the alliance was signified by the willingness of the United States to resolve territorial issues left over from World War II. In 1968 the United States restored the Bonin Islands to Japanese possession, and in 1969 agreed to the eventual reversion of Okinawa to Japanese sovereignty. By the end of the decade the slate was wiped clean, and Premier Satō announced the "end of the postwar era."

Epilogue:
Japan in the 1970s

The Japanese entered the 1970s in a mood of national optimism and renewed national self-confidence that had been growing since the middle of the previous decade. There was pride that Japan had emerged as the world's third largest industrial power, and quiet self-satisfaction that foreign experts predicted the emergence of a prosperous "Japanese superstate" in the 1980s. The most obvious symbol of the new mood was Expo '70, a world's fair held on the outskirts of Osaka. Thousands of foreign tourists streamed into the country to visit the exposition, but Japanese visited it by the millions, enthralled as much by their own technological accomplishments as by the foreign exhibitions. It was not difficult to imagine that the twenty-first century might well be the "Japanese century," for Japan now possessed wealth and power beyond the wildest dreams of the Meiji leaders. But with the upsurge in national pride came a renewed sense of doubt and questioning: To what end was all this wealth and power to be directed? What were to be Japan's future goals? What was to be its national purpose?

This ambivalence deepened as new international currents began to buffet Japan. As the decade wore on it became clear that Japanese success as an economic power was imposing strains on the Japanese-American alliance. Despite all the talk about Japanese-American partnership, many officials in Washington had come to feel that the booming Japanese economy was getting a free ride militarily as a result of the mutual security treaty (renewed without incident in 1970). Many American businessmen also complained that although Japanese goods were flooding American markets, the Japanese kept down competition at home by protectionist barriers against American goods and capital. In the summer of 1971 the Nixon administration, faced with an overall balance of payments crisis, announced the imposition of a 10 percent surcharge on all imports and took the dollar off a fixed international exchange rate. Although these moves were intended to deal with a worldwide problem there was little doubt that one of their chief purposes was to reverse an unfavorable balance of trade with Japan. The Japanese business community was irritated that the United States was trying to solve its economic problems by exporting them, but the Satō government responded to the "Nixon shock" by a revaluation of the yen and the liberalization of restrictions on import of goods and capital to Japan.

A second "Nixon shock" came a few weeks later when the American government announced that the president would make an official visit to the People's Republic of China in 1972. Save for the conservative pro-Chiang elements in the LDP, most politicians, officials, and ordinary Japanese citizens welcomed this sudden access of pragmatism in American Asia policy. However, since the American initiative toward China was undertaken without prior consultation with Japan, the United States' closest ally in the region, many Japanese feared that American rapprochement with Peking might lead to American estrangement from Tokyo. The American government quickly moved to assure the Satō government that it planned to make no deals behind Japan's back and hastily fixed a date for the final return of Okinawa. But lingering doubts were hard to contain. A great many politicians and commentators began to question the adequacy of Japan's security arrangements, which depended so heavily on the American nuclear umbrella. Some began to advocate greater Japanese self-sufficiency in conventional weaponry, and a few even began to talk about the development of a Japanese nuclear capability.

In the short run, the chief casualty of the "Nixon shocks" was neither the favorable Japanese trade balance (which continued to grow) nor the American alliance (which remained battered but firm), but rather Premier Satō, who finally resigned from office in the sum-

mer of 1972. As a token of the changing times, his successor was
Tanaka Kakuei, a brash, rough-hewn ex-businessman, who had
never gotten more than a technical high school education. Nick-
named "the computerized bulldozer," Tanaka was an exuberant
member of the self-made postwar generation, who had struggled to
the top first by accumulating a personal fortune in the construction
business and then working his way up in the LDP hierarchy. Blessed
with a common touch—he once garnered public attention by singing
Japanese folk songs on television—he was immediately popular with
a Japanese public weary of well-modulated, formal, and restrained
public figures like Satō, Ikeda, and Kishi. His popularity soared even
further when in September 1972—after first conferring with President
Nixon—he visited Peking to establish formal diplomatic relations.
Newspaper commentary, echoing the residual resentment of earlier
American actions, spoke of a "Tanaka shock" for the United States.
Although this was clearly a misnomer the new Japanese initiative
toward China reflected once again the growing desire of the Japanese
to move on the world stage as more than a "nation of transistor
salesmen."

If the Tanaka government helped resuscitate Japan's self-confidence
in its ability to deal with the outside world, it soon found that new
and urgent problems were eroding optimism and complacence at
home. The adverse effects of rapid economic growth and affluence
became increasingly visible in the early 1970s. The huge industrial
complex built up in the 1950s and 1960s poured industrial pollu-
tants into sky and sea on a horrendous scale. In the industrial belt
stretching along the Pacific side of the archipelago, a soupy veil of
smoke, smog, and exhaust fumes usually lay heavy in the sky. In
other parts of the country there were crueler manifestations of industrial pollution, such as the hideously crippling Minamata disease
caused by industrial effluents in coastal waters. Rapid urbanization,
accompanying economic growth had also crowded over half the
population of the country into the Tokyo-Yokohama and Osaka-
Kobe areas, bringing with it a host of problems. Commuter lines and
traffic arteries were jammed at rush hour, the price of urban land
soared steadily, and housing grew scarcer and more expensive. A third
of the country's families, most of them in the city, were forced to
live in dwellings too small for each member to have one room.
Finally, inflation, the companion of postwar prosperity, continued

to accelerate at a rate higher than any other major industrial country in the world. Apart from the effects this had on ordinary household budgets the inflationary spiral raised the possibility (especially after yen revaluation) that Japanese exports might price themselves out of the competition in world markets.

The most sobering shock to renewed national self-confidence came with the oil crisis of 1973–1974. The imposition of the Arab oil embargo underlined the fragility of both Japan's prosperity and international position. At a stroke the Japanese economy found itself hostage to an international conflict in which it had no interest and over which it had no control. Although the oil soon began to flow again the implications of the crisis were clear. Imported natural resources, like oil, on which "miraculous growth" depended, might someday be too expensive or too scarce for Japan to buy in the quantity it needed. Indeed, according to one estimate, if the energy-dependent heavy industries, which accounted for three-quarters of Japan's exports, continued to grow at the same rate as they had during the late 1960s and early 1970s, they would require nearly a third of the world's current oil supplies by the 1980s. Clearly this meant that the future of the "Japanese miracle" was limited. Not surprisingly, one of the most popular best-sellers in 1973 was *Submerging Japan* (*Nihon chinbotsu*), a science fiction tale about the disappearance of the Japanese archipelago in a cataclysm of earthquakes, volcanic eruptions, and tidal waves.

Just what pollution, urban crowding, energy shortages, and inflation would mean in the decade to come was by no means certain. As one 1974 New Year's Day editorial noted: "Everything seems to be enshrouded in mist, and apparently the uncertainty and fears besieging Japan are growing worse."[1] The economic growth rate was certain to slow down, but no one could say for sure whether this meant a mild recession, zero economic growth, or major economic collapse. A growing disillusionment with "GNPism" was spreading, cutting across older divisions between right and left and between conservative and socialist. Yet what was to replace affluence as a basis for national pride and self-confidence was equally uncertain. On the one hand, there was a revulsion against the materialism of the postwar period and a nostalgia for older Japanese values. As the leader of a band of antimainstream young LDP members told an American reporter:

> If we get too rich, prosperous, and materialistic, all we do is create more unhappiness. We must therefore return to the true

Japanese moral standards, including respect for our ancestors, compassion, gratitude, courage, cooperation, and obligation—all virtues neglected since the war. Only in this way will we regain the confidence of the people.[2]

(The hero's welcome accorded Lt. Onoda, a former intelligence officer who finally emerged from the Philippine jungles to surrender twenty-nine years after the war had ended, indicated such sentiments might be widely shared.) On the other hand many also felt that although prosperity and material comfort were not bad in themselves, it was wrong to devote national energies exclusively to building the economic growth rate. As the editors of one major Tokyo newspaper noted:

Our country's economic policy in the past has emphasized high production, but there is no reason, internal or external, why this emphasis must be continued. The most urgent task Japan faces today is to shift to an economy which emphasizes social welfare, one that will solve long-ignored inadequacies in our social environment and will provide equal social guarantees to all citizens.[3]

In short, in this view, the problem that Japan faced was not a decline in the older virtues, but the need to reorder national priorities.

Once again Japan stood at a crossroads, as it had so often during the modern century, but how it would eventually meet the hard new challenges of the 1970s was still anyone's guess.

Notes

Introduction

[1] The foreign observer was Gustav Lebon, whose remarks are quoted in the introduction to Yosaburo Takekoshi, *The Economic Aspects of the History of the Civilization of Japan,* 3 vols., George Allen and Unwin, London, 1930.

[2] The American publication was the *American Annual Cyclopedia.* Quoted in William I. Neumann, *America Encounters Japan: From Perry to MacArthur,* Harper and Row, New York, 1963, p. 66.

[3] Lafcadio Hearn, *Japan: An Interpretation,* Charles E. Tuttle, Rutland, Vt. and Tokyo, 1955, pp. 461–462.

[4] For more information on Homer Lea, see William L. Neumann, *America Encounters Japan,* pp. 128–129.

[5] Norman's classic work is E. Herbert Norman, *Japan's Emergence as a Modern State,* Institute of Pacific Relations, New York, 1940. A selection of Norman's most important writings have been anthologized in *Origins of the Modern Japanese State: Select Writings of E. H. Norman,* ed. John W. Dower, Pantheon Books, New York, 1975.

Chapter 1

[1] Okakura Kakuzō, *The Awakening of Japan,* The Century Co., New York, 1905, p. 187.

[2] See Masao Maruyama, *Nihon no shisō,* Iwanami shoten, Tokyo, 1961, pp. 159–163.

[3] A brief discussion of the four-class theory may be found in Eijirō Honjo, *The Social and Economic History of Japan,* Russell and Russell, New York, 1965, pp. 188–202.

[4] The "ideology of merit" is discussed in Thomas C. Smith, " 'Merit' as Ideology in the Tokugawa Period," in *Aspects of Social Change in Modern Japan,* ed. R. P. Dore, Princeton University Press, Princeton, N.J., 1967, pp. 71–90.

[5] Kaibara Ekken is quoted in David John Lu, *Sources of Japanese History,* McGraw-Hill, New York, 1974, I, pp. 248–249.

[6] Fukuzawa Yukichi is quoted in Masao Maruyama, *Thought and Behaviour in Modern Japanese Politics,* Oxford University Press, New York, 1963, p. 18.

[7] The quotation is from Ihara Saikaku, *The Japanese Family Storehouse, or the Millionaires' Gospel Modernised,* tr. G. W. Sargent, Cambridge University Press, Cambridge, 1959, p. 144.

[8] Dore's comments on the "collectivity ethic" may be found in R. P. Dore and Tsutomu Ōuchi, "Rural Origins of Japanese Fascism" in *Dilemmas of Growth in Modern Japan,* ed. James W. Morley, Princeton University Press, Princeton, N.J., 1971, pp. 181–209.

[9] A famous puppet play based on this tale has been translated by Donald Keene. *Chūshingura: The Tragedy of Loyal Retainers,* Columbia University Press, New York, 1971.

[10] The quotation is from Kenjirō Tokutomi, *Footsteps in the Snow,* tr. Kenneth Strong, George Allen and Unwin, London, 1970.

[11] Ninomiya is quoted in Robert N. Bellah, *Tokugawa Religion: The Values of Pre-Modern Japan,* Free Press, New York, 1957, p. 128.

[12] Ibid., p. 130.

[13] The quotation from the craftsman's handbook may be found in Charles J. Dunn, *Everyday Life in Traditional Japan,* B. T. Batsford, London, 1969, p. 92.

[14] The observation on the dual nature of Japanese character may be found in Zbigniew Brzezinski, *The Fragile Blossom: Crisis and Change in Japan,* Harper and Row, New York, 1972, p. 5.

[15] The quotation from Yamazaki may be found in Ryusaku Tsunoda, et al., *Sources of Japanese Tradition,* Columbia University Press, New York, 1958, pp. 369–370.

[16] The quotation from Matsudaira Sadanobu may be found in R. P. Dore, *Education in Tokugawa Japan,* University of California Press, Berkeley, 1965, p. 46.

Chapter 2

[1] John W. Hall, "The Nature of Traditional Society," in *Political Modernization in Japan and Turkey,* eds. Robert E. Ward and Dankwart A. Rustow, Princeton University Press, Princeton, N.J., 1964, p. 27.

[2] Sir Rutherford Alcock, *The Capital of the Tycoon: A Narrative of a Three Years' Residence in Japan,* 2 vols., Macmillan, New York, 1863.

[3] See John W. Hall, "The Nature of Traditional Society," in *Political Modernization in Japan and Turkey,* p. 34.

[4] See Thomas C. Smith, " 'Merit' as Ideology in the Tokugawa Period," in *Aspects of Social Change in Modern Japan*, ed. R. P. Dore, Princeton University Press, Princeton, N.J., 1967, pp. 71–90.

[5] The quotation is from Sugita Gempaku, whose views may be found in *Yuragu hōkensei*, Yomiuri shimbunsha, Tokyo, 1963, p. 165.

[6] See Harry D. Harootunian, *Toward Restoration: The Growth of Political Consciousness in Tokugawa Japan*, University of California Press, Berkeley, 1970.

Chapter 3

[1] Thunberg's observations on Japan may be found in his *Travels in Europe, Africa, and Asia*, F. and C. Rivington, London, 1795, IV.

[2] Quoted in Johannes Hirschmeier, *The Origins of Entrepreneurship in Meiji Japan*, Harvard University Press, Cambridge, 1964, p. 23.

[3] See Eijirō Honjo, *Economic Theory and History of Japan in the Tokugawa Period*, Russell and Russell, New York, 1965, pp. 31–32.

[4] See Thomas C. Smith, "The Land Tax in the Tokugawa Period," *Journal of Asian Studies*, 18, No. 1 (November 1958).

[5] Quoted in Thomas C. Smith, *The Agrarian Origins of Modern Japan*, Stanford University Press, Stanford, Ca., 1959, p. 176.

[6] Conrad Totman, *Politics in the Tokugawa Bakufu*, Harvard University Press, Cambridge, Mass., 1967, p. 77.

[7] Fujita is quoted by Harry D. Harootunian, *Toward Restoration: The Growth of Political Consciousness in Tokugawa Japan*, University of California Press, Berkeley, 1970.

[8] For Motoori's views see Shigeru Matsumoto, *Motoori Norinaga, 1730–1801*, Harvard University Press, Cambridge, Mass., 1970, pp. 144–156.

[9] Honda Toshiaki is quoted in Thomas C. Smith, " 'Merit' as Ideolody in the Tokugawa Period," in *Aspects of Social Change in Modern Japan*, ed. R. P. Dore, Princeton University Press, Princeton, N.J., 1967.

Chapter 4

[1] Aizawa Seishisai is quoted in Ryusaku Tsunoda et al., *Sources of Japanese Tradition*, Columbia University Press, New York, 1958, p. 602.

[2] A fuller treatment of the Russian view of Japan may be found in George Alexander Lensen, *The Russian Push toward Japan, 1697–1875*, Princeton University Press, Princeton, N.J., 1959.

[3] *Meiji ishin*, Yomiuri shimbunsha, Tokyo, 1968, pp. 19–20.

[4] The comment is quoted in Konishi Shirō, *Kaikoku to jōi,* Chūō kōron sha, Tokyo, 1966, p. 8.

[5] Perry's views on the Japanese are dealt with in Samuel Eliot Morison, *"Old Bruin": Commodore Matthew Calbraith Perry,* Little, Brown, and Co., Boston, 1967.

[6] See Harry D. Harootunian, *Toward Restoration: The Growth of Political Consciousness in Tokugawa Japan,* University of California Press, Berkeley, 1970, Chapter 6.

[7] Quoted in W. G. Beasley, *The Meiji Restoration,* Stanford University Press, Stanford Ca., 1972, p. 261.

[8] See Thomas C. Smith, "Japan's Aristocratic Revolution," *Yale Review,* 50, No. 3 (Spring 1961), 370–383.

Chapter 5

[1] The journalist was J. R. Black. See his book *Young Japan. Yokohama and Yedo. A Narrative of the Settlement and the City from the Signing of the Treaties in 1858 to the Close of the Year 1879,* 2 vols., Trubner and Co., London, 1880–1881.

[2] The text of the Charter Oath may be found in Ryusaku Tsunoda, et al., *Sources of Japanese Tradition,* Columbia University Press, New York, 1958, pp. 643–644.

[3] Quoted in Joseph Pittau, *Political Thought in Early Meiji Japan, 1868–1889,* Harvard University Press, Cambridge, Mass., 1967, p. 33.

[4] Ibid., p. 23.

[5] Quoted in Ienaga Saburō and Inoue Kiyoshi, *Kindai Nihon no sōten,* Mainichi shimbunsha, Tokyo, 1967, I, p. 177.

[6] Ibid., p. 186.

[7] Ōkubo's comments on the need to industrialize may be found in *Meiji Japan through Contemporary Sources,* III, The Centre for East Asian Cultural Studies, Tokyo, 1970, pp. 18–23.

[8] See Thomas R. H. Havens, *Nishi Amane and Modern Japanese Thought,* Princeton University Press, Princeton, N.J., 1970, pp. 78–85.

[9] See Donald Keene, *Modern Japanese Literature,* Grove Press, New York, 1956, pp. 31–33.

[10] Quoted in Carmen Blacker, *The Japanese Enlightenment: A Study of the Writings of Fukuzawa Yukichi,* Cambridge University Press, Cambridge, 1964, p. 31.

[11] Nakamura Keiū is quoted in ibid., p. 29.

[12] Ibid.

[13] The edict on the school system is quoted in Joseph Pittau, *Political Thought in Early Meiji Japan, 1868–1889,* pp. 24–25.

Chapter 6

[1] Quoted in *Meiji Japan through Contemporary Sources*, II, The Centre for East Asian Cultural Studies, Tokyo, 1970, p. 168.

[2] *Meiji ishin*, Yomiuri shimbunsha, Tokyo, 1968, p. 240.

[3] The text of this memorial may be found in *Meiji Japan through Contemporary Sources*, II, pp. 134–141.

[4] Quoted in Ienaga Saburō and Inoue Kiyoshi, *Kindai Nihon no sōten*, Mainichi shimbunsha, Tokyo, 1967, I, pp. 131–141.

[5] A discussion of Ueki's views may be found in Nobutaka Ike, *The Beginnings of Political Democracy in Japan*, Johns Hopkins Press, Baltimore, 1950, pp. 129–137.

[6] Quoted in George Akita, *Foundations of Constitutional Government in Modern Japan*, 1868–1900, Harvard University Press, Cambridge, Mass., 1967, p. 25.

[7] Kido's memorial may be found in *Meiji Japan through Contemporary Sources*, II, pp. 99–110.

[8] *Ibid.*, pp. 69–70.

[9] Motoda is quoted by Donald Shively in David S. Nivison and Arthur F. Wright, eds. *Confucianism in Action*, Stanford University Press, Stanford, Ca., 1959, p. 327.

[10] Quoted in Carmen Blacker, *The Japanese Enlightenment: A Study of the Writings of Fukugawa Yukichi*, Cambridge University Press, Cambridge, 1964, p. 134.

Chapter 7

[1] Iwakura's views are cited in Thomas C. Smith, *Political Change and Industrial Development in Japan: Government Enterprise 1868–1880*, Stanford University Press, Stanford, Ca., 1955, pp. 97–98.

[2] The text of the Imperial Precepts for Soldiers and Sailors may be found in Ryusaku Tsunoda et al. *Sources of Japanese Tradition*, Columbia University Press, New York, 1958, pp. 705–707.

[3] The quote from Itō may be found in *Meiji Japan through Contemporary Sources*, II, The Centre for East Asian Cultural Studies, Tokyo, 1970, pp. 121–123.

[4] Quoted in Ienaga Saburō and Inoue Kiyoshi, *Kindai Nihon no sōten*, Mainichi shimbunsha, Tokyo, 1967, I, p. 379.

[5] Ibid., p. 381.

[6] Mori is quoted in Herbert Passin, *Society and Education in Japan*, New York, Columbia University Press, 1965. p. 81.

Chapter 8

[1] The peace party's view was summarized in a memorial written by Ōkubo Toshimichi. See Ryusaku Tsunoda, et al., *Sources of*

Japanese Tradition, Columbia University Press, New York, 1958, pp. 658–662.

2 Sugita Teiichi's views are quoted in *The Emergence of Imperial Japan: Self-Defense or Calculated Agression,* ed. Marlene Mayo, D.C. Heath, Lexington, Mass., 1970, p. 6.

3 Yamagata's views are summarized by Marius B. Jansen in *Political Development in Modern Japan,* ed. Robert E. Ward, Princeton University Press, Princeton, N.J., 1968, p. 182.

4 Ōkuma is quoted in *Kindai Nihon shisōshi kōza: Sekai no naka no Nihon,* ed. Takeuchi Yoshimi, Chikuma shobo, Tokyo, 1961, p. 140.

5 Itō Miyoji is quoted in Edwin Baelz, *Awakening Japan,* Viking, New York, 1932, p. 243.

6 Okakura's views are outlined in *Japanese Thought in the Meiji Era,* ed. Kōsaka Masaaki, Pan-Pacific Press, Tokyo, 1958, pp. 217–224.

Chapter 9

1 Quote is from Ronald P. Dore, *Land Reform in Japan,* Oxford University Press, London, 1959, p. 51.

2 Morimura is quoted in Byron K. Marshall, *Capitalism and Nationalism in Prewar Japan,* Stanford University Press, Stanford, Ca., 1967, p. 36.

3 See Arthur Tiedemann, "Big Business and Politics in Prewar Japan," in *Dilemmas of Growth in Prewar Japan,* ed. James W. Morley, Princeton University Press, Princeton, N.J., 1971, pp. 267–316.

4 Ibid. The remark was made by Ikeda Seihin.

5 The quotation may be found in *Aspects of Social Change in Modern Japan,* ed. R. P. Dore, Princeton University Press, Princeton, N.J., 1967, pp. 120–121.

6 Quoted in Byron K. Marshall, *Capitalism and Nationalism in Prewar Japan,* pp. 57–58.

Chapter 10

1 The anonymous candidate is quoted in R. H. P. Mason, *Japan's First General Election: 1890,* Cambridge University Press, Cambridge, 1969, p. 127.

2 Wakatsuki is quoted in Ōshima Fujitarō, *Kokutetsu,* Iwanami shoten, Tokyo, 1961, pp. 50–51.

3 Hoshi Tōru quoted in Masumi Junnosuke, *Nihon seitōshiron,* II, Tokyo daigaku shuppan kai, Tokyo, 1966, p. 225.

4 Quoted in Peter Duus, *Party Rivalry and Political Change in*

Taisho Japan, Harvard University Press, Cambridge, Mass., 1968, p. 24.

[5] Ibid., p. 111.

[6] Quoted in Nobuya Bamba, *Japanese Diplomacy in a Dilemma,* University of British Columbia Press, Vancouver, 1972, p. 70, n. 48.

[7] Quoted in ibid., p. 76

Chapter 11

[1] Quoted in Koji Taira, *Economic Development and the Labor Market in Japan,* Columbia University Press, New York, 1970, p. 132.

[2] Quoted in Ienaga Saburō and Inoue Kiyoshi, *Kindai Nihon no sōten,* Mainichi shimbunsha, Tokyo, 1967, III, p. 149.

Chapter 12

[1] Tagore is quoted in D. MacKenzie Brown, *The Nationalist Movement: Indian Political Thought from Ranade to Bhave,* University of California Press, Berkeley, 1970, p. 9.

[2] Yoshino is quoted in *What Japan Thinks,* ed. Karl Kiyoshi Kawakami, Macmillan, New York, 1921, p. 88.

[3] Quoted in Takahashi Kamekichi, *Taishō-Shōwa zaikai hendōshi,* Tokyo, 1954, pp. 1179–1180.

Chapter 13

[1] Quoted in Masao Maruyama, *Thought and Behaviour in Modern Japan,* Oxford University Press, 1963, p 45.

[2] Quoted in Takahashi Masae, *Shōwa no gunbatsu,* Chūō kōron sha, Tokyo, 1969, pp. 163–164.

[3] General Araki is quoted in Ben-Ami Shillony, *Revolt in Japan: The Young Officers and the February 26, 1936 Incident,* Princeton University Press, Princeton, N.J., 1973, p. 36.

Chapter 14

[1] Roberta Wohlstetter, *Pearl Harbor: Warning and Decision,* Stanford University Press, Stanford, Ca., 1962, p. 353.

[2] Masuo Kato, *The Lost War: A Japanese Reporter's Inside Story,* Alfred A. Knopf, New York, 1946, p. 157.

[3] Quoted in Shinobu Seizaburō, "From Party Politics to Military Dictatorship," *The Developing Economies,* 5, No. 4 (December 1967), 682.

[4] Masuo Kato, *The Lost War,* p. 193.

Chapter 15

[1] Quoted in Kōsaka Masatake, *100 Million Japanese: The Postwar Experience,* Kodansha International, Tokyo, 1972, p. 45.

[2] Quoted in Kōsaka, *100 Million Japanese,* pp. 106–107.

Chapter 16

[1] R. P. Dore, *Aspects of Social Change in Modern Japan,* p. 141.

Epilogue

[1] New Year's Day editorial quoted in *The Wheel Extended,* 3, No. 4 (Spring 1974), 29.

[2] Quoted in "Letter from Tokyo," *The New Yorker,* May 20, 1974, p. 117.

[3] New Year's Day editorial quoted in *The Wheel Extended,* 3, No. 4 (Spring 1974), 33.

Further Reading

Books dealing with the development of modern Japan have increased in number and quality over the past decade. Some have been written by historians and others by social scientists, but all contribute to more complete understanding of Japanese modernization.

Students who know little or nothing about Japanese history and culture might find it useful to consult some general works. A good place to begin is John W. Hall and Richard K. Beardsley, *Twelve Doors to Japan* (McGraw-Hill, New York, 1965). Two suggestive interpretive works on Japanese cultural style are Ruth Benedict, *The Chrysanthemum and the Sword* (Houghton Mifflin, Boston, 1946), and Chie Nakane, *Japanese Society* (University of California Press, Berkeley, 1970). A classic work on the pre-1800 period is G. B. Sansom, *Japan: A Short Cultural History* (Appleton-Century-Crofts, New York, 1962). A brief treatment of pre-modern institutional developments is Peter Duus, *Feudalism in Japan* (Knopf, New York, 1969), while more detailed coverage of the same material can be found in John W. Hall, *Government and Local Power in Japan, 500–1700* (Princeton University Press, Princeton, N.J., 1966). There are also two excellent anthologies dealing with pre-modern literature and thought: Donald Keene (ed.), *Anthology of Japanese Literature from the Earliest Time to the Mid-Nineteenth Century* (Grove, New York, 1955); and W. T. deBary, R. Tsunoda, et al. (comp.), *Sources of Japanese Tradition* (Columbia University Press, New York, 1965).

For the Tokugawa period, there are several excellent works: Robert N. Bellah, *Tokugawa Religion: The Values of Pre-Industrial Japan* (Free Press, New York, 1957); Harold Bolitho, *Treasures Among Men: The Fudai Daimyō in Tokugawa Japan* (Yale University Press, New Haven, Conn., 1974); Ronald P. Dore, *Education in Tokugawa Japan* (Princeton University Press, Princeton, N.J., 1964); Charles James Dunn, *Everyday Life in Traditional Japan* (Stanford University Press, Stanford, Ca., 1969); John W. Hall and Marius B. Jansen, *Studies in the Institutional History of Early Modern Japan* (Princeton University Press, Princeton, N.J., 1968); Thomas C. Smith, *The Agrarian Origins of Modern Japan* (Stanford University Press, Stanford, Ca., 1959); Conrad Totman, *Politics in the Tokugawa Bakufu, 1600–1853* (Harvard University Press, Cambridge, Mass., 1967); William B. Hauser, *Economic Institutional Change in Tokugawa Japan: Ōsaka and the Kinai Cotton Trade* (Cambridge University Press, Cambridge, Mass., 1974).

The Meiji Resotration, of course, has attracted the attention of many scholars. The classic work is E. H. Norman, *Japan's Emergence as a Modern State* (Institute of Pacific Relations, New York, 1940). The interpretations presented in this work have been questioned by many more recent writers, but it remains stimulating reading. The most recent general work on the Restoration is W. G. Beasley, *The Meiji Restoration* (Stanford University Press, Stanford, Ca., 1973), a thorough and judicious book. Somewhat more uneven in quality is Paul Akamatsu, *Meiji 1868: Revolution and Counter Revolution in Japan* (Harper and Row, New York, 1972). Other works dealing with particular aspects of the Restoration and the events leading up to it are: W. G. Beasley, *Select Documents on Japanese Foreign Policy, 1853–1868* (Oxford, New York, 1955); Albert M. Craig, *Chōshū in the Meiji Restoration* (Harvard University Press, Cambridge, Mass., 1961); H. D. Harootunian, *Towards Restoration: The Growth of Political Consciousness in Tokugawa Japan* (University of California Press, Berkeley, 1970); Marius B. Jansen, *Sakamoto Ryōma and the Meiji Restoration* (Princeton University Press, Princeton, N.J., 1961).

There is no single work giving an overview of the Meiji period. A readable if dated account of the early Meiji decades can be found in G. B. Sansom, *The Western World and Japan: A Study in the Interaction of European and Asiatic Cultures* (Knopf, New York, 1950). Meiji political developments are dealt with in George Akita, *Foundations of Constitutional Government in Modern Japan, 1868–1900* (Harvard University Press, Cambridge, Mass., 1967); Nobutaka Ike, *The Beginnings of Political Democracy in Japan* (Johns Hopkins, Baltimore, 1950); Joseph Pittau, *Political Thought in Early Meiji Japan, 1868–1889* (Harvard University Press, Cambridge, Mass., 1967); and Robert Scalapino, *Democracy and the Party Movement in Prewar Japan: The Failure of the First Attempt* (University of California Press, Berkeley, 1953); R. II. P. Mason, *Japan's First General Election: 1890* (Cambridge University Press, Cambridge, 1967). A masterful description of the early industrialization effort is to be found in Thomas C. Smith, *Political Change and Industrial Development in Japan: Government Enterprise, 1868–1880* (Stanford University Press, Stanford, Ca., 1955); also interesting on Meiji economic developments are Johannes Hirschmeier, *The Origins of Entrepreneurship in Meiji Japan* (Harvard University Press, Cambridge, Mass., 1964); Byron K. Marshall, *Capitalism and Nationalism in Prewar Japan: The Ideology of the Business Elite, 1868–1941* (Stanford University Press, Stanford, Ca., 1967); James Nakamura, *Agricultural Production and the Economic Development of Japan, 1873–1922* (Princeton University Press, Princeton, N.J., 1966). Three stimulating works on Meiji intellectual history are: Kenneth B. Pyle, *The New Generation in Meiji Japan: Problems of Cultural Identity, 1885–1895* (Stanford University Press, Stanford, Ca., 1969); Carmen Blacker, *The Japanese Enlightenment* (Cambridge University Press, Cambridge, 1964); Irwin Scheiner, *Christian Converts and Social Protest in Meiji Japan* (University of California Press, Berkeley, 1970). A more intimate and personal view of how it felt to live through the tumultuous years of Meiji may be found in Yukichi Fukuzawa, *The Autobiography of Yukichi Fukuzawa* (Columbia University Press, New York, 1966), the memoir of one of the leading Meiji intellectuals, or Kenjirō Tokutomi, *Footsteps in the Snow* (George Allen Unwin, London, 1970), a Japanese version of *David Copperfield*.

The first three decades of the twentieth century have attracted less attention than other periods of modern Japanese history, but a number of useful works have appeared recently. Political developments are treated in: Peter Duus, *Party Rivalry and Political Change in Taishō Japan* (Harvard University Press, Cambridge, Mass., 1968); Tetsuo Najita, *Hara Kei in the Politics of Compromise, 1905–1915* (Harvard University Press, Cambridge, Mass., 1967); George O. Totten, *The Social Democratic Movement in Prewar Japan* (Yale University Press, New Haven, Conn., 1966). Aspects of Japanese foreign policy during this period have been treated in: Akira Iriye, *After Imperialism: The Search for a New Order in East Asia* (Harvard

University Press, Cambridge, Mass., 1965); James W. Morley, *The Japanese Thrust into Siberia, 1918* (Columbia University Press, New York, 1957); Shumpei Okamoto, *The Japanese Oligarchy and the Russo-Japanese War* (Columbia University Press, New York, 1970); Marius B. Jansen, *The Japanese and Sun Yat-sen* (Harvard University Press, Cambridge, Mass., 1954). Aspects of social and intellectual history are covered in: Tatsuo Arima, *The Failure of Freedom: A Portrait of Modern Japanese Intellectuals* (Harvard University Press, Cambridge, Mass., 1969), and Henry D. Smith, *Japan's First Student Radicals* (Harvard University Press, Cambridge, Mass., 1972). An excellent collection of essays on the early twentieth century is Bernard S. Silberman and H. D. Harootunian (eds.), *Japan in Crisis: Essays on Taishō Democracy* (Princeton University Press, Princeton, N.J., 1974). For literary treatments of the period, students are directed to the translated works of authors such as Natsume Sōseki, Mori Ōgai, and Tanizaki Junichirō, as well as Donald Keene (ed.), *Modern Japanese Literature from 1868 to the Present Day* (Grove, New York, 1956).

There is a rich literature on the 1930s and early 1940s, much of it revolving around Japan's expansion and involvement in World War II. Some of the more interesting works are: Robert C. Butow, *Tōjō and the Coming of the War* (Princeton University Press, Princeton, N.J., 1961); James B. Crowley, *Japan's Quest for Autonomy: National Security and Foreign Policy, 1930–1938* (Princeton University Press, Princeton, N.J., 1966); Nobutaka Ike (ed.), *Japan's Decision for War: Records of the 1941 Policy Conferences* (Stanford University Press, Stanford, Ca., 1967); Roberta Wohlstetter, *Pearl Harbor: Warning and Decision* (Stanford University Press, Stanford, Ca., 1962); Ben-Ami Shillony, *Revolt in Japan: The Young Officers and the February 26, 1936 Incident* (Princeton University Press, Princeton, N.J., 1973); Robert J. C. Butow, *Japan's Decision to Surrender* (Stanford University Press, Stanford, Ca., 1967); Dorothy Borg and Shumpei Okamoto (eds.), *Pearl Harbor as History* (Columbia University Press, New York, 1973).

Two collections of exciting and perceptive essays on Japanese nationalism by Japanese authors are Masao Maruyama, *Thought and Behaviour in Modern Japanese Politics* (Oxford University Press, London, 1963), and Kazuko Tsurumi, *Social Change and the Individual: Japan Before and After Defeat in World War II* (Princeton University Press, Princeton, N.J., 1970). A collection of interpretive essays by American authors, dealing mainly with the 1930s, is James W. Morley (ed.), *Dilemmas of Growth in Prewar Japan* (Princeton University Press, Princeton, N.J., 1971).

Students of economic history tend to ignore political periodization, so most works dealing with the development of the prewar economy cut across the conventional chronological boundaries. Three excellent analytical works are: William W. Lockwood, *The Economic Development of Japan: Growth and Structural Change, 1868-1938* (Princeton University Press, Princeton, N.J., 1955); William W. Lockwood (ed.), *The State and Economic Enterprise in Japan* (Princeton University Press, Princeton, N.J., 1965); and Kazushi Ohkawa and Henry Rosovsky, *Japanese Economic Growth: Trend Acceleration in the Twentieth Century* (Stanford University Press, Stanford, Ca., 1973).

Other works dealing with developments throughout the entire modern period are: Marius B. Jansen (ed.), *Changing Japanese Attitudes Toward Modernization* (Princeton University Press, Princeton, N.J., 1965); R. P. Dore (ed.), *Aspects of Social Change in Modern Japan* (Princeton University Press, Princeton, N.J., 1967); Robert E. Ward, *Political Development in Modern Japan* (Princeton University Press, Princeton, N.J., 1968); Donald H. Shively (ed.), *Tradition and Modernization in Japanese Culture* (Princeton University Press, Princeton, N.J., 1971); Albert M. Craig and Donald H. Shively (eds.), *Personality in Japanese History* (University of California Press, Berkeley, 1970).

The post-1945 period has yet to be studied systematically by historians. A useful overview, however, can be found in the appropriate chapters of E. O. Reischauer, *Japan: The Story of a Nation* (Knopf, New York, 1970). Most books on postwar Japan have been written by social scientists. A few of the more interesting and readable volumes are the following: Kazuo Kawai, *Japan's American Interlude* (University of Chicago Press, Chicago, 1960); Ronald P. Dore, *Land Reform in Japan* (Oxford University Press, London, 1958); Ronald P. Dore, *City Life in Japan* (University of California Press, Berkeley, 1958); Ezra F. Vogel, *Japan's New Middle Class: The Salary Man and His Family in a Tokyo Suburb* (University of California Press, Berkeley, 1967); R. P. Dore, *British Factory, Japanese Factory: The Origins of National Diversity in Employment Relations* (University of California Press, Berkeley, 1973); Nathaniel P. Thayer, *How the Conservatives Rule Japan* (Princeton University

Press, Princeton, N.J., 1969); Haruhiko Fukui, *Party in Power·
The Japanese Liberal-Democrats and Policy-Making* (University of
California Press, Berkeley, 1970); Gerald P. Curtis, *Election Cam-
paigning Japanese Style* (Columbia University Press, New York,
1971); Bradley Richardson, *The Political Culture of Japan* (Univer-
sity of California Press, Berkeley, 1974); Nobutaka Ike, *Japanese
Politics: Patron-Client Democracy* (Knopf, New York, 1972);
Kozo Yamamura, *Economic Policy in Postwar Japan: Growth versus
Economic Democracy* (University of California Press, Berkeley,
1967); Kurt Steiner, *Local Government in Japan* (Stanford Univer-
sity Press, Stanford, Ca., 1965); Robert E. Cole, *Japanese Blue
Collar: The Changing Tradition* (University of California Press,
Berkeley, 1971); Martin E. Weinstein, *Japan's Postwar Defense
Policy, 1947–1968* (Columbia University Press, New York, 1971);
Donald C. Hellman, *Japanese Domestic Politics and Foreign Policy*
(University of California Press, Berkeley, 1969); George R. Packard,
Protest in Tokyo: The Security Treaty Crisis of 1960 (Princeton
University Press, Princeton, N.J., 1969); M. Y. Yoshino, *Japan's
Managerial System: Tradition and Innovation* (MIT Press, 1971).

Index